Improving Outcomes: Disciplinary Writing, Local Assessment, and the Aim of Fairness

Improving Outcomes: Disciplinary Writing, Local Assessment, and the Aim of Fairness

Edited by

Diane Kelly-Riley and
Norbert Elliot

The Modern Language Association of America
New York   2021

MLA and the MODERN LANGUAGE ASSOCIATION are trademarks owned by the Modern Language Association of America. For information about obtaining permission to reprint material from MLA book publications, send your request by mail (see address below) or e-mail (permissions@mla.org).

Library of Congress Cataloging-in-Publication Data

Names: Kelly-Riley, Diane, editor. | Elliot, Norbert, editor.
Title: Improving outcomes : disciplinary writing, local assessment, and the aim of fairness / edited by Diane Kelly-Riley, Norbert Elliot.
Description: New York : The Modern Language Association of America, 2021. | Includes bibliographical references. | Summary: "Covers fairness in assessment of writing in various disciplines, such as nursing, architecture, engineering, and computer science. Strategies discussed include feedback analytics for peer learning; socio-cognitive perspectives; faculty collaboration; trajectory-based responses to writing; and culturally responsive assessment applicable in technical schools, two-year and four-year colleges, and online and hybrid courses"— Provided by publisher.
Identifiers: LCCN 2020022633 (print) | LCCN 2020022634 (ebook) | ISBN 9781603295123 (hardcover) | ISBN 9781603295130 (paperback) | ISBN 9781603295147 (EPUB) | ISBN 9781603295154 (Kindle)
Subjects: LCSH: Technical writing—Study and teaching (Higher). | Technical writing—Evaluation. | English language—Rhetoric—Study and teaching (Higher)
Classification: LCC T11 .I47 2021 (print) | LCC T11 (ebook) | DDC 808.06/66—dc23
LC record available at https://lccn.loc.gov/2020022633
LC ebook record available at https://lccn.loc.gov/2020022634

Published by The Modern Language Association of America
85 Broad Street, Suite 500, New York, New York 10004-2434
www.mla.org

Contents

Part Three: Disciplinary Writing

Part Four: Location

Foreword

Anne Ruggles Gere

The Modern Language Association's first book on writing studies, Jasper Neel's *Options for the Teaching of English: Freshman Composition*, announced in its title and contents that composition instruction makes an important contribution to the learning of students in English departments, to a liberal arts education, and to the humanities more generally. Produced against a background of "Johnny Can't Write" commentaries, the descriptions of twelve different writing programs in Neel's collection launched a program of publication in writing studies that has continued over the past forty years.

During this time the questions and perspectives have changed. The MLA's book list in the 1980s attended, as Neel's book did, to ways of teaching. In the 1990s, a number of publications explored the relations between composition and areas like feminism, critical theory, and postmodernism. In 1996, questions about assessing student writing were addressed in *Assessment of Writing: Politics, Policies, Practices* by Edward M. White, William D. Lutz, and Sandra Kamusikiri. As the standards movement and its attendant tests were gathering steam, the questions addressed in that volume centered on political issues, policy questions, and, to some degree, equity. The volume you are about to read comes at just the right time, because the growing inequities in our society make questions about fairness urgent, and the increasing number of students constructing their own programs of study raises questions about disciplinary discourses.

In one way, *fairness* seems an easy concept to define, but since its meaning is inflected with concepts like *justice* and *equity*, it becomes quickly evident that the idea of fairness does not yield to easy answers. As the definition offered by the *Standards for Educational and Psychological Testing*, quoted in the introduction to this volume, explains, "the term *fairness* has no single technical meaning" (49). That is exactly the point. There can be no technical, portable definition of fairness because it does not mean the same thing in all cases. Defining fairness is an ongoing process, shaped by the contexts, persons, and projects at any given location and time, always guided by principles of justice and equity. This process calls for the sort of focused engagement described in the pages of this book, and it is part of the large conversation we call the humanities, a conversation about what it means to be human, what we value, and what we understand about our own experiences and those of others.

In the context of writing instruction, the concept of fairness takes on particular significance since it is through the processes of writing that students learn to speculate, imagine, and understand what it means to be human. The assignments given and the responses to them contribute to the ways students see themselves and their world. Students who feel assessment of their writing is capricious or unfair will develop a very different view of the world than do students who feel that assessment of their writing is just, fair, and equitable. The outcomes featured in this collection speak to what students learn to value in writing, what they come to understand as quality, and what they recognize as fairness.

This volume's attention to discipline-focused writing reminds us of the many different contexts in which fairness can be employed. By recognizing and valuing the discourses of a given discipline, writing assessment can enact fairness in assessment rather than applying inflexible standards to all fields. As the authors included in this volume make clear, the best assessment is constructed locally, and, for college students, the disciplines in which they enroll become a local context. Writing assessment informed by the discursive norms of a given discipline conveys a powerful message about fairness to students.

Viewing writing assessment in terms of specific disciplines is especially important in the current moment, when many students carry multiple majors or a combination of majors and minors. Whether to hedge their opportunities on the job market, satisfy long-standing questions or desires, or take advantage of multiple opportunities, students frequently take up more than one disciplinary focus during their undergraduate careers. As they enter the multiple discourse communities of their areas of interest, students can find their way much more easily when writing assessment reflects the values and conventions of each locale.

One of my goals as the 2018 president of the MLA was to underscore the possibilities of more alliances between faculties in writing studies and literature. This volume, with its emphasis on the concept of fairness, helps accomplish some of that work by showing how the processes of reading and writing are inextricably linked in writing assessment. It demonstrates how the assessment of writing engages the same kinds of questions about justice and equity as literature does, and it makes clear how crucial it is to put students at the center of pedagogical decisions.

Introduction

Diane Kelly-Riley and Norbert Elliot

This is a book about public good advanced through written communication. By improving writing outcomes, we enrich cultures, educational institutions, and student lives. The authors in this collection emphasize dual advantages when writing occurs within and beyond disciplinary settings: instructors apprentice students in the conventions of their communities of rhetorical practice, and students thrive, developing personal and professional identities when exposed to multiple disciplinary genres. This mutual relationship demonstrates the benefits of the long-held belief that writing instruction is the responsibility of everyone. Because language is deeply situated, these authors also emphasize the importance of localism and the benefits of conducting research at specific and varied institutional sites in which educational transformation occurs. Because equality of opportunity is a primary aim of education in a participatory democracy, fairness is central as a governing concept in contemporary scholarship of instruction and assessment. Within this collection, fairness operates as an integrative principle.

Working across the curriculum, academic communities have demonstrated meaningful, equitable ways to teach and assess learning outcomes associated with written communication. This edited collection features voices of "scholars of field-appropriate rhetoric" (68)—those colleagues Charles Bazerman, writing in 1992, hoped would emerge and who are now present thanks to three decades of collaborative work in education in the United States. This introduction begins with the background leading to the present volume and the demographic shifts that make approaches such as ours relevant. We conclude with an overview of the volume.

Background

Nearly thirty years ago, the Modern Language Association published Anne Herrington and Charles Moran's edited collection, *Writing, Teaching and Learning in the Disciplines*; soon after, *Assessment of Writing: Politics, Policies, Practices* appeared, edited by Edward M. White, William D. Lutz, and Sandra Kamusikiri. Published in 1992 and 1996, respectively, both volumes presented state-of-the art scholarship by leading researchers working in the fields of disciplinary

writing and writing evaluation. Although the present edited collection is indebted to these two landmark volumes, the difference nearly three decades
makes is readily apparent. When the series Research and Scholarship in Composition was launched, disciplinary writing and writing assessment were two
different areas of study and were rarely seen in terms of each other. Beyond
first-year essay writing, little was known in detail about the role of process and
product in professional settings, where genres such as proposals were central to
knowledge distribution. As for writing assessment, accountability forces external to educational settings—especially those associated with federal and state
programs—had become so ubiquitous that a volume was needed to sort out the
issues, from empirical to legal. Assessment was singularly associated with testing. The need for local adaptation of national, regional, and state curricular and
assessment initiatives were just starting. The realities of student differences and
language settings were not well documented, and the aim of education as the advancement of opportunity was little more than a slogan. In the 1990s, situated
writing pedagogy and writing assessment were not integrated concepts, but in
the last thirty years they have evolved to be mutually influential. Today, as our
educational structures diversify, this integration holds a great deal of possibility
when these efforts are focused on the concept of fairness.

This volume relies on three interwoven principles: the achievement of outcomes as a way to structure opportunity, the use of disciplinary writing as a way
to broaden student perceptions as distinct individuals and members of disciplinary communities, and the pursuit of fairness as a unifying aim of curricular
initiatives.

Historically, *outcomes* was a term first used the year after the creation of
the Servicemen's Readjustment Act of 1944 (Good 404; "Outcome," N. def. 3d).
As postsecondary education was reconceptualized in terms of surging enrollment—in fall 1949, about 2.4 million students enrolled in colleges, or about
fifteen percent of eighteen- to twenty-four-year-olds, a rise from seven percent
in 1930 (Snyder 65)—educators began efforts to articulate learning goals and
design curricula based on those goals. By the early 1960s, edited collections such
as Paul L. Dressel's *Evaluation in Higher Education* provided handbooks of institutional research that emphasized the unifying function of assessment, exempli-
fied in this case at Michigan State College, to help administrators and instructors understand the policy implications of establishing and evaluating outcomes.
By the time Michael F. Middaugh published his guide *Planning and Assessment in
Higher Education* in 2010, outcomes were viewed as vehicles for the achievement
of institutional missions, and assessment was linked to the advancement of student learning through emphasis on information use to refine site-based curricula and improve local student learning. Viewed as a study of outcomes, Cathy N.
Davidson's 2017 book, *The New Education: How to Revolutionize the University to*

Prepare Students for a World in Flux, analyzes challenges to designing and achieving outcomes in a world filled with contingency. Davidson emphasizes faculty
members' obligation to students. In terms of outcomes, Davidson proposes, our
aims must be operationally achieved: "Where do we teach those deep reading
and critical thinking and communication skills? These are not just rhetorical
questions but structural ones" (712).

With an emphasis on outcomes, writing in the disciplines became a phenomenon in the twentieth-century United States. The rise of big science was
accompanied by the need to document findings for funding justification and
initiating research programs. In the postwar years, literacy became increasingly
important in the United States, as large-scale research demanded literate scientists and engineers who could assemble bodies of knowledge in their disciplinary specializations—and articulate that knowledge to nonspecialists (Bazerman et al., *Reference* 18–21; Russell 240). In this process of knowledge creation
and dissemination, genre became especially important. Following the emphasis
first articulated by Carolyn Miller in 1984 ("Genre") on form as a mediating and
flexible cultural artifact, genre came to be recognized as a symbol of social action. By experimenting with writing processes and products used in their chosen
profession, individuals learned to be members of their fields. In that tradition,
Herrington and Moran followed their earlier volume with a second edited collection, *Genre across the Curriculum*, in 2005. Today, genre is understood as a way to
recognize writing expectations and to help students succeed in meeting them.
As many of the authors in this volume note, to understand the constitutive nature of genre is to understand a profession. As such, curricular efforts involving writing in the disciplines—"having students learn the ways of writing and
reasoning assumed to be characteristic of academic contexts" (Herrington and
Moran, *Genre* 9)—are usefully conceptualized under genre. Emphasis on genre
moves broad concepts into directions for writing instruction in terms of audiences identified, aims implied and articulated, processes and forms used, and
self-efficacy gained. Assessment processes have evolved, and so has the need to
accommodate and understand our much more diverse student population.

The concept of fairness serves as a touchstone for such instructional and assessment efforts. Although the concept is definable, its historical instantiation
is complex. Following social and policy development initiated by the Civil Rights
Act of 1964, assessment specialists increasingly turned to evidence related to
fairness. Along with validity and reliability, fairness evidence became important
to influential legal and measurement frameworks (Poe and Cogan, Jr.). The 2014
edition of the *Standards for Educational and Psychological Testing* positions fairness as a core consideration to protect those who take and use tests in all aspects. The authors of the revised *Standards* assert "the term *fairness* has no single
technical meaning and is used in many different ways in public discourse . . . a

full consideration of the topic would explore the multiple function of testing in relation to many goals, including the broad goal of achieving equality of opportunity in our society" (49). In philosophy, John Rawls, influenced by the events of the 1960s, focused on fairness in a body of work published between 1971 and 2006 and collected in his volumes *A Theory of Justice* and *Justice as Fairness: A Restatement*. For Rawls, fairness was a governing principle, and justice followed. Very recent work has examined both the measurement applications and theory-building involved with claiming fairness as a primary aim of writing assessment (Kelly-Riley and Whithaus, *Theory* and *Two-Year College Writing*; Poe et al., *Writing*). These three tropes—legal, statistical, and philosophical—suggest the conceptual range and historical development of fairness. At any given moment, fairness is a contingent concept. Made manifest by contexts, individuals, and aims, fairness becomes a concretizing principle that shifts across time yet yields a demonstrable end through solidarity.

At the present, attention to fairness in its various forms is increasingly being used to challenge reductionist practices of teaching and assessing writing. As authors of this collection illustrate, attention to fairness has made us consider opportunity structures across multiple institutional settings: vocational training programs, private undergraduate institutions, community colleges, R1 Carnegie-classified research institutions, institutions that predominantly serve underrepresented populations, private and public liberal arts colleges, and regional college and university accreditation agencies. Distributed learning is the order of the day, and attention is needed to the varied contexts in which teaching and assessing writing appear. For language scholars, these changes are very important and help us reconceptualize the ever-present, high-stakes discussions around assessment and accountability and, perhaps more significant, demonstrate the power of humanities education in an educational environment of ever-increasing utilitarian values. Although writing studies scholars have had an early influence in broadening the scope of curricular assessment beyond technical concerns since the 1990s, these debates and discussions continue to unfold. Building on recent scholarship in disciplinary writing, local assessment, and fairness used in this edited collection, humanities scholars can continue to shape this area by imagining new ways of improving outcomes through our collective expertise about language and what it means to be human.

Population Shifts

The pursuit of fairness must be rooted in language study grounded in disciplinary experiences within and beyond the curriculum. Our work can broaden the focus and emphasis of assessment to wider issues of humanity and society. As the nation continues to be more diverse, studies of language practices within disciplinary settings will become increasingly important. Although diverse in membership, ours remains a common future. The link between what the authors have established in this volume and the need for such scholarship is revealed in terms of shifting demographic populations. In its most recent projections, the National Center for Educational Statistics (NCES) in the United States estimates that in K–12 settings Hispanic, Asian / Pacific Islander, and other students of two or more races will experience dramatic enrollment shifts. Between 2016 and 2028, there will be a twenty percent rise for students who are Asian / Pacific Islander; an eight percent rise for students who are Hispanic; and a fifty-one percent rise for students who are two or more races. In terms of high school graduation rates, by 2028–29, there will be a twenty-three percent rise for students who are Asian / Pacific Islander, a forty-nine percent rise for students who are Hispanic, and a 199 percent rise for students of two or more races. Along with these shifts for K–12 students, NCES predicts similar race/ethnicity changes in postsecondary enrollment. Between 2016 and 2028, there will be an increase of eight percent for Black students and an increase of fourteen percent for Hispanic students (Hussar and Bailey).

Calls for fairness extend beyond simply considering the seismic demographic shifts in language and ethnicity in the United States. We must consider the many intersections that form individual identity, including socioeconomic status, ability, gender, race, and other characteristics. In the seventeen essays that follow, our authors return time and again to the desire to improve outcomes, the willingness to explore writing in the disciplines in order to identify academic and professional opportunities for students, and the courage to use local assessments to ensure students are evaluated in meaningful ways. In all these efforts, the aim of fairness provides a unifying concept that remind us of what we are doing and why, and for whom our efforts are undertaken in the first place.

Structure of This Collection

As editors of this collection, we strove to create a volume that reflects the most recent evolutions in scholarship that now combine writing in the disciplines and writing assessment as mutually informing fields across multiple disciplines. To that end, we sought contributors who represent the diversity of postsecondary settings where this work is conducted. No longer is writing assessment or writing in the disciplines housed solely in English departments. Our collection reflects a snapshot of the present moment of approaches to situated writing instruction and assessment that put fairness at the center.

In the foreword, the recent MLA president Anne Ruggles Gere situates the collection within the present moment of humanities and language study. She reminds us that fairness is an ongoing process and stresses the importance of alliances. In her focus on deliberation and community, she captures the essence of this volume. To provide exposition, we have structured this collection in four parts, and a more explicit framing of each part here will be useful to readers.

Part 1 explores values associated with fairness as the aim of disciplinary writing instruction and assessment. These essays demonstrate the multidimensional ways fairness is enacted across various contexts. Although an entire volume might be given to a discussion of values, it is significant that this is the first collection of its kind to showcase the enactment of fairness in teaching and assessing writing in disciplinary settings, thus demonstrating that the term itself is far more than simply a technical construction, as we witness the values it evokes in diverse classroom settings. In an age of contingency, values emerge in interaction. In examining connections between disciplinary writing and local assessment, we see how field-situated language instruction and institutional context can improve instructional experiences for diverse students in our classrooms. In the past thirty years, disciplinary writing and the distributed sites of learning have become mainstay issues in postsecondary settings. At the same time, we have started to understand more intricately the complex needs of students within our institutions and how our values may be aligned with those needs. In this section, authors make explicit curricular, attitudinal, and cultural values associated with the pursuit of fairness.

In the opening essay, Mya Poe traces the evolution of scholarship associated with writing in the disciplines by emphasizing research traditions employing cognitive models, sociocultural studies, and corpus-based studies to demonstrate the deeply situated nature of language. Today, researchers in a wide array of disciplines are attentive to ways that language is essential to professional practice. Such attention provides the kairotic moment—the occasion of opportunity—that Poe believes is within our grasp. Turning her attention to assessment for program accountability, she notes that such genres of evaluation, while valuable, often neglect issues of subgroup and individual student impact. To expand evidence related to consequences, she calls for increased attention to fairness functioning along a continuum from the technical to the philosophical. Taxonomies of fairness deserve attention as our scholarship becomes increasingly alert to difference. Issues of access, cultural responsiveness, and justice are advanced when program accreditation and classroom research acknowledge and use such analyses.

In the next essay, Ruth Osorio argues that the transdisciplinary field of disability studies offers the opportunity to consider political, social, and cultural dimensions of ability within our courses and at our institutions. Because disability studies frames variation of ability as a source of discovery, Osorio offers a disability-as-insight approach to multimodal assessment. She accounts the ways in which an understanding of disability can broaden our understanding of all students and their capabilities. In setting aside the concept of accommodation, Osorio reveals the benefits that occur when difference is seen as the object of our attention. With special attention to writing in digital environments, disability-as-insight focuses attention on how composers of multimodal texts leverage accessibility and difference to ethical and persuasive ends. Using disability as a way to reimagine our instructional and assessment practices, we can develop informed ethical, material, aesthetic, and rhetorical approaches to accessibility—values that will enhance educational experiences for all students.

Concluding part 1, Brooke Carlson and Cari Ryan explore working with Native Hawaiian students at a religiously affiliated, private institution. They reckon with the postcolonial legacy of teaching and assessing writing at a Catholic university in the Marianist tradition, one with an explicit mission for community and service. They highlight the ongoing tensions between structuring student success in college settings and acknowledging the effects of a colonial past of linguistic imperialism. Their work demonstrates the ways students' education can be enhanced through a twenty-first-century pedagogy embracing three trajectories that increase localization, knowledge transfer, and fairness: mobile learning, writing tasks, and task-aligned rubrics. Carlson and Ryan use these trajectories to examine theories of power and hegemony and, in doing so, help students realize the force of literacy in their lives. Theirs is a curriculum designed to strengthen student accountability and self-assessment through content, voice, and textuality.

Part 2 focuses on foundational issues for fairness, identification of opportunity structures, and use of evidence-based assessments. Because fairness must be pursued with a keen awareness of student identity, the authors in this section document approaches to facilitating fairness through views of assessment as a deeply contextualized activity. This section outlines transformations emerging in educational measurement regarding the socially situated roles of assessments and explores how this reconceptualization is fostered in a variety of educational environments with a diversity of students at multiple, postsecondary levels. Written communication is a sociocognitive, deeply situated human activity. Instruction and assessment are at their best when integrated and informed through multidimensional efforts. Writing involves planned encounters with multiple cognitive and affective domains in which student proficiency can be demonstrated and improved through robust construct representation. In these encounters, transparently communicated outcomes afford explicit instruction, and formative feedback to students becomes an important part of assessment used to inform instruction. In this section, authors explore these foundations for teaching and assessing writing as a way to advance opportunity to learn.

In the first essay, the psychometrician Robert J. Mislevy attends to the direct relation between representation of the writing construct and adoption of a socially situated perspective on written communication. Integrating a socio-cognitive psychological perspective with traditional psychometric traditions has implications for writing in the disciplines that, in turn, provide a coherent rethinking of writing assessment responsive to developing research in student learning. Setting aside the prevailing, but limited view of assessment as a form of testing, Mislevy offers a new one proposing that we see assessment as an evidentiary argument. Assessment, he argues, is most valuable when situated in social contexts, centered on students' emerging abilities as observed in real-world writing activities shaped by value and aim. He proposes that fairness and opportunity to learn extend assessment by providing information important to instructional design through traditional categories of evidence related to validity and reliability.

By emphasizing dignity and respect for students who most need support in learning to write, Ruth Benander and Brenda Refaei in the next essay provide an agentic view of basic writers at an open admissions community college. Their approach recognizes that social circumstances must be considered when teaching and assessing writing in two-year college settings. Often, basic writing courses are noncredit classes where principles of writing are based on skills and correctness. As such, students in these courses are often victims of facially neutral policies that are, in effect, related to discriminatory practices that frustrate identity creation through diverse language practices. To ensure that these practices do not occur, Benander and Refaei emphasize self-regulation and self-efficacy as integral to writing success. Using both performance measures and student surveys, the authors demonstrate how their e-portfolio strategy contributes to the fairness of the course assessment by allowing broad engagement with writing. As they show, robust exposure to varied forms of writing is associated with opportunities to learn.

Emphasizing writing assessment in digital environments, William Hart-Davidson and Melissa Graham Meeks focus on the important role that peer feedback plays in instruction. Using information extracted from a Web-based platform that helps instructors run feedback-centric writing classrooms, they find students' contributions as reviewers predict classroom success. Through a concept Hart-Davidson and Meeks call "giver's gain," peer review advances student knowledge about writing processes and products and tempers writer isolation. Innovatively, the authors believe that the reciprocity of peer review contributes to virtuous behavior. As students learn to understand criteria and associated outcomes in communal digital environments, they create new identities as both readers and writers, learn to revise according to explicit aims, and participate in a community dedicated to learning. The use of large-scale data analysis provides real-time, formative assessment so teachers can better identify and respond to students. Harvesting data from the intricate interactions in peer learning, the authors use algorithms—designed to identify patterns of peer review associated with successful writing—to provide instructors with just-in-time intervention reports. Associated with fairness, real-time feedback to instructors emphasizes the planning and revision processes needed to promote writing success for all students.

Erick Montenegro focuses on culturally responsive assessment and details ways in which such assessment can operate at institutional, program, and course levels. Understood as assessment that is mindful of language and cultural differences affecting student performance, he examines applications of culturally responsive assessment through the "Transparency Framework" developed by the National Institute for Learning Outcomes Assessment (NILOA)—an educational assessment initiative based at the University of Illinois and Indiana University. To illustrate the significance and benefits of culturally responsive assessments, Montenegro provides a case study of their use at North Carolina Agricultural and Technical State University—a historically Black university and a leader in producing Black engineers. Montenegro extends the concept of culturally responsive assessment as way to modify programmatically the Council of Writing Program Administrators' "WPA Outcomes Statement for First-Year Composition," often viewed as a gold standard of outcomes. He concludes the essay with discussions of how Davidson's negotiated course outcomes and Asao B. Inoue's labor-based contract grading practices offer ways to implement culturally responsive assessment within classroom settings.

In the final essay of this section, Jeremy Schnieder and Valerie M. Hennings describe a project that envisions assessment as an opportunity for key stakeholder learning at a small liberal arts college. On their campus, faculty members across the curriculum worked to transform distinct disciplinary perspectives into a new vision of assessment where shared goals are identified and assessment becomes faculty-member-driven. More than an idealized framework, faculty and administrators developed a component model of transdisciplinarity emphasizing negotiated boundaries, goal-centered problem-solving, reframing of received assessment outcomes, development of shared language, and fairness-centered reflexivity. This model is, in turn, administratively operationalized so future assessments would no longer be conducted by a solitary figure isolated from faculty members and students and reliant on purchased tests. The results are unique and beneficial to those who reject conformative practice.

In part 3, scholars of field-appropriate rhetoric demonstrate how their contexts have enabled them to think reflectively about their disciplinary writing, formative assessment practices, and fairness. These scholars have designed instructional contexts that elevate specific values of their disciplines, with special attention to genre as both a form of writing and a vital component of disciplinary competence. Recognizing that language is a deeply situated human activity, they have designed assessments aligned with specific educational aims. This section moves from foundational issues to empirical studies situated across distinct contexts and institutions, each with diverse student populations. The authors in this section illustrate how disciplinary writing and local assessment facilitate fairness for a variety of students through multiple means.

For many readers, part 3 will be the most memorable and significant section of the book, and so we note some stark differences from Herrington and Moran's collection and that of White and his colleagues from thirty years ago. At that time, all the authors discussing writing in the disciplines were from English departments. Along with those in English, the authors in this part of the collection represent social science, architecture, nursing, engineering, and computer science; the influence of humanities through writing studies is evident in every single discipline here and throughout this volume. Likewise, thirty years ago, writing studies scholars and educational measurement specialists focused on issues of placement and technical representations of the construct of writing. Today, new authors highlight the broadened possibilities that arise when writing instruction and assessment are situated within local contexts with a focus on fairness. They demonstrate widened opportunities for students, disciplines, and society.

Such opportunities begin with collaborations, including high schools. In the first essay in this section, Christine Farris argues for enlarging the focus on genre in postsecondary, first-year writing to include reading, thereby strengthening the bridge between secondary and postsecondary education through use of both literary and nonliterary texts. Farris reports on a collaborative project with secondary teachers in Indiana in which academics in English play an expanded role in college readiness. Her focus is on the disjuncture between close reading and written communication. As she observes, there is a bifurcation of reading and writing in the Common Core State Standards Initiative (CCSSI), a large-scale assessment initiative embedded within many K–12 settings throughout the United States. She argues that the focus on career readiness of the CCSSI does students a disservice, as it emphasizes written skill over broader literacy abilities, including reading, intellectual inquiry, and appreciation for textual complexity. English and other disciplines rooted in languages, she reminds us, have the responsibility to encourage wider application of a contextualized, intertextual, multigenre approach to reading as the basis for the sort of writing students will encounter in college. Farris's essay also reminds us that we must work across the educational spectrum—K–20—to ensure broader expectations are promoted and articulated in collaboration with our elementary and secondary school colleagues.

Extending attention to postsecondary education in the next essay, Beth Buy-serie, Tialitha Macklin, Matt Frye, and Patricia Freitag Ericsson detail the use of a programmatic portfolio assessment of student first-year writing to inform faculty development. The authors describe the implementation and results of the Portfolio Outcomes Project, a formative assessment of local first-year composition portfolio outcomes as adapted from the "WPA Outcomes Statement for First-Year Composition." Defining fairness as the effort to develop pedagogical responses to assessment results, they explain the design of their training program for their instructional faculty—comprised largely of graduate teaching assistants and adjunct faculty members at a large public research university. They describe a process that assesses strengths and weaknesses of students' writing performance using professionally informed but locally implemented standards. In terms of assessment, they design training to help their instructional faculty attend to language, knowledge, and power within classroom settings. The authors foreground how language is used to describe assessment to explore the communication of programmatic values and disciplinary knowledge that are the core of their ongoing professional development training with instructors. As a result, their teaching corps embraces situated knowledge by collectively examining the connections among race, language, and writing studies. In their approach to fairness, they also frame design and assessment of multimodal assignments as ways to advance new possibilities for student learning.

The next four essays focus on studies involving field-appropriate rhetoric—knowledge of aim, audience, and genre necessary for disciplinary writing success—outside the humanities. Such scholars of rhetoric often teach large, general education courses and struggle to meaningfully engage students in course content. Such is the case of Karen Singer-Freeman and Linda Bastone, faculty members in psychology at a large regional university that is a primary access point to higher education for low-income and racially diverse students living outside New York City. Singer-Freeman and Bastone describe how they embedded reflective writing within their course on child development to leverage fairness, provide substantive opportunities for writing engagement, increase conceptual retention, and support overall student wellness. In doing so, they argue, their use of culturally responsive pedagogy, including reflective writing assignments, used to personalize and widen pedagogical approaches in these large classes, strengthens learning and improves student engagement. Because general education courses are lecture based and often detrimental to diverse student populations, the authors provide examples of strategies to engage students in meaningful ways leading to deep subject matter understanding. The authors further illustrate how intensive self-reflective writing used to increase conceptual retention can be enhanced through genre-specific rubrics. As such, the authors complicate current perceptions about rubrics as checklists and propose instead that task-specific rubrics can be used to link success on assignments to clearly articulated learning outcomes.

The final three essays in this section present programs where disciplinary experts emphasizing the conventions of their professions assess student work. The first looks at an effort undertaken collaboratively by architecture and humanities instructors. Jeffrey Hogrefe and Vladimir Briller explore ways their program engages the disciplines of humanities and architecture at a private institution with a special focus on art and architecture. In studio courses, students are introduced to concepts of writing and architecture informed by design practices and contemporary critical theory; in turn, students are apprenticed to expectations of their field. Emphasizing that new information in architecture is based on graphic forms of representation, Hogrefe and Briller demonstrate how concepts of the built environment and critical theory link studio and seminar through genre. Attention to literary figuration, rhetoric, and situational genre is woven through their curriculum.

Continuing the emphasis on the constitutive nature of genre, Rhonda Maneval and Frances Ward trace the evolution of writing and genres within the field of nursing as an important component of professional preparation. In this essay, genre in nursing practice is presented both as a case study of the varied forms of writing used in the profession and as a historical analysis of the role of language in health care practice. Maneval and Ward present a program in which specific assignments that acculturate nursing students with genres of their profession are also evaluated using complementary rubrics. As such, the authors establish the essential role of writing in professional life, one that defines the scope of the work of nursing and illustrates the shifting relations between nurse and society.

Hogrefe, Briller, Maneval, and Ward all have designed writing assessments to function within program accreditation demands. Within these processes, these scholars of architecture and nursing have found ways to transform accountability reporting into occasions to transform student learning. In similar fashion, Julia M. Williams details the long-standing e-portfolio assessment developed at a small private college specializing in Science, Technology, Engineering, and Math (STEM). Such programs often have additional accreditation requirements driven by their professional societies that require demonstration of certain learning outcomes. Williams and her colleagues used such a mandate to evaluate students' communication competencies across the disciplines. Central to the assessment is its humanistic view of students as agents of disciplinary expertise displaying boundary-crossing competencies, global understanding, and communicative ability. Such a view results in informed, research-based classroom pedagogy, with increased attention to ethics and preparation for roles as technically aware, skilled graduates.

Part 4 considers the central role of language beyond the traditional scope of four-year postsecondary education. In varied ways, each author examines the role that local adaptation plays in teaching and assessing writing. As the study of place, geography is traditionally described in terms of exact location (mapping longitude and latitude) and relative location (identifying cultural association across physical boundaries). Applying this classification renders traditional views (that teaching and assessing writing is best conducted in English departments, where essays are the privileged genre of academic writing) susceptible to transformative ones (that common aims are likely to be achieved across disciplines when genres best known to subject matter experts are used). In this final section of our collection, authors focus on technical education students in two-year colleges, distributed learning, and distributed assessment. Each essay in this section challenges us to reconsider our sense of location in teaching and assessing writing.

Angela B. Rasmussen and Andrea Reid turn to the two-year college in a case study of technical education students. First-year writing at Spokane Community College has a blended population: students who seek career and technical education that does not extend beyond credentialing or certification and students who intend to complete the curriculum, earn an associate's degree there, and then transfer to a four-year college. Attention to genre is therefore related to student success. For most first-year composition classes, the academic essay remains a standard writing form. Rasmussen and Reid note that relying solely on that genre can work against institutional goals of engaging and preparing students for a wide variety of discipline-specific transfer courses and workplace communication skills—especially when many students are unlikely to use or transfer the knowledge of how to write an academic essay beyond first-year composition. In order to create a curriculum that includes transparent, real world, and reflective writing tasks, the authors describe a discussion protocol aimed at creating a fair and inclusive curriculum that exposes students to varied disciplinary genres. Linking genre exposure to fairness, Rasmussen and Reid approach fairness in terms of curricular design—innovation that builds all students' knowledge of writing, rather than privileging one type of writing over another. For a classroom to be fair, the authors argue, all students must have an equal opportunity to succeed, which cannot be attained if the genres associated with workplace success are denied to them.

Continuing the theme of innovation, Carl Whithaus showcases research at the intersection of localized writing assessments and large-scale assessments:

distributed learning technologies and their impact on the development of students' writing abilities. As a general term, *distributed learning* describes curricular delivery methods ranging from fully online instruction to face-to-face instruction supplemented with online modules. In a study describing an assessment of student learning outcomes in first-year composition courses delivered in online, hybrid, and face-to-face formats, Whithaus records a troubling finding: although curriculum and instruction were working effectively across all different course delivery formats, external factors impacted cross-campus students in the online sections to such a degree that administrators decided to discontinue offering these sections until these factors were identified. Although effective use of technologies that connect writers to each other and to their readers is recognized as central to professional discourse, the specific impact of these technologies is yet to be fully understood.

This section closes with an essay by Terrel L. Rhodes of the Association of American Colleges and Universities (AAC&U). He presents the origin and development of an assessment approach entitled Valid Assessment of Learning in Undergraduate Education—the VALUE collaborative. In 2007, AAC&U issued calls for higher education professionals to help develop a paired set of learning outcomes and rubrics that could be used across institutional boundaries. Since the fall of 2009, when the rubrics were released, more than six thousand unique organizations have accessed and downloaded the sixteen rubrics both within the United States and internationally. At the present writing, the multistate collaborative to test the VALUE initiative stands as the only nationwide effort to systematically address the challenge of demonstrating through direct evidence progressive levels of student learning across essential learning outcomes. Embracing the intersection of local and distributed assessment, Rhodes envisions a future in which the point of accreditation is to be able to affirm institutional commitment to fairness for students' access to and achievement of quality learning. There must be, he argues, no value dualism of local versus distributed assessment: benefit occurs when one is seen in terms of the other.

The volume concludes with an afterword that reaffirms the importance of writing in the disciplines as a sustainable and necessary site for significant educational reform. As editors, we emphasize the need for specific action to be initiated through the lens of fairness to advance student learning through written communication. Now more than ever, scholar-teachers and scholar-administrators with specific backgrounds in languages and a broad humanities orientation to education must continue to engage in the ongoing scholarly and societal conversations around student learning and assessment. We have in hand distinct programs of research, principled frameworks, and evidence-centered practices. For the sake of our students, we cannot afford to cede our places at the table.

Part One

Values

A Matter of Aim: Disciplinary Writing, Writing Assessment, and Fairness

Mya Poe

Perspective

This chapter takes an expansive approach to review the literature on writing across the disciplines, with special attention to the influence of three research traditions in the study of writing: cognitive models, sociocultural studies, and corpus-based studies. Turning to assessment research, I examine two common frames for writing assessment in the disciplines—program accreditation and classroom research. In my review of research related to these traditions and accountability, it becomes clear that considerations about students related to fairness are often ignored, primarily because of the restricted aims of such research. As I argue, foundational issues in writing assessment surrounding collaboration, access, cultural responsiveness, and the achievement of justice are integral to improving student outcomes. The identification of outcomes is, in fact, an illustration of an articulation of fairness in the curriculum; the fulfillment of these outcomes is evidence of the creation of opportunity through education.

Introduction: Boundary Crossings

In higher education in the United States, writing is the learning outcome most often cited by universities and colleges. According to a 2009 survey of the Association of American Colleges and Universities, seventy-seven percent of universities and colleges surveyed indicated that writing is one of their top general education outcomes (Hart Research Assoc.). Writing (or, more broadly, communication) is also frequently named in disciplinary outcomes through regional and program accreditation associations. Given the ubiquity with which writing is a named in undergraduate learning outcomes, it is not surprising that research on writing has garnered interest across disciplinary boundaries.

In framing questions about the teaching and assessment of writing at the college level, scholars bring a set of interests that illustrate their own exigencies for the teaching and assessment of writing. As is the case with writing studies instructors, those in other disciplines have an interest in the genres and purposes of writing in their respective field, are invested in assessment from a desire to understand how classroom evaluation can help students learn disciplinary ways of writing, and are invested in understanding what demographic shifts in student populations mean for the ways we teach and assess writing. In this chapter, I explore the research on and assessment of writing in disciplinary contexts to position the value of practices related to fairness, identification of opportunity structures, and use of evidence-based disciplinary writing assessments. Integrating these concepts, I argue, will substantively advance the teaching and assessment of writing in light of the complexity of both disciplinary language and student identities today.

Research on Writing in the Disciplines: Cognitive Models, Sociocultural Studies, and Corpus-Based Studies

For the purposes of this collection, three traditions have been especially useful in research on writing in the disciplines: cognitive models, sociocultural studies, and corpus-based studies. Cognitive modeling of writing, introduced by researchers such as rhetorician Linda Flower and psychologist John R. Hayes, as well as education researchers Carl Bereiter and Marlene Scardamalia, would change our understanding of composing. Vital to their research was the use of think-aloud protocols, a tool well suited to cognitive modeling in its ability to capture a detailed record of what transpires in the writer's mind during the act of composing itself. To collect their protocols, Flower and Hayes gave their undergraduate college students constructed response tasks and invited them to compose out loud near a tape recorder. The think-aloud tool enabled model building—a taxonomy of the major elements and subprocesses of writing, along with the interaction of these elements and subprocesses. By 1994, Flower had created one of the seminal studies in the field, *The Construction of Negotiated Meaning: A Social Cognitive Theory of Writing*. Emphasizing the power of language to shape meaning, Flower identified the significance of the task environment, planning, translating, reviewing, and memory of the writer in the composing process. Flower argued that individual personal representations—what she termed "personal cognitive constructs" (53)—must be understood in their complexity if we were to teach writing in ways that aligned with student capabilities. The story, however, does not end there. In 2013, Mariëlle Leijten, Hayes, and their colleagues used a new technique to study process data—keystroke logging—on a professional writer working with digital sources (Leijten and Waes; Leijten et al.). In the workplace, the professional writer searched for other organizational content that could be used to suit aim, construct visual content, and expertly manage his attention and motivation. Since content reuse, aesthetic design, and self-efficacy were not part of the original model, the researchers recast the cognitive model. In 2018, psychometrician Robert J. Mislevy continued to advance research in sociocognitive modeling in order to plan instruction and design assessments (*Sociocognitive Foundations*).

Accompanying cognitive research, sociocultural studies of writing have long been appealing to writing researchers who study writing in disciplinary contexts because they have revealed how students learn disciplinary writing, the role of writing in disciplinary enculturation, and the development of expertise. Through more than fifteen naturalistic studies of writing across undergraduate years, ranging from Barbara Walvoord and Lucille McCarthy's examination of students in four disciplines to Anne Beaufort's studies of Tim, a history and engineering major ("Developmental Gains"), as well as numerous studies of students in the disciplines, we have learned students generally improve in writing abilities over their undergraduate years—especially in the areas of rate of production, understanding of how disciplinary writing is organized, and of disciplinary voice (Haswell, *Gaining*; Lavelle and Bushrow; Lavelle and Zuercher; Lavelle et al; Gilbuena et al.). Whereas students' histories of writing inform their development as writers in the disciplines (Prior; Roozen), how much knowledge they transfer from first-year writing remains disputed (Wolfe et al.). Beaufort has shown that once students arrive in the disciplines, they must acquire knowledge in the areas of genre, rhetoric, and process, in addition to subject-area expertise (Beaufort, *College Writing*; see also Artemeva and Fox; Patton; Poe et al., *Learning*). One of the most important changes in students' writing development in college is exposure to new genres and new ways of using writing (Carroll; Thaiss and Zawacki), yet certain metagenres may operate across disciplines (Carter et al.). For students' enculturation into disciplinary writing, the most important factors are effective mentoring and modeling and the opportunity to engage in authentic writing activities (Blakeslee; Paretti and Powell, *Assessment*). And finally, as disciplinary scholars such as James Clifford and George Marcus in *Writing Culture: The Poetics and Politics of Ethnography* and Dorothy Smith in *Writing the Social: Critique, Theory, and Investigations* have demonstrated, becoming attuned to the social and political dimensions of writing in their fields is very much a part of being in the profession.

Researchers today look to corpus-based studies of intertextuality, circulation, and reception for further insights into writing in the disciplines. For example, the applied linguist Ken Hyland's well-cited research includes mining thirty research papers from eight disciplines in the sciences, engineering, social sciences, and humanities, yielding 1.4 million words (195), for findings related to citation use, stance (hedges, boosters, attitude markers, and self-mention), and engagement (reader mention, directives, questions, knowledge references, and asides) (198). Through such analysis, he has been able to demonstrate that "writers in different disciplines represent themselves, their work and their readers in different ways, with those in the humanities and social sciences taking far more explicitly involved and personal positions than those in the sciences and engineering" (203). Other textual analysis studies have clear pedagogical aims. For example, in "Systematic Literature Reviews in Engineering Education and Other Developing Interdisciplinary Fields," researchers conducted a genre analysis of fourteen exemplary systematic review articles—"a collection of evolving research methodologies for synthesizing existing studies to answer a set of research questions formulated by an interdisciplinary team" (Borrego et al. 66). The goal of the researchers was not merely to describe textual features but also to introduce a methodology for conducting systematic reviews. Such scholarship continues in work by Laura Aull, whose *How Students Write: A Linguistic Analysis* has been recently published by the MLA. Informed by a linguistic analysis of school genres and student discourse, Aull provides educators with principled strategies to improve writing instruction and assignment design.

Research involving cognitive models, sociocultural studies, and corpus analysis has contributed to the body of knowledge that informs this book. Important to remember is that these techniques are extraordinarily sensitive to language use in context. If the researchers discussed here could be asked for one element that unites their efforts, they would undoubtedly agree on the following statement: Written communication is a deeply situated behavior, and to understand how that deeply human activity works, we must understand context as more than a flat surface against which writing happens. Writing—and the assessment of writing—in disciplinary contexts is complex, for it is tied to the shifting historical, political, and social landscapes of the disciplines themselves. Today, the globalization of scholarly research and shifting demographics of students (and faculty members) in the disciplines are dramatically remaking disciplinary landscapes (Englander; Englander et al.). Research on writing in the disciplines must attend to these shifting landscapes if writing assessment in the disciplines is to be fair.

Assessing Writing in the Disciplines: Accreditation and Classrooms

Without attention to today's shifting disciplinary landscapes, it is unlikely that assessment can be marshaled for practices related to fairness, identification of opportunity structures, and use of evidence-based disciplinary writing assessments. One potential barrier to this work is accreditation, which, although sensitive to local context, does not require disaggregation by student demographics.

In their present form, institution and program accreditation call for precise outcomes associated with a variety of standards, from those calling for statements of institutional mission and sound fiscal planning to those leading to advancement of student learning. Writing and communication proficiency is named by various disciplinary accreditors, including the Accreditation Board for Engineering and Technology, the Association to Advance Collegiate Schools of Business, and the Commission on Collegiate Nursing Education. As Edward White, Norbert Elliot, and Irvin Peckham point out in *Very like a Whale: The Assessment of Writing Programs*, the genre (or genres) of program assessment requires close attention to local definitions of the writing construct and the ecologies with which program assessment operates (24–33). Although localization is a powerful means to reveal how outcomes are articulated and enacted at a specific institution, localization itself may not reveal the need for additional opportunity structures because it does not demand student-level data. As a result, it is difficult to ascertain how such research is designed or its implications beyond accreditation reporting. Indeed, the chapters treating program accreditation demands in this volume are welcome exceptions.

Published program assessment reveals where these tensions may lie. For example, Chris Anson and Deanna Dannels describe how a model of disciplinary-based assessment at North Carolina State University known as "the departmental profile" (1)—a process that has corollaries at the University of Denver and the University of Massachusetts—led departments to more formative assessment practices. In previous iterations of disciplinary assessment at North Carolina State, each department "generate[d] communication outcomes specific to its discipline and to students' needs, then decide[d] how it [would] assess those outcomes and what it [would] do internally to help to achieve them" (1). In a follow-up formative approach to assessment, each department generated a self-study profile: "a profile based on internal, consultative study of a program" that "result[ed] in a report representing the department's current status: how writing and speaking are used, where, to what ends, and in what relationship to broader curricular, pedagogical, and career goals" (2). Departmental profile products included a grid showing where and how strongly various departmental outcomes were being met or textual narratives, drawn from interview data (7).

In another example, Terry Myers Zawacki and colleagues at George Mason University demonstrated how accreditation assessment elided seeing differential outcomes within the disciplines. In 2008, Zawacki and colleagues came together following the Virginia State Council of Higher Education task force, which mandated that institutions conduct value-added assessment that "indicate[d] progress, or lack thereof, as a consequence of the student's institutional experience" (qtd. in Zawacki et al. 1; for a description of state-mandated assessment and WAC at George Mason prior to 2008, see Zawacki and Gentemann). The state-mandated plan challenged the deeply disciplinary model of assessment that had been in place prior to 2008, in which outcomes were defined in the context of the discipline. For the George Mason researchers, the challenge was to "demonstrate that our writing instruction itself was adding value to students' overall educational experience—while still retaining the discipline-focused and workshop-based assessment process" they had been using for the last six years (1). To satisfy the state council, they developed "a pool of commonly used criteria" from which instructors could select to assess writing (6).

Unlike accreditation assessment, classroom assessment is typically driven by teacher or local concerns and, thus, potentially more sensitive to questions of fairness. For instance, in "Outcomes Assessment of Case-Based Writing Exercises in a Veterinary Clinical Pathology Course," Leslie Sharkey and colleagues compared traditional multiple-choice versus free-response case-based assessments "to predict future academic performance and to determine if the perceived value of the case-based exercises persists through the curriculum" (396). They found that "after holding multiple-choice scores constant, better performance on case-based free-response exercises led to higher GPA and better class rank in the second and third years and better class rank in the fourth year" (396). Moreover, they found that even two years later students valued the writing exercises and found them "an efficient use of their time" (396).

In the *Journal of Engineering Education*, Heidi A. Diefes-Dux and colleagues set out to "develop a framework to analyze instructor feedback on team responses to open-ended mathematical modeling problems and to demonstrate the use of the framework in investigating formative assessment systems" (375). Their intent was to understand patterns in feedback and "the impact of feedback on student performance and learning" (378). Drawing on rubric responses by ten graduate teaching assistants (GTAs) in a first-year engineering course, they yielded 541 feedback comments on the fifty pieces of student work. They then coded the data by *form* and *substance*. Four codes for *form* feedback included prompt change through questioning, prompt change through open suggestions, prompt change through direct suggestions, and not to prompt change (389). They concluded that their framework was generalizable under certain conditions. For *form* comments, the scheme is "generalizable to a much broader range of open-ended work including the design of models and objects, laboratory reports, and writing assignments" (399). For *substance* comments, the scheme is "generalizable to any mathematical modeling or design or other type of problem solving episode where students need to develop a model and describe their model and reasoning so that someone else can understand their work enough to apply, replicate, or modify it" (399). Regarding the impact of feedback from GTAs on student work, the results were inconclusive, leading to the conclusion that "such research will need to focus on whether GTAs interpret students' work correctly (understand the students' models and respond appropriately) and whether or not the GTAs' comments prompt the change they seek in student work" (400).

What we can take from the discussion on assessment research on writing in the disciplines is not just that assessment occurs for different purposes and audiences but that researchers go about assessment research with the intent of improving learning and teaching in the disciplines, not merely to fulfill an administrative demand. Moreover, the systematic approaches of the researchers reveal that great care is taken to collect evidence related to validity, reliability, and fairness. Such assessment research requires disciplinary expertise, for, as Mislevy reminds us in this collection, "writing assessment in the professions requires understanding the deep interconnections among skills, knowledge, identities, values, and the very epistemology of the domain."

Yet, unlike the cases offered throughout this collection that attend to difference, such as Ruth Osorio's work on disability, instruction is often advanced without attention to impact on diverse students. As a result, it becomes difficult to surface unequal outcomes for students from underrepresented groups or to determine how institutional structures might be altered to advance opportunity for more students. More must be done.

Fairness: Opportunity in Disciplinary Writing Assessment

Within the fields of educational measurement and writing assessment, there has been a renewed interest in questions of fairness, a point made apparent in the *Standards for Educational and Psychological Testing*, a jointly published set of standards for the American Educational Research Association, the American Psychological Association, and the National Council on Measurement in Education. The 2014 revision to the *Standards* made fairness an evidentiary category on par with reliability and validity. Although discussion about the impact of test score use had circulated in the measurement community since the 1950s, the *Standards* had traditionally sidestepped the debate about social impact and the professional responsibility of test designers that played out in measurement journal articles. As a result, design and social impact resided on opposite poles; if a test was designed to predict equally for all subgroups, then it was fair; social impact was beyond the duty of those involved in test design.

Today, we find a number of venues in which researchers are working through questions about fairness in writing assessment. One thread—access—looks to universal design (Mislevy and Haertel). Other threads—interpretation and impact—look to sociocognitive theories (Mislevy, *Sociocognitive Foundations*) and legal studies (Poe et al., "Legal"). For example, in research that I conducted with colleagues (Poe et al., "Legal"; Poe and Cogan, Jr.), we were interested in looking beyond the immediate design or effects of placement testing to downstream effects on graduation. To do so, we drew on legal scholarship related to disparate impact—"facially neutral policies that are not intended to discriminate based on race, color, or national origin, but do have an unjustified, adverse disparate impact on students based on race, color, or national origin" (United States, Dept. of Education, *Dear Colleague* 8). By connecting placement testing results to subsequent graduation rates for populations of students—for example, African American students placed in basic writing—we were able to determine that the placement resulted in an undue harm to those students, because their graduation rates were lower than similarly admitted students who had not been placed into basic writing.

As a result of the work that has been done on the concept of *fairness* in writing assessment recently, one definition that has arisen is that offered by Elliot: "In teaching and assessing writing, fairness may be defined as the identification of opportunity structures created through maximum representation of varied writing constructs as they are used in various disciplinary settings" ("Theory"). Elliot's definition is valuable because it draws attention to four features of fair assessment: defining the construct of writing; ensuring there are multiple instances of writing to be assessed; ensuring the construct is sufficiently broad to obtain a meaningful measurement of writing; and identifying teaching support, institutional resources, and structures that might complement assessment decisions.

In comparison to research on universal design and impact, Elliot's work illustrates the range of work on fairness. As Anne Ruggles Gere observes in her foreword to this volume, although fairness seems easy to define, its meaning is inflected with concepts like *justice* and *equity*. As such, it becomes quickly evident that questions of fairness do not resolve into simplistic answers. Tropes of fairness fall along a continuum from the technical (fairness as absence of bias) to the philosophical (fairness as justice). Each is deserving of our attention as our scholarship becomes increasingly alert to difference, and each is needed if we are to create inclusive ways of teaching and assessing writing.

In taking an expansive view of writing research in the disciplines and the ways it is assessed, researchers can better see how articulations of fairness in assessing disciplinary writing are similar to those in writing studies and educational measurement. For example, what demographic categories are most meaningful to interpret data obtained at a particular site? Or, what institutional structures influence the results that we are seeing in assessment outcomes, and what structures are or are not changeable to provide opportunities to a greater number of students? Moreover, drawing attention to disciplinary writing assessment, it should be noted that in disciplinary environments, foundational issues surrounding collaboration, access, cultural responsiveness, and justice are related to improving student outcomes. The identification of outcomes is, in fact, an illustration of an articulation of fairness in the curriculum.

As the authors in this volume realize, the identification of outcomes may indeed be an instance of the obsession in the United States with standardization and accountability. But this identification of goals for learning may also be an occasion for an articulation of fairness in the curriculum. Further, the fulfillment of these outcomes is evidence of the creation of opportunity through education. Here, then, is that which has been too often lacking: the aim of fairness that unifies our efforts to advance each student so that equality of opportunity is universally achieved.

As readers engage the seventeen essays in this volume, they will be taken with the hopeful perspective of each author. Each imagined that the improvement of outcomes related to student learning was inextricably related to writing in the disciplines, assessment of that writing, and the advancement of fairness. As it is often implied in this volume, we are at a kairotic moment in education in general and in writing studies in particular: in the fullness of time, now is the moment for actions that will accompany the dawn of a new era in education. If this is true, then putting students at the center of our efforts is, as the authors in this book well know, a good place to begin.

A Disability-as-Insight Approach to Multimodal Assessment

Ruth Osorio

Perspective

Students with disabilities face numerous daunting obstacles in obtaining college degrees. Writing instructors have thus turned to the transdisciplinary field of disability studies for guidance on how to make their classrooms more accessible for disabled students. Disability studies frames disability as a source of insight, and in this chapter I propose a disability-as-insight approach to multimodal assessment. Disability as insight focuses attention on how composers of multimodal texts leverage accessibility and difference to ethical and persuasive ends. Through a disability-as-insight approach to multimodal assessment, students and faculty members encounter multiple opportunities to engage with disability in broad and powerful ways through instruction, assessment, and reflection—creating more accessible classrooms, texts, and futures.

Introduction

According to the National Center for Education Statistics, nearly twenty percent of undergraduate students report having a disability ("Fast Facts")—and due to difficulties in obtaining official diagnoses and the stigma surrounding disability, disability studies scholars imagine that number is higher (Dolmage, *Academic Ableism* 22). Sixty percent of high school students with disabilities enter higher education. And yet, despite the high number of disabled students entering higher education, and despite federal laws asserting the right of disabled students to attend college, nearly two-thirds of disabled college students will not graduate within six years (s. smith). A 2012 study conducted by Rankin and Associates may explain why: 33.7 percent of college students with disabilities in their study had experienced "exclusionary, intimidating, offensive, or hostile experiences on campus, compared to only 17.1 percent of nondisabled students" (qtd. in Harbour and Greenberg 5). Higher education seems to be sending a loud message to disabled college students: you are not welcome here.

As these numbers show, if you teach in higher education in the United States, chances are you have at least one student with a disability in your course. Furthermore, our disabled students face daunting barriers in their pursuit of college degrees. In response to structural and cultural barriers disabled students face, assessment scholars and creators have paid increasingly close attention to designing fair writing assessments that account for students' diverse ways of movement, thought, and expression (White et al., *Very* 75–76). As scholar-teachers increasingly recognize disability's centrality in the writing process, many have proposed Universal Design for Learning (UDL) as a framework for designing writing assessments with disability in mind (Cohen et al.; Elliot; Mislevy et al., "Design"). Universal Design for Learning provides the tools to "structure the design of the learning environment to consider from the outset the tremendous variability of individuals in a given classroom," often leading to robust options for student engagement, representation, and expression (Cohen et al. 131). As signaled by its inclusion in the 2014 *Standards for Educational and Psychological Testing*, UDL has been widely embraced as a tool to ensure fairness in assessment. Given the barriers faced by students with disabilities in higher education, the push for faculty and administrators to design assessments that aim to affirm student difference rather than pathologize it is a welcome one.

This chapter extends conversations about accessibility, disability, and writing assessment by imagining a disability studies approach to multimodal assessment. The transdisciplinary field of disability studies envisions disability not as an individual deficit or embodied failure but rather explores the political, social, and cultural dimensions of disability (Linton 518). Writing instructors increasingly incorporate disability studies in their pedagogy to make space for students who move, communicate, and process information in nonnormative ways (Price; Yergeau et al.; Janine Butler, "Where" and "Embodied Captions"; Walters; Brueggemann; Brueggemann et al.). I further this conversation by mapping the prominent concept in disability studies of disability as insight onto conversations about multimodal assessment. A disability studies approach to teaching and assessing multimodal projects, I argue, can encourage disabled and nondisabled students to tap into disability as a source of wisdom and possibility. Such a powerful shift can affirm the value of disabled perspectives—an affirmation desperately needed in higher education. Furthermore, disability as insight invites students to consider the ethical, material, and aesthetic dimensions of accessibility—leading to, ideally, arguments that are more accessible for diverse audiences and more rhetorically powerful.

I make this argument by first providing an overview of disability studies as a theoretical framework. In this section, I focus on the concept of disability as insight, which positions disability as a powerful inventional source for meaning making. I follow that section by imagining a disability studies approach to multimodal assessment. Focusing on assessment at the classroom level, I envision assessment as a practice of recursive, collaborative, and ongoing feedback: "the kind of assessment that can be used as a part of instruction to support and enhance learning" (Shepard, "Role" 4). I outline five principles of a disability-as-insight approach to multimodal assessment, illustrating how disability as insight can spark meaningful conversations about the rhetorical dimensions of multimodality, accessibility, and embodied difference. Throughout the essay, I honor the different preferences within the disability community by alternating between language that is person-first (students with disabilities) and identity-first (disabled students) (Liebowitz).

Disability as Insight: A Theoretical and Activist Framework

Disability studies grew from disability activism, both emerging in response to the centuries of exclusion of disabled people from higher education and broader society. In 1976, the activist group the Union of the Physically Impaired against Segregation introduced the social model of disability to discourse, describing disability not as a problem with the individual's body but with society's ableist attitudes (*Fundamental Principles*). The social model has been taken up (and revised, critiqued, affirmed, and adapted) in the field of disability studies, which rejects the idea that disability is a failure of the body or mind or both. As Alison Kafer writes in her book *Feminist, Queer, Crip*, "the problem of disability no longer resides in the minds or bodies of individuals but in built environments and social patterns that exclude or stigmatize particular kinds of bodies, minds, and ways of being" (6).

A central project of disability studies, then, is to destigmatize disability. In the words of Simi Linton, disability studies provides analytic frameworks to "examine how disability as a category was created to serve certain ends" and, significantly, to establish a political objective "to weave disabled people back into the fabric of society, thread by thread, theory by theory" (518). Instead of being a source of shame, within a disability studies perspective, disability is a source of insight. After all, moving through the world with a nonnormative bodymind in a world built for the (ever elusive) normative bodymind often cultivates flexible, creative, and embodied rhetorical movement (Dolmage, *Disability* 160). As Rosemarie Garland-Thomson argues, disability is "a potentially generative resource rather than unequivocally restrictive liability" (341).

Writing studies scholars have theorized how disability as insight can shape pedagogical practices. For instance, Brenda Jo Brueggemann centers disability in her writing classes, even classes not focused thematically on disability, because "disability enables insight—critical, experiential, cognitive, sensory, and pedagogical insight" (795). Brueggemann and others are careful not to provide a checklist of specific pedagogical practices, fearful that prescriptive checklists reduce disability to a static identity and life experience. Rather, scholars invested in disability and writing studies push teachers to see disability as "a central, critical and creative lens for students as well as teachers" (Wood et al. 148). Disability as insight has prompted writing instructors to rethink common pedagogical practices, transforming how they approach classroom policies, activities, and assignments (Brueggemann et al.; Dunn and Dunn De Mers; Price). As our pedagogical practices evolve to embrace disability as insight, our assessment practices must as well.

Disability-as-Insight Principles for Multimodal Assessment

Disability studies aims to remake the world to embrace the diverse ways people move, communicate, and process information—a disability-as-insight approach to assessment, then, would encourage students and faculty members to tap into disability as a source for rhetorical invention. Similarly, disability as insight rejects the deficit model that reduces bodies, minds, and texts to a measure of correctness. I see disability as insight as a path that merges fairness—designing assessments that allow for diverse and flexible methods for achieving the primary goals of an assignment—and social justice. As Mya Poe and Asao B. Inoue argue, fairness and social justice "are always ongoing, mutually beneficial projects, not competing traditions" (123). Social justice emphasizes "creating equitable relationships, distribution of resources, and decision-making among these and other communities" in writing assessment, striving for the advancement of "opportunity for all" (Poe et al., "End" 11, 15). As my analysis below illustrates, disability as insight powerfully brings together fairness and social justice. Through a disability-as-insight approach, assignments are designed to allow for diverse and divergent ways of making meaning (fairness) and to foster an equitable learning community devoted to relational learning across difference (social justice).

As a central construct, disability as insight values accessibility as an ethical stance, a rhetorical analysis, and a design framework. In this section, I imagine how disability as insight can transform an always evolving, and often contested, site of assessment: multimodal composition. I outline five principles of disability as insight—not an exhaustive list, of course, as accessibility, disability, and difference are fluid, impossible to categorize into objective identities or strategies. Furthermore, disability as insight builds on moves already considered best practices in the field of writing assessment, such as the focus on process and formative assessment. Disability as insight does not reinvent the wheel, but rather, reorients it to emphasize embodied difference and accessibility as critical components to multimodal design assessment.

Principle 1: Disability as Insight Envisions Multimodal Assessment as a Site of Possibility

Traci Fordham and Hillory Oakes assert, "Multimodal communication environments, by definition, require broader, more integrated epistemologies: one must be able to entertain multiple perspectives and multiple strategies for communication" (315). Multimodality and disability both embrace broadness and multiplicity, making them potentially powerful constituents in a disability-as-insight approach to assessment. Despite the excitement surrounding multimodal composition in writing studies, many scholar-teachers feel uncomfortable assessing multimodal projects—and a significant number avoid teaching multimodal instruction completely because of that discomfort (Murray et al.). Scholar-teachers ask, do we assess multimodal projects using the same framework we do for print projects (Borton and Huot; Murray et al.), or do we, in the words of Kathleen Blake Yancey, "invent a language that allows us to speak to these new values" of multimodal composition ("Looking" 89)?

In ongoing conversations about multimodal assessment, concerns about fairness, social justice, and embodiment are often overlooked. Poe observes this discrepancy, asserting that "research on digital writing assessment has conventionally adopted a color-blind, homogenizing approach" and thus has ignored the "impact of [dominant models of multimodal] assessments on students of color, working class students, and students with disabilities" ("Making"). Therefore, we need a new way of approaching and assessing multimodal composition, one that reflects writing studies' investment in the matrices of power in both multimodal composition and rhetorical concepts. In his essay in this collection, Carl Whithaus proposes focusing on fairness in developing a conceptual framework for assessing student work composed in multiple environments. I agree, and I further assert that disability as insight's commitment to fairness and social justice can transform multimodal assessment.

By naming disability as insight as a value of multimodal composition, teachers can emphasize the political, ethical, and embodied nature of multimodal texts. Multimodal composing is not a neutral act: it often embodies the assumptions, biases, and values of the composer—and consequently, very often, multimodal texts are inaccessible to people with different disabilities (Ellis and Kent 77). As Stephanie Kerschbaum observes, "[M]any multimodal texts exclude disabled audiences because they are not commensurable across multiple modes, thus rendering the text inaccessible." A focus on disability as insight when teaching multimodal composition underscores the ethical dimensions of multimodal composing. Students examine how whole groups of people are left out of vital avenues for communication: who is excluded from audio texts without captions, from visual projects that lack image descriptions and alt text? Instead of focusing on the presence of rhetorical concepts in isolation, a disability-as-insight approach to multimodal assessment asks students to consider diverse audiences and to imagine, as Kerschbaum proposes, "ways that information can be available in multiple modes, and be flexible and adaptable within a variety of situations for a variety of users." Thus, disability as insight provides tools for not just faculty members but also students to incorporate accessibility and UDL into their projects, creating a new generation of multimodal composers invested in accessible, ethical design.

Principle 2: Disability as Insight Positions Accessibility as a Rhetorical Asset

Disability studies scholar-teachers argue that, in addition to serving an ethical imperative, accessibility can be a rhetorical asset. Indeed, as composers reflect on the generative possibilities of disability, they can sharpen their awareness of purpose, situation, and audience. Significantly, too, accessibility is inherently multimodal, with composers using visuals to describe sound and sound and text to describe visuals. Janine Butler asserts, "synchronizing multiple modes—visual, digital, gestural, spatial, aural, linguistic—strengthens the aesthetic and rhetorical message of a composition and increases the chances of meaning being accessed through different modes" ("Where"). Access, aesthetics, and argument are thus interconnected. Just as multimodality contains the risk of hostility toward disabled audiences, as Kerschbaum notes, it also contains possibilities for richer, more creative forms of access.

Through a disability-as-insight approach to multimodal composition, teachers evaluate multimodal projects by how fully and richly accessible they are. Sean Zdenek's and Janine Butler's work on captioning illustrates the rhetorical possibilities of integrating accessibility. Zdenek argues that, in addition to providing a critical accessibility function, "captioning [is] a rhetorical and interpretative practice" (Butler, "Embodied Captions"). Composers can write—and even design, as Butler argues—captions that amplify the meaning of audio material. By designing captions, multimodal projects can be accessible and more visually persuasive for hearing and nonhearing audiences (Butler, "Where" and "Embodied

Captions"). Accessibility is not a separate category but, rather, one interconnected with the multimodal argument, style, and delivery. In this framework, then, a disability-as-insight approach to multimodal assessment does not distract from but instead amplifies the other constructs multimodal scholar-teachers have named before, such as rhetorical sensitivity (Shipka), metaphor and metonymy (Sorapure), and standard rhetorical concepts (Borton and Huot; Murray et al.). Assessing multimodal projects through a disability-as-insight lens allows faculty members to value equally the ethical, embodied, aesthetic, and rhetorical dimensions of a project.

Principle 3: Disability as Insight Integrates Ongoing, Recursive Feedback throughout the Semester

Disability as insight, then, broadens our conception of accessibility, and thus, our approach to assessing accessibility in a multimodal text. A disability-as-insight approach to multimodal assessment must move beyond simple checklists that ensure the presence of accessibility features without evaluating the quality or rhetorical implementation of those features. This conceptualization poses a challenge, of course, as there is no singular, universal, correct approach to accessibility. Disability is dynamic and fluid, therefore there is no universal, objective approach to access; as Elizabeth Brewer, Cynthia Selfe, and Melanie Yergeau assert, "access is a moving target" (151). What provides access to one person may preclude it for another—for instance, visually designed captions for people with hearing disabilities may not be accessible for someone with a visual disability—and a disabled person's needs may change over time. Since there is no one correct way to do accessibility, a disability-as-insight approach to assessment refuses a static, summative, objective assessment framework. Rather, a disability-as-insight approach to assessing multimodality requires ongoing and recursive learning, feedback, and reflection.

As a field, writing studies largely embraces the weaving multiple checkpoints for feedback and revision through the semester; disability as insight extends this practice by using ongoing, recursive feedback as opportunities for the ethical, social, and political development of students. Here, disability as insight echoes John Pryor and Barbara Crossouard's conception of divergent formative assessment, "an on-going dialogue between and amongst learners and teachers where learners initiate as well as respond, ask questions as well reply" (5). Pryor and Crossouard describe divergent formative assessment as a site of identity construction, and thus, an opening for examining issues of power, agency, and identity (9). Disability as insight similarly engages with social, collaborative forms of assessment as strategies to bolster not only rhetorical awareness but also disability awareness. We are asking students to push aside dominant notions of disability—that disability is a deficit, an error in need of a cure, charity, or social isolation—and to approach disability as a source of insight (Dolmage, *Disability* 34–37). Undoing dominant ideologies takes time, practice, and reflection, and therefore, a disability-as-insight approach to assessment does so as well.

Janine Butler provides a model for ongoing, recursive feedback in her article "Embodied Captions in Multimodal Pedagogies," which analyzes her experience teaching captioning in a first-year writing course. From the beginning of the semester, she shares her commitment to accessibility and discusses the pedagogical insight gained from her identity as a Deaf woman. Disability as insight is woven throughout the semester's activities, assignments, and assessments in Butler's course. During a module on video arguments, students craft creative captions; this work is done in class over multiple class periods, so she and the students "could work through the new experience of using video captioning technologies together." Finally, students complete their own self-assessments in the form of reflective letters, explaining their design choices and describing their affective and embodied responses to the captioning work. Captioning is a socially situated, contextually rich writing task—one that calls for the sociocognitive approach to assessment as outlined by Robert J. Mislevy in his essay in this volume. Butler's approach illustrates the importance of ongoing, recursive instruction, feedback, and reflection. Since captioning was new to all her students, they needed constant feedback and opportunities to assess, reflect, and revise not only their projects but also their overall thinking about deafness, disability, and captions.

Principle 4: Disability as Insight Embraces the Visibility of Difference

Within a disability-as-insight model, the goal of accessibility isn't to remove the traces of disability in the writing processes or products. Rather, disability as insight embraces the visibility and presence of difference. Melanie Yergeau discusses the stakes of assessing writing based on normative ideas of correctness, asking:

> *What makes good writing, and who/what makes it so?* I wonder how composing the standard, white, male, neurotypical essay affects autistic writers: what do they have to give up in order to write—or try to write—in this manner? In what ways does the academy devalue their ways of knowing, thinking, and making sense of the world?

Plenty of scholar-teachers have constructed sharp critiques of models of assessment that prioritize an elusive concept of "correctness" (Alexander; Poe and

Inoue; Poe et al., "End"). Yergeau extends these by highlighting the detrimental impact measurements of good writing have on autistic writers, who feel as though they have to erase signs of autism in college writing. A disability-as-insight approach to assessment, then, invites disabled students to incorporate nonnormative forms of expression into their projects—in this framework, stimming, lisping, signing, and limping communicate meaning rather than error.

Difference can be made visible in multimodal projects in a variety of enriching ways. Shannon Walters rejects the notion that multimodal projects should be evaluated based on wholeness. She examines a multimodal text that, instead of "editing out the ruptures and discontinuities . . . in favor of wholeness and coherence," emphasizes the ruptures, discontinuities, and difficulties of collaborating across disabled and nondisabled identities. She calls for writing teachers to question normative concepts of coherence, collaboration, and process, and thus question assessment frameworks that strive to erase the presence of disability. In this way, disability as insight reflects Jonathan Alexander's vision for queering writing assessment. Alexander invites writing faculty members to "see our students' many language and writing differences and experiences as a powerful asset, not a deviation from the norm" in their approach to assessment (205). Disability as insight similarly embraces the presence of difference—in terms of disability, of course, but also other markers of identity like gender, race, sexuality, language—as powerful rhetorical assets for multimodal argumentation. Thus, instructors must develop assessment strategies for interpreting signs of difference as sites of meaning making.

Principle 5: Disability as Insight Values Reflective Models of Assessment

There is no one right way to enact accessibility, disability, or difference in a text; therefore, there can be no singular rubric to objectively evaluate how a student integrates disability into a multimodal project. Reflective writing, then, provides key insights into how students think through the rhetorical possibilities of disability in their writing processes and products. For Jody Shipka, students' discussions of "their writerly choices [and the] visual, material, and technological aspects of their texts and practices" guide her "generous reading" of student multimodal texts, allowing her to focus on the intentions behind students' choices (W355). Shipka argues that reflective writing can activate what Anne Wysocki calls "generous reading," approaching "different-looking texts with the assumption not that mistakes were made but that choices were made and are being tried out and on" (qtd. in Shipka W353). Since the presence of disability is often coded as mistake or error, student reflective writing provides essential space for students to explain innovative accessibility features and nonnormative expressions as rhetorical choices.

Through a disability-as-insight approach, reflection becomes a space for students to not only justify their rhetorical moves but also grapple with their embodied responses to the text, explain the risks they took to make disability present, and consider ethical and rhetorical concerns about accessibility. Steph Ceraso asks students to "address how their thoughts and actions relate to a constellation of materials, people, technologies, knowledge, environments, and more" in their reflective writing for their embodied sonic project—an auditory project that invites deaf, hearing, and hard of hearing students to consider sound as a multisensory, whole-bodied experience (55). With their projects, students submit an artist statement, in which they reflect on how they attended to accessibility in the creation and implementation of the project as well as on their own embodied relation to the text (54). Ceraso's artist statement emphasizes the importance of accessibility in students' projects, as they are prompted to assess their own implementation of disability as insight in their texts. Importantly, Ceraso's expansive notion of embodied listening, alongside Janine Butler's group captioning activity, demonstrates that students do not need to identify as disabled in order to successfully integrate disability as insight into their multimodal projects. In each study, both disabled and nondisabled students demonstrated richer understandings of disability, multimodality, and access in their reflective writings. Through a disability-as-insight approach, then, reflection becomes not just a space for students to justify their rhetorical choices but also one where they grapple with their embodied responses to the text, explain the risks they took to make disability present, and consider ethical and rhetorical concerns about accessibility.

Conclusion

Discussing the value of integrating disability into writing classrooms across disciplines, Tara Wood and colleagues ask,

> In what ways should and could disability actually be central and centered in all classrooms? How does disability better help us to understand the learning process and the writing process? Disability sharpens our focus on important concepts including adaptation, creativity, community, interdependency, technological ingenuity and modal fluency. Could such a focus replace traditional pedagogical ideals like correctness, the autonomous writer, bootstrapping, and reverence for final drafts? (148)

I grapple with these questions throughout this essay, as I imagine what a disability-as-insight approach to multimodal assessment could look like. Following their lead, I do not prescribe a universal, objective rubric but rather outline five potential principles of a disability-as-insight framework for assessment. Though I focus on the principles of disability as insight in the classroom setting, I believe they can also be used as starting points for writing program administrators to critically reflect on how they position disability, accessibility, and difference in their writing assessment. One model for a disability-as-insight approach to writing program administration is that of the University of Pennsylvania's Critical Writing Program, an award-winning writing program that embraces "the importance of recognizing differences, particularly in the area of neurodiversity" (Ross and Browning).

The work of critically evaluating our classroom and programmatic assessment practices—and which students they serve and which they don't—offers a small yet potentially significant step toward creating a culture of access throughout higher education. Disabled students face numerous barriers that make higher education appear hostile to disability. As teachers, we can ask ourselves, How can we each remake our classroom to welcome disabled students? In her examinations of race and disability in the academy, Christina V. Cedillo calls for academics to "move beyond acknowledging bodily diversity and its value as mere trademark [and to instead become] active makers of spaces that accommodate diverse experiences." We may not be able to solve all the problems students with disabilities face in higher education. But as writing faculty embedded in departments across institutions of higher education, we can become "active makers of spaces that accommodate diverse experiences" by transforming our assessment practices. A disability-as-insight approach can make assessment less scary for disabled students and can make the experience of making knowledge and meaning across difference richer for all students.

Fairness as Pedagogy:
Uniformity, Transparency, and Equity through Trajectory-Based Responses to Writing in Hawai'i

Brooke A. Carlson and Cari Ryan

Perspective

Influenced by our institution's Native Hawaiian–serving and Marianist mission to educate for justice, service, and peace, we share our postcolonial pedagogy for teaching and assessing writing. To this end, we build our pedagogy on three trajectories: mobile learning, writing tasks, and rubrics. Each trajectory is aimed at increasing localization, knowledge transfer, and fairness. Because we believe our students construct knowing by writing, our creation of a digital learning space for instruction and assessment has allowed us to support equitable opportunity structures that cultivate dynamic action.

Introduction

At Chaminade University of Honolulu, culturally responsive assessment is necessary to support retention and successes of Native Hawaiian and Pacific Islander students and Chaminade's Native Hawaiian values. Chaminade University is a Native Hawaiian–serving institution, where most students are women, first-generation college students, and people of color and largely come from lower socioeconomic groups, with ninety-eight percent of students receiving some form of financial aid. To be identified as a Native Hawaiian–serving institution requires that ten percent of the university's population be Native Hawaiian, and such a designation allows for funding from the United States federal government under Title III of the Higher Education Act of 1965. Chaminade currently has a Title III grant that funds many efforts across campus toward retention of Native Hawaiian students. Chaminade is also a Catholic university in the Marianist tradition, which means the mission of the school includes a focus on social justice, commitment to change and adaptation, belief in service, and strengthening of community.

Demographically, Chaminade is a small, private, not-for-profit, master's level university that provides over twenty-three undergraduate and seven graduate programs to almost 2,500 students with ninety-one full-time faculty members. Its Carnegie classification is master's university, and the school is accredited through the Western Association of Schools and Colleges Senior College and University Commission. More than one-third of the students identify themselves as Asian, about a quarter identify as Native Hawaiian or Pacific Islander, and the rest identify as white, Hispanic, African American, or other ethnicity or ethnicities (*Carnegie*). Our mission is reflective of such diversity.

Our students at Chaminade do not arrive at the university with a great deal of knowledge or practice for postsecondary reading and writing. Most of our students have limited to no experience with traditional, individual workshopping as part of the writing process, and know academic writing in its more restricted forms, such as the five-paragraph essay. Metacognition and reflection are usually not part of their educational experience. Hawaiʻi is a diverse linguistic space featuring English, Pidgin (Hawaiʻi Creole), Hawaiian, Tagalog, Ilocano, Japanese, Spanish, Chinese, and Korean. Many of our students speak English as a second language, if not a third. Writing in high school is taught primarily through the reading of literature, which means students are accustomed to repurposing literary analysis as academic writing. Rhetorical voice, rhetorical appeals, and critical thinking are challenging for many of our students who come from communities and cultures where a communal voice of elders is privileged over the individual. Indeed, writing as an individual practice challenges our students, who have generally worked and learned together in collaborative and community efforts.

Although some of these missing experiences may be cultural, others may be related to restrictive standards. There is a lack of emphasis, for example, in the Hawaiʻi State Common Core Standards for Language Arts, for grades 11–12, in terms of metacognition and reflection. The standards pertaining to writing emphasize the composition of arguments, informative or explanatory texts, and narratives. Reflection is largely viewed as a narrative tool, and not one for assessment or metacognition (*Common Core*). Within this cultural and educational context, our entering first-year college students generally enter the space of postsecondary composition as true novices. In this new space, our students are asked to be more analytic than informational and to support their critical thinking with secondary sources. They are asked to be metacognitive in their practice and reflective in their approaches. In this new space, students are limited by their lack of prior knowledge about and experience with writing practice.

Knowledge of our students and the experiences and values they bring with them into our classrooms allows faculty and staff members to create a more just, equitable, and effective learning environment. The recent life span movement suggests the complexity of teaching writing requires greater pedagogical clarity and depth. Charles Bazerman and colleagues, for example, caution us that "high-stakes decisions about curriculum, instruction, and assessment are often made in unsystematic ways that may fail to support the development they are intended to facilitate" ("Taking" 353). It is important to acknowledge Hawaiʻi's colonial history and the unique dynamics of students and faculty at a small, private university located on a Pacific island thousands of miles from the mainland.

Our work in this essay moves in the direction of a postcolonial systematic structure. Teaching composition in the middle of the Pacific today means asking how we can help students transfer knowledge and practice in writing so they can develop ways to take these skills along with them across both their college experience and careers. We seek ways to generalize the skills we teach in composition so our students are capable of repurposing these skills as a flexible and effective knowledge and writing practice. These writing skills are critical not only to college and jobs but also to twenty-first-century life. We have renewed interest in focusing on the importance of academic reading, thinking, and writing in the classroom; engaging students with the knowledge they already bring into it; and, in so doing, improving our composition pedagogy to better account for a postcolonial world.

Justice and Postcolonial Pedagogy

Our writing pedagogy is ground in notions of social justice, built on an understanding of social structure and the power relations between individuals. We have been influenced by the work of Michael Reisch, John Rawls, Iris Marion Young, Norbert Elliot ("Theory"), Mya Poe (Poe et al., "Legal"; Poe and Inoue, "Toward"), and Asao B. Inoue ("Community-Based Assessment"). These are foundational texts for postcolonial pedagogy which, following David Huddart, we take as "the connection between World Englishes and hegemony." In examining this connection, Huddart asserts we must become "interested in the reception of English; we become interested in audiences, and what they do with the culture around them" (95). In a postcolonial approach for teaching writing, this interest in culture and audience can be associated at the granular level with fairness as a robust construct representation. As Elliot argues in "A Theory of Ethics for Writing Assessment," fairness is the result of opportunity structures created through maximum construct representations. In practice, this interpretation of fairness means that the construct of writing—its genres; its cognitive, interpersonal, and intrapersonal domains; its power to respond to and shape audiences—is to be strongly represented in assignments. In this way, writing instruction is not yet another form of linguistic imperialism but, rather, a way for our students to shape knowledge. Robust curricular construct representation is therefore agentic.

In particular, mobile learning in today's twenty-first-century classroom allows faculty members new opportunity structures that support agentic, collaborative, and communal learning. We argue for the use of the learning management system (LMS) and social media platforms that bolster community and allow for transparency in writing. At the same time, these platforms create spaces of greater equity and rely on students' prior knowledge in an increasingly digital world. As Douglas M. Walls and Stephanie Vie make clear in their edited collection *Social Writing / Social Media: Publics, Presentations, and Pedagogies*, scholarship on writing in digital environments is yielding valuable information that attends to the ways public authors engage in and across networked social writing platforms to achieve their goals.

Scaffolding writing through clear writing tasks in these networked environments furthers the instruction of writing as a process. This scaffolding is best achieved through what Doug Baldwin calls constructed response tasks that require a writer to provide a structured response rather than write to a prompt. Designed to invoke audience and context, such tasks invite very specific rhetorical moves that can yield actionable feedback for students.

Rubrics accompanying these tasks, when used intentionally in conjunction with clear tasks, can create opportunity structures of equity and fairness. We acknowledge, with Bob Broad, that rubrics may be "at odds with our ethical, pedagogical, and political commitments" (2), and we concede that when misused by others for punitive purposes they may not necessarily promote fairness and equity. In our efforts, however, we use them as tools to support fairness and equity. Here, we follow Ellen Cushman, who proposes that the praxis of assessment can benefit by participatory action, as students, teachers, and designers collaborate to create rubrics that best represent generic conventions. As described by Don J. Kraemer in "The Good, the Right, and the Decent: Ethical Dispositions, the Moral Viewpoint, and Just Pedagogy," we promote fairness as pedagogy through task-specific rubrics designed to capture the genre at hand rather than through potentially unfocused narrative responses to student writing. Analytic rubrics provide faculty members with transparent and more focused responses to students' prior knowledge and writing. Instructors can use rubrics the better to focus both directions within tasks and feedback for student improvement. Y. Malini Reddy and Heidi Andrade argue a student-centered approach to assessment is created when rubrics are used not only to grade students' work but also to provide them with clear expectations on the quality of the work and to facilitate a student's own judgment and revisions of that same work. Students, in return, will receive more just, equitable, and instructive responses to their work: not merely a score or label, but clear feedback. When rubrics are used with backward course redesign, universal design for learning, and scaffolding tasks, pedagogy can become more uniform and transparent. Such student-centered, active, and dynamic learning pedagogy strengthens place-based and culturally responsive education at Chaminade, and more effectively serves our entering Hawaiian and Pacific students.

At its broadest, the field of rhetoric and composition has been influenced by a number of key shifts, starting with the application of linguistics in the 1950s. In the 1960s and '70s, writing as a process became central to the teaching of writing. This privileging of process led to the establishment of writing programs in the 1980s and '90s. It is not coincidental that during this period postcolonial studies emerged. As Simon During notes, literary criticism turned to thinking about literature as "a vehicle of cultural-political identities, or as a resistance to ideology, or, more neutrally, as articulated into broader signifying or social structures" (498). Although space does not allow us to recount the history of postcolonial theory in writing studies, readers can find no better guide than *Crossing Borderlands: Composition and Postcolonial Studies* by Andrea A. Lunsford and Lahoucine Ouzgane.

In this reconceptualization of the relation between knowledge and power in higher education in the United States, this concentration on process resulted in a divisional split between English literature as a discipline and writing studies as its own area of study. The study of English literature was affixed to English departments and the literary canon, whereas writing studies produced writing centers, composition faculty (often viewed as deserving of a lesser status than those who taught and wrote about literature), and new writing foci, along with writing requirements in new general education curricula. This important history is outlined in the introduction of Judith H. Anderson and Christine R. Farris's collection, *Integrating Literature and Writing Instruction*.

In the last five years, we have seen yet another evolution in writing studies—this time, with attention to genre itself and a renewed interest in the expansion of scholarship on how, what, and why we teach. Much credit goes to Ernest Boyer and his call for more scholarship on teaching and learning, as well as on discovery, integration, and application. In "Notes toward a Theory of Prior Knowledge and Its Role in College Composers' Transfer of Knowledge and Practice," Liane Robertson, Kara Taczak, and Kathleen Blake Yancey argue that composition pedagogy benefits from a model of transfer of knowledge—one that does not fixate on any single genre or writing episode but, rather, envisions teaching for transfer. Yancey, Robertson, and Taczak fully articulated their theory in *Writing across Contexts*, which details a theory and practice for preparing students to transfer writing abilities from one context to the next. To allow students to write more effectively beyond the first-year writing class, Yancey, Robertson, and Taczak have created a new kind of writing class: teaching for transfer. At Chaminade, we stress knowledge transfer through another route, one that emphasizes postcolonial pedagogy as a way to interrupt hegemony. We champion a robust, student-centered, active learning approach along three trajectories: mobile learning, writing tasks, and rubrics. Although many may find our approach a common sense way to challenge English as an imperial tool, we have found that our practical emphasis allows precise inroads in a complex terrain.

Mobile Learning

Dynamic, student-centered, active learning allows students to learn through doing, particularly using writing in their day-to-day lives. By the time our students arrive in the classroom, they have been writing for at least twelve years in elementary and secondary school settings. Most of our students have grown up living in two worlds, the digital and the real, and they spend more time reading, thinking, and writing online than we did in books or libraries. We give low-stakes writing assignments and provide formative feedback in a variety of different places that depend on students' wielding prior knowledge in new ways. Low-stakes writing is writing that is not qualitatively assessed and is employed as a practice space for academic voice, awareness of audience, and knowledge of genre. Students earn credit for doing the writing, regardless of the quality. Providing students the social space and structure for low-stakes writing is a more just and equitable way to create room for success. We have adapted journaling to digital platforms in an effort to repurpose spaces our students are familiar with and already use. The employment of digital discussion and social media apps improves on and changes the journal model. Student writing is now more visible, and students may read and learn from their peers.

While many college faculty members view learning management systems as constrictive, we view our LMS, *Canvas*, as a key tool to situate all students equally on a shared platform. In *Canvas*, we use the discussion feature to pose open questions, ones that do not require content knowledge or preparation in advance. Students write in an academic voice that is seemingly objective, authoritative, and informative. The voice they are asked to assume is not that of text messaging, but is more similar to blog writing and e-mail, or other, more formal messaging platforms. The more effective students are thinking and reflecting about the words they choose and the voice they wield as they practice digitized prose in a somewhat familiar space.

This sense of formative practice is congruent with the three kinds of student models Robertson, Taczak, and Yancey describe as necessary for transfer of knowledge. The "assemblage" student pieces together new information atop old knowledge (8). A second student "remixes" the new and the old in more fluid ways (11). In the "critical incident" (14), a student incapable of melding prior knowledge with new information fails in ways that lead the student to reflection and change. We have witnessed each type of student as they assemble, remix, and fail productively. But we also view writing as a collaborative process and so use *Google Drive* to invite students in small groups to work in a shared *Google* document, and then present from the same page, which encourages collaborative learning. In the low-stakes space of discussion, and even online in mobile learning, failure is unlikely, unless a student opts not to participate. In terms of trends, we have noticed that the most effective students tend to follow the remix model. These students generally come with more digital experience.

Students new to the discussion feature in *Canvas*, or something similar in a different LMS, and new to the mobile learning apps *Twitter* and *Instagram*, are just as capable of remixing and success. In "Tracing Discursive Resources: How Students Use Prior Genre Knowledge to Negotiate New Writing Contexts in First-Year Composition," Mary Jo Reiff and Anis Bawarshi describe a similar model with two types of learners: "boundary guarders" and "boundary crossers" (325). *Boundary guarders* tend to be resistant to new technology, afraid of trying, and uncomfortable working within such platforms. *Boundary crossers* move more fluidly across apps and platforms. Indeed, twenty-first-century living and the rapidly increasing digital world will require us to continually learn how to use the latest app. Social networking systems provide the same equitable space for users. *Instagram*, for instance, provides a common space for students to present visual material. Any picture posted appears within the same digital framing and size, and any editing or filtering is the same for all users. *Twitter* limits tweets to 280 characters, and the structure of the app is applied to all who use it. Hashtags allow faculty members and the public to group, see, and follow students, and students, similarly, can view and connect with their peers in the same way. Successful students quickly wield hashtags in new and creative ways, and in so doing open their work up to a greater audience. Students bring prior knowledge that can be either detrimental or advantageous, but our working with such spaces contributes to a blending of new skills with the old. These apps can be accessed for free on phones, tablets, and computers.

The space of digital communication privileges community building and collaborative work. Cultural Pacific values rank the community over the individual, so students see and learn from one another in the process of responding to one another. *Twitter* is used to focus instruction in open platforms. Students are introduced to the MLA formats for integrated and block quotations and par-enthetical citations; they are then asked to tweet passages of importance from literary and expository texts using correct punctuation and parenthetical cita-tion of an integrated quotation. The character limit on *Twitter* pushes students to think critically and punctuate properly in a space that is not normally used under such conditions. The *Twitter* platform creates an opportunity structure by which students can see citations digitally on their own time by following their peers. We like those tweets that provide proper punctuation and parenthetical citation, a form of assessment that allows students to see and learn from their peers. Students must also respond directly to their peers' tweets of selected pas-sages of importance with their own analysis. In this context, we rely on students' using their prior knowledge of examples and explanations in a new context. Again, previous texting experience may be disruptive here unless students are comfortable blending new information with old.

In an effort to teach critical thinking and close reading, we ask that stu-dents respond to passages of importance with literary analysis, limited to the 280-character limit available on *Twitter*. In this space, students are encouraged to forgo academic contextualization or argumentative prose so as to maximize content in terms of felt experience. Forgoing academic and interpretive prose structures also allows students to engage in writing as a process. Moreover, freed from academic constraints when presenting a quotation from a text, students can blend the spaces of prior and new knowledge. Voice is of key importance here, and students are able to see and read the tweets of their peers, who are at the same level. In contrast to reading literature as if it must be first interpreted by experts who seem far above them (the imperial gaze), our students are see-ing, reading, thinking with, reflecting, and writing to each other. This process also allows them to evaluate others' writing and identify areas of improvement within their own. The asynchronous component of smart phone apps creates room for thinking and reflection as students engage with the app throughout the week. Seeing others post before they do helps them think about their own posts before they actually post. We see this space as dialogic and as an exten-sion of the classroom. We hope that the flexibility involved in the ways we use the *Twitter* platform will lead students toward a more reflexive and thoughtful writing process, as well as one that wields greater critical thinking and a more engaged local community.

Students are also supplied with essential learning objects (ELOs) that model best tweet responses, to be viewed on their own time. The ELOs allow students to watch or experience a lesson around a skill on their own time and machine, and this kind of individualized learning experience is derived from universal de-sign, in which there are many ways to an end. There are many kinds of learners in our classroom, and we hope that, through using a variety of different learning experiences, we create an effective opportunity structure that is also fair. Moreover, practicing critical thinking across multiple platforms or writing in different spaces encourages reflection and metacognition. Students are thinking in between their writing, and the rupture created by writing in different places (classroom, home, work, library, and other settings) and at various times produces greater depth. This structure thus ensures students access writing as a process. We substantiate the process with tasks that scaffold writing.

Writing Tasks

Although prompts are one way to describe the assignments we give students, we prefer *constructed response tasks*, a more exact term used by Randy Elliot Bennett. These tasks provide a structure for the assignment expectations as well as specify audience and context. The following is an example of such a task:

STUDENT LEARNING OUTCOMES

Upon completion of this course, students will be able to

use prewriting strategies and techniques
identify and implement structured and effective rhetorical writing techniques
write clear and effective claims or thesis statements
demonstrate organizational development in a written text
identify, create, and edit using correct grammar, punctuation, word choice, mechanics, and sentence structure in a written text
cite written works using MLA citation

ASSIGNMENT

Select a story or a song and write an argument using the two texts as support. Your three- to five-page analytic essay should comprise an introduction, body paragraphs built around quotations from the text as support, and a conclusion.

You may wish to use a question as a starting point: What does family mean? Or, How do these songs and stories make an argument about children, their parents, and families?

Please remember that form matters, and you will be using a song and a short story to make an argument. Stories and songs are read here as literary texts. You will do a close reading of them. Songs work above and beyond mere narrative because they involve sound, which will complement the meaning in some way. Peter Brooks, Roland Barthes, and Tzvetan Todorov help us better understand stories using narrative engines, narrative threads, or states.

>This essay asks that you engage in discussion of and cite the two works. Because you will be citing both a story and a song, include a works-cited page with your essay.

The design of the task is related to the learning outcomes which described in both the task and the syllabus. The framing of the task provides information and asks students to situate the task in terms of academic content and audience. The language used to describe the writing teaches students about the structure of academic prose as a genre. Referring to MLA citation similarly reinforces writing conventions at the college level. The language of citation is itself new to many of our students, and ELOs help students better understand this part of the writing and researching process. A series of questions may be offered to help students focus, but too many questions often confuse students, leading them to believe they are to answer all of them in the paper. As a result, we encourage a single question or a statement. A flexible schedule that allows for at least a week of writing is more equitable. A week or more gives students room to create a structure for writing as a process, and deadlines for specific pieces ensure students are writing constructed responses.

Such emphasis on flexibility is important because many of our students are working, commuting on an island that is difficult to navigate at rush hour, and have family responsibilities in multigenerational homes. We scaffold writing assignments to distribute the workload over time and multiple due dates. This writing fits discourse described by Anne Beaufort in *College Writing and Beyond*, which includes five overlapping spaces or types of knowledge: discourse community knowledge, rhetorical knowledge, genre knowledge, composing process knowledge, and subject matter knowledge (5–58). Tasks such as those we describe touch on those five types of knowledge. With our students, writing outcomes about the knowledge involved and the scheduled, scaffolded tasks render the classroom not only more fair but also more dialogic.

Task-Aligned Rubrics

Rubrics are central tools for us in the teaching of writing, and we share writing tasks with rubrics in the LMS, allowing students free, equal, and transparent access to evaluative methods. We promote fairness by intentionally sharing the rubric early in the semester and then using it throughout the term. We acknowledge that simply using rubrics does not ensure fair practice, but our intentional work around the language and values of the rubrics promotes fairness by ensuring students understand the design of the task and the ways the criteria are aligned with the task for evaluation. In our classroom discussion, we unpack the embedded values of postsecondary expectations within the context of our Pacific setting. Moreover, rubrics create opportunity structures rooted in fairness, limiting the instructor's potential bias in evaluation and providing common language to talk about students' writing. Because so many of our students in Hawai'i have been taught using rubrics at the high school level, we take this opportunity to build on their familiarity with the genre to take advantage of their prior knowledge. Aligned to tasks, these rubrics also provide a vehicle for a more robust construct representation. As shown in table 1, our rubrics describe four levels of performance (emerging, developing, competent, mastery) and outline criteria areas along the left column.

Our criteria are adapted for each task and allow for writing about the genre (expository writing and poetry), rhetorical knowledge (voice), subject matter knowledge (grammar and mechanics, critical content, and textual content). In addition, sharing more with students on and in writing provides space for them to turn back to what they already know before taking in new and challenging ideas about writing for the college classroom. Providing students with opportunities throughout a course—like contributing to the construction of a rubric, or allowing students to self-assess and determine the evidence that will demonstrate the achievement of course learning outcomes—increases students' engagement with and ownership of the course content. Working with our students, we create a variety of spaces for writing that allow students to integrate, adapt, and wield prior knowledge in new ways.

In essence, the rubric is a reminder that textual evidence is part of a learning process that grounds our students in reading and writing about writing. In cultures that still privilege the spoken word, as do many of our Pacific cultures, this reliance on textual evidence may be new, and our tasks invite students to remix what they learn about citation in the classroom with prior knowledge of how examples should be incorporated in expository writing. Rubrics craft space for self-reflection and regulation. Criteria deemed essential for our students' success include content, voice or tone, and textual evidence. Content allows us space to build on prior knowledge using language students recognize as academic discourse. In terms of summative assessment, the four levels employed here can be replaced with letter grades, D through A. As such, rubric design is direct. Critical to our pedagogy, scaffolding throughout the semester includes but is not limited to shared documents and collaborations; the practice of citation through *Twitter*; ELOs to help explain bibliographies, annotated bibliographies, and parenthetical citation; and the use of *RefWorks*. Discussion of the task and rubric at the outset of each assignment helps students situate and understand these terms. Examples of such writing are also instrumental in showing and sharing student writing that fits these levels. This collaborative effort is particularly important for our students and their Pacific cultures.

Table 1. Sample Task-Aligned Rubric

	Emerging	Developing	Competent	Mastery
Content	The writer does not explore the topic explained in the task and ineffectively writes about something else.	The writer offers an introduction introducing the two primary texts but no argument. Body paragraphs are present but are predominantly summary. The conclusion suggests a main idea.	The writer offers an introduction that contextualizes the primary sources, a claim, body paragraphs, and a conclusion. Although not always clear, the body does support a main idea.	The writer leads the reader with a claim-driven introduction, then on through insightful analysis in point-led body paragraphs. In conclusion, the writer expands on the topic and closes with brilliance.
Voice, tone	The writer writes as though the reader were a friend, using "you" and "I" repeatedly. Slang, informal expressions, and contractions abound.	The writer writes as though the reader were there listening but also sometimes finds a more academic voice.	The writer occasionally slips into "I" but generally offers a voice that is focused and acceptable in academic writing.	The writer offers a clear and objective voice that does not interrupt the reading process.
Textual evidence	The writer does not offer quotations or a works-cited page.	The writer offers quotations but misquotes the text and does not understand or wield integrated and block quotations appropriately, in addition to leaving out parenthetical citations. Only one essay is used. A works-cited page is included but is incorrect.	The writer cites the text correctly, uses integrated and block quotations effectively, and offers correct parenthetical citations. Both essays are cited and a correct works-cited page is included.	The writer uses summarization to introduce the quotations from both essays, skillfully employs integrated and block quotations, and offers correct parenthetical citations. A correct works-cited page is included.
Grammar and mechanics	Errors in syntax make for a difficult and disruptive read.	Errors are troublesome, but the writer is successful in parts too.	There are one or two errors, but the paper is a smooth read.	There are no errors, and the paper is a pleasure to read.
Format	The writer does not use the proper format. No peer review.	The writer seems to be trying to follow directions but still has multiple mistakes. No peer review or an incomplete effort.	The format is correct, as indicated in the syllabus. The peer review is complete.	The writer employs the required format and does so well, offering a catchy title in the proper space. A helpful and insightful peer review is included.

Conclusion

In closing, we are reminded of Huddart's observation that "postcolonial theory's seductive vocabulary of the hybrid and the marginal distracts us from the necessary task of contextualization and specification" (102). Our three trajectories are meant to lend focus to an important emphasis on writing studies by using theories of power and hegemony to help students realize the force of literacy in their lives. We construct knowing by writing. In our experience, faculty can build equitable opportunity structures in writing classrooms that privilege the transfer of the diversity of student experience and knowledge. We can create experiences to strengthen students' own accountability and self-assessment through content, voice, and textuality. Building on the skills and knowledge students already have, our dynamic writing process increases student ownership and confidence. With our emphasis on mobile learning, writing tasks, and rubrics, we have found that culturally responsive assessment can be achieved, in part, through collaborative practice and transparency.

Part Two

Foundational Issues

Assessing Writing: Construct Representation and Implications of a Sociocognitive Perspective

Robert J. Mislevy

Perspective

Advances in cognitive and social psychology invite a reconception of educational assessment. From my perspective as a psychometrician, I discuss how a sociocognitive view of learning and activity changes the way we design and use assessments, highlighting implications for writing in the professions. Instead of seeing assessment primarily as measurement, we can view it as evidentiary argument, situated in social contexts, centered on students' developing competencies in valued activities, and shaped by purposes and values—chief among them validity, fairness, and opportunity to learn.

Introduction

In this essay I discuss an overdue development in educational assessment and consider its implications for assessing writing in the disciplines. Two decades ago, I noted that along with tests and quizzes, teachers have always drawn on evidence from projects, conversations, and classwork, as well as background information about students and the schooling context (Mislevy, "Postmodern Test"). The power of these informal assessments comes from their intimate connection to particular students in specific contexts at certain points in time, in contrast with the formal assessments typified by large-scale standardized tests. Yet precisely because they are contextualized, the rationale and results of informal assessments are harder to communicate beyond the classroom. Standardized tests do communicate across time and place, but only by so constraining the information that it holds less value for learning. "The challenge now . . . is to devise assessments that, in various ways, incorporate and balance the strengths of formal and informal assessments by capitalizing on an array of methodological, technological, and conceptual developments" (Mislevy, "Postmodern Test" 189).

The development of which I speak is a reconception of the very foundations of assessment. At its heart are a sociocognitive perspective on peoples' capabilities and a framing of assessment as evidentiary argument. This is where I have arrived after wrestling with the challenge (Mislevy, *Sociocognitive Foundations*), and this is why: a sociocognitive perspective changes how we understand both what is being assessed and the roles that assessment plays in educational systems. An argument framing helps us build on underlying principles across assessment practices, uses familiar forms more effectively, and devises new forms around developments in learning psychology. This synthesis helps us use assessments to better support students' learning and facilitates designing and employing assessment in ways that are more valid and fair.

I must start by sorting out the terms *assessment*, *test*, and *measurement*. Their conflation over the past century distorts education policy and hampers opportunities to learn. I then turn to the core ideas of a sociocognitive perspective, highlighting implications for assessment. This perspective is not new to the writing community, of course, with a literature including titles such as *The Construction of Negotiated Meaning: A Social Cognitive Theory of Writing* (Flower) and "Critical Discourse Studies: A Sociocognitive Approach" (Dijk). I then zero in on assessment, considering the interplay among constructs, contexts, purposes, and constraints in assessment design. We see how substantially different forms of assessment can be derived from the same overarching construct for different uses and contexts. Design decisions must be made in light of purposes, contexts, and constraints, as we strive to instantiate the abstract values of validity and fairness in particular circumstances.

An assessment-argument schema based on the respective writings of Stephen E. Toulmin and John H. Wigmore is a rhetorical device for sorting out issues of assessment design, interpretation, and use. It proves useful in organizing multiple strands of inference, adapting to assessment contexts, and employing measurement-modeling tools. I sketch its structure and then illustrate its use with the discipline-specific writing genre of critical incident reports (CIRs) in nursing.

There is more going on in writing assessment than meets the eye, and there always has been. There are many choices we must make and justify when we design and use assessments of all types, from informal discussions of classroom work to high-stakes selection and placement tests. Each choice has an impact on validity and fairness. I close by underscoring the overarching role of these values in designing and using assessments responsibly.

Assessments, Tests, and Measurements

Defined broadly as gathering and interpreting information about students' capabilities for some educative purpose, the term *assessment* spans the formal and informal assessments mentioned above. A *test* is a particular genre of assessment, a predetermined set of tasks and scoring procedures administered to test takers under specified conditions. *Measurement* is process that can be applied across assessment genres, situating results in a quantitative framework to characterize the evidence they provide for interpretations and inferences.

Aspects of two familiar writing assessment practices help clarify the terms. The first is a wholly contextualized formative assessment (itself an assessment genre) concerning CIRs. The instructor in a nursing practicum evaluates each student's initial draft of a CIR on a situation they have observed, offering suggestions on what to include and omit, always underscoring the intended readers, specifically what they need to know and how they will use the information. Rhonda Maneval and Frances Ward show in their essay in this volume how the instructor's comments can be individualized to students but draw on common ways of thinking and talking about writing in this disciplinary genre. There are no scores, no statistics, no reliability coefficients. These informal, personalized assessments are more like coaching than testing.

The second example is the GRE Analytical Writing measure. Thousands of examinees write their essays on a common theme, independently, in a timed and proctored sitting. This assessment is a test: it acquires information using standardized tasks with little context and under standardized conditions, evaluates all performances with the same procedures, and reports all results in a common framework. Evaluation is reported as a numerical rating that emphasizes quality of exposition. Moreover, GRE writing scores are treated as measures, estimates of location on an underlying scale. Scores are analyzed statistically, reliability coefficients are calculated to gauge their usefulness for comparing test takers, and standard errors of measurement quantify the uncertainty about each individual's score. The GRE writing score is meant to provide information about aspects of students' writing capabilities in a manner that is economical and can be communicated to distant users for their own purposes. These test procedures and the statistical analysis were adapted from the physical sciences a little more than a century ago: standardized tasks, evaluated and interpreted in the same way for all test takers, as a means of obtaining transportable information. Brian Huot, Peggy O'Neill, and Cindy Moore provide a useful review of its history in writing assessment.

So not all assessments are tests, and not all assessments are analyzed in terms of measurement. Further confusion ensues from the fact that *measurement* is variously used to mean the procedures for producing and analyzing numbers and the purported referents of those numbers. These distinct meanings appear in physical sciences as well, but attributes of, say, electrons—hence patterns in data about them, hence inferences based on standardized procedures—are not culturally and historically contingent in the way patterns in human behavior are. Although analogous models can be useful to investigate the properties of test scores, it can be misleading to interpret scores as measures of relatively stable characteristics of persons, which are consistently manifested to some degree when relevant, despite considerable variation in the range of settings and circumstances. This is, however, the interpretation under the trait psychology perspective that produced educational measurement, which persists among policy makers and the public at large. This understanding encourages, for example, the belief that there exists a quantitative writing proficiency attribute, in much the same sense as length and weight; essentially the same capability across people who have more or less of it, manifest across a wide variety of assessment situations and real-world situations that involve writing. This reading disregards the particular knowledge bases and contextual demands of writing in different settings and circumstances and distorts policies and instructional practices.

The efficiency and transportability of large-scale testing thus comes at a cost. Viewing writing as a unitary ability and scoring writing products as if it were misses much that we value—and need to help students learn. Yes, writing in almost any genre and context displays sequences of words arranged in grammatical forms to convey meanings, and, yes, students' difficulties and successes in one genre and one context can hold information about how they might fare in another. And any genre and context requires writers in disciplines to put themselves in the mind of the reader: knowing something about their knowledge base; likely purposes; and expectations as to the language, structures, and conventions in the genre that support comprehension in the genre. Writing GRE essays for an audience of GRE essay raters (humans and computers) is but one particular genre and context. What can be learned from such an essay offers limited information to help students improve in other genres and contexts, such as writing CIRs or engineering proposals. (Also see Williams, this volume.)

A Sociocognitive Perspective

A synthesis is emerging across cognitive science, social psychology, linguistics, and many other fields as to the nature of how humans develop and use capabilities to act and interact in the physical and social world—a sociocognitive perspective (Gee, *Social Mind*). *Socio-* highlights the interpersonal, or across-person, knowledge and activity patterns that structure individuals' interactions with the world and others, regularities among the myriad unique interactions among people. These include the structures and ways of using language, knowledge representations, and cultural models, as well as the patterns of activities of communities, personal interactions, classrooms, workplaces, and so on (Wertsch)—linguistic, cultural, and substantive (LCS) patterns for short. *Cognitive* highlights within-person mental patterns. These intrapersonal patterns are traces over an individual's experiences, continually assembled, adapted, and revised to make meaning and guide action in each new situation. Richard F. Young uses the term *resources* to describe individuals' acquired cognitive patterns of knowledge, relationships, actions, feelings, and motives (88). We assemble resources in the moment to make our way through the world, extending and adapting them in the process. Our experience in a given situation blends the particulars of that situation and the activation of resources from previous experiences.

The heart of the perspective is the dynamic interplay of persons acting through within-person resources, in situations organized around across-person LCS patterns—LCS patterns of many kinds, at many layers, combined and recombined in new ways in new situations. In the present case, words and syntax, tailored to domains and situations, and conversation structures and written forms, tailored to roles and purposes, enable individuals to coordinate their thoughts and actions.

Resources are unique to individuals, for every person's lived experience is unique. Similarities among individuals' resources depend largely on the similarities in the LCS patterns involved in situations they have experienced; it is these similarities that make it possible for us to interact in recurring social situations. Architects, for instance, communicate with blueprints and site maps with common conventions to describe unique projects and use them to work with clients and contractors in recurring patterns throughout design and construction.

The Writing Construct

These sociocognitive themes appear in writing practices, and in writing in the disciplines in particular. Genres, as LCS patterns, "embrace both form and content, . . . [and] the use of genres simultaneously constitutes and reproduces social structures; and . . . genre conventions signal a discourse community's norms, epistemology, ideology, and social ontology" (Berkenkotter and Huckin 475). Writing a project proposal or completing an insurance form structures individuals' thinking and acting in a network of activity that extends over time, people, and institutions. Developing proficiency to create, communicate, and use knowledge in such forms is integral to becoming an engineer or a nurse, for it is woven into the very fabric of how one thinks and acts in these roles. The considerations of forms, purposes, substance, and audience that a writer must manage (Hayes) are inextricable from the realm of practice.

This view of embedded language holds strong implications for our efforts to help students develop competency in profession-specific writing genres. To be sure, a writer can adapt certain resources that from one context to another, such as broadly used conventions, metacognitive resources for structuring and revising, and an awareness that one must connect with readers' knowledge and expectations. But *awareness that* is not knowing *what* and *how*, which differ with substance, contexts, and purposes. Disciplinary writing demands integrating genre with not only disciplinary knowledge but also disciplinary values, identities, situations, and purposes, even for a writer skilled in other genres and disciplines.

Edward M. White, Norbert Elliot, and Irvin Peckham's representation of the writing construct helps us apply the sociocognitive view to writing assessment (White et al., *Very* 75). Figure 1 suggests social and cognitive factors involved in every episode of writing, each specific to that episode. The matchup between an assessment and its uses determine its usefulness, validity, and fairness (Mislevy and Elliot).

The top row spans the environments in which writers and readers interact: digital, print, and blurred (i.e., merged with each other or other media). The second row captures a language arts framework, including writing, reading, and speaking, as many episodes of writing are part of a larger communicative activity. The third row identifies rhetorical conceptualization in its attention to language and its sources of knowledge. The fourth and fifth rows identify the cognitive domain of writing, as sources of knowledge a writer draws on. The sixth row delineates the interpersonal domain of writing, and the seventh the intrapersonal domain. The eighth row attends to the neurological, attention, and vision capacities necessary to perform language tasks. Together, these social and cognitive factors establish a *construct space* for writing, across all its forms and contexts. The arrow suggests the drawdown of the factors into a particularized writing construct for designing assessments or instruction, or describing real-world situations. The resulting particularized construct is remarkably small compared to the span of all writing; no single assessment can be anything like an assessment of writing in toto.

The matchups between assessment situations and those of real-world use can be identified in this model. For a given assessment, a designer creates an instantiated construct by specifying a configuration of artifacts and activities from the unbounded universe of writing-related situations that could provide evidence about the complex of capabilities that are meant to be assessed in the

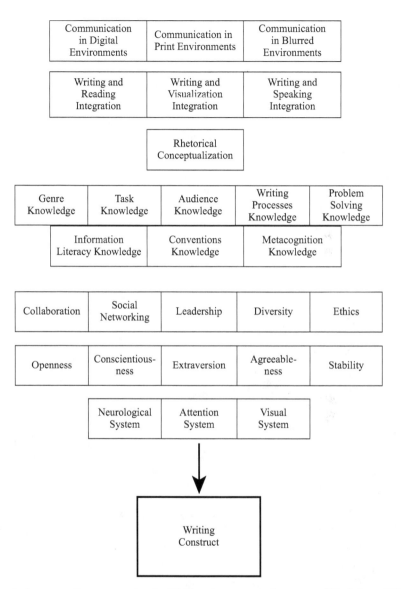

Figure 1. Construct Representation for Writing Assessment (courtesy of Utah State UP).

kinds of situations that call for them. See, for example, Julia M. Williams's discussion in this volume of assessments that draw down to focus on different aspects of written communication in engineering. The targeted real-life situations, such as particular kinds of writing in a discipline or instructional activities that offer opportunities to improve, can be similarly described. The argument framework helps a designer work through these matchups, to establish validity and fairness and to identify threats to them.

Assessment Arguments

Lee J. Cronbach introduced the argumentation framework to assessment in the 1980s, writing "Validation speaks to a diverse and potentially critical audience; therefore, *the argument must link concepts, evidence, social and personal consequences, and values*" (4). An assessment design argument sees assessments as evidentiary arguments, instantiated in social and historical contexts, meant to provide information to some users about peoples' capabilities for some educative purposes, cast in some (possibly tacit) psychological perspective, and developed and carried out under constraints.

Figure 2 is an assessment argument. It extends Toulmin's general schema for reasoning from data to claims, through warrants, with qualifiers. This same structure applies to informal classroom assessments, standardized tests with measurement-model analyses, and conversations between students and teachers as they work through drafts of, say, engineering proposals. A conception of proficiency shapes all the elements in the argument and the rationale that connects them: the kinds of things we want say about persons (claims), and the kinds of things we need to see them say or do (data), in what kinds of situations (also data). A particular situated conception of proficiency also shapes purposes, contexts, individuals, and constraints, none of which appear in measurement models but all of which are essential to instantiate the argument in a real-world application. A situated conception accommodates discussions of assessment design and use for special populations and diverse student groups. These factors enable us to balance the tradeoffs inherent in design and identify alternative explanations (qualifiers) and take them into account or mitigate them.

Figure 2 actually portrays two connected arguments. The lower rectangle concerns designing an assessment and interpreting results, whereas the upper rectangle concerns using the results for further inferences, such as evaluations or instructional guidance. The next section illustrates how to use this argument frame to reason about elements of an assessment through a sociocognitive lens, but first, some orienting comments.

The cloud at the very bottom of the figure represents the student's performance. The data concerning the performance are themselves interpretations: what we identify and characterize, given the capabilities of interest and practical constraints. Equally important data are the features of the situation. From a sociocognitive perspective, actions make sense only in terms of context, purpose,

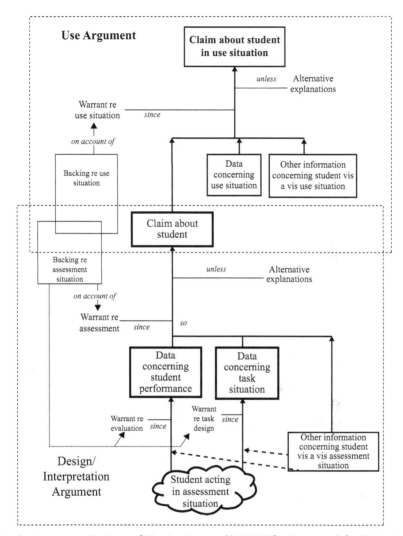

Figure 2. Assessment Design and Use Arguments (© 2006 The Regents of the University of California; used with permission).

and relevant LCS patterns and practices. Discerning the salient aspects of a performance and situation are subarguments that require their own warrants and backing and are subject to alternative explanations.

Also critical, though usually tacit, is the user's information about the relation between the student and the assessment situation, such as students' prerequisite knowledge or familiarity with the evaluation standards. This information helps a user rule in or rule out alternative explanations, increasing validity and fairness. The lack of such information in large-scale testing renders the same task less useful than it would be in a classroom.

The assessment claims in the middle express, at a more general level, inferences about students based on their performances. A contemporary understanding of learning now warrants the inferences from students' performances (backed, for example, by cognitive, sociocultural, and corpus-based research: see Poe in this volume). These claims are data that enter the use argument. It is not performances that drive assessment uses, but interpretations of performances.

Measurement models and statistical methods play greater roles in assessments with higher stakes, more test takers, or more-distant users. Users have little information about test takers and must rely more heavily on information from the assessment. The modeling supports the reasoning laid out in the argument, characterizing the weight of the evidence and highlighting anomalous patterns. When measurement models are used, they are nested within assessment arguments, which are nested within purposes and contexts, which are nested in turn within practices and institutions (Oliveri et al.).

Application to a Discipline-Specific Writing Genre

To see how the sociocognitive perspective and argument framing support assessment design and use, consider three scenarios concerning CIRs, a writing genre in nursing (see Maneval and Ward, this volume). A CIR is a written record of an unexpected occurrence (e.g., a patient's fall or a technician's accidental exposure to hazardous material) or a lapse in procedures that affect patient care (such as the administration of an incorrect medication or a failure of equipment to receive scheduled maintenance). A nurse should complete a CIR as soon as practicable. The primary purposes of CIRs are risk management and quality improvement. They include information on what, when, where, and how the incident occurred, who was involved, and any injuries or damages that occurred, but not speculations or recommendations. CIRs are usually structured around forms that support nurses, not only in filling out a CIR for given incidents that occur but also as a lens to see all care activity all the time.

Although writing a CIR requires disciplinary knowledge, as a communication node connecting many professionals, it also necessitates understanding what is expected and what is not. It calls for structuring the narrative in styles and language that help administrators spot patterns across incidents, as well as satisfy legal and procedural requirements. Sometimes, as with neglected maintenance, an incident is something that did not happen but should have. Becoming a competent writer of CIRs is thus interwoven with learning to see and act in the world as a nurse. The following assessment scenarios all concern the capabilities of nursing students to write CIRs. Their particular purposes, contexts, and constraints shape the forms the assessments take and bear on their validity and fairness.

Scenario 1: Critical Incident Reports in a Live Simulation Practicum

This scenario is inspired by the live simulation experience in the nursing program at the University of South Australia (Warland). The students have completed course work, and the aim is to draw their knowledge into a (simulated) chaotic ward environment. Because the other professionals and patients are playing roles, a variety of preplanned challenging situations can arise. Incidents that should prompt CIRs are introduced to see if students recognize these occasions and write CIRs, whose qualities are then evaluated. The assessment is complex and resource-intensive but provides authentic experiences that support learning and offer valid evidence about correspondingly complex capabilities.

This assessment is formative because the main purpose is learning. Instructors can give students feedback on recognizing and interpreting incidents and for revising their CIRs. This individualized feedback can be structured around pretested rubrics such as those Maneval and Ward discuss: say, twelve dimensions described abstractly, such as the clarity of the description and the degree to which necessary information has been included. Note that the latter is critical for competence but is not addressed in general writing courses. This assessment optimizes the opportunity-to-learn aspect of fairness; the circumstances of performance and the evaluation are well matched to the targeted competency of writing in the discipline-specific CIR genre.

Although the only statistics needed for learning and feedback are overall CIR scores to track progress, more sophisticated studies and analyses like those Maneval and Ward describe could be carried out to develop the rubrics. A measurement model called generalizability analysis can be applied with data from multiple raters, dimensions, incidents, and students to examine the completeness and clarity of the scoring dimensions, study rater agreement, and improve the rubrics and support for using them.

The preplanned incidents involve medical and patient care situations that instructors know are already familiar to students. The tasks are thus designed so that lack of necessary disciplinary knowledge is not a strong alternative explanation for poor performance. The focus is squarely on integrating knowledge with the situated activity—a critical aspect of nursing practice revolving around this discipline-specific writing genre.

Scenario 2: A Critical Incident Report in a Licensure Examination

Now consider a nursing licensure examination—a high-stakes decision, requiring accurate scores for reliable decisions, as authentic and complete coverage as can be attained under tight constraints on cost and testing time. A licensing agency includes a task based on a video clip of a confused patient taking a tube of nitroglycerin ointment from an unattended medication cart and rubbing it onto a patch of dry skin. A CIR is to be written in a provided form.

The CIRs are scored holistically, most by a single rater, synthesizing the twelve aspects that were separated out in scenario 1. A random twenty percent are scored by a second rater. A generalizability analysis of these data provides information about the consistency of scoring across raters. The task scores are entered into another measurement model (from item response theory) that combines information across tasks more accurately than total scores. This increases the fairness of decisions from the limited information that is available. The statistical analysis is used not to measure a trait but to understand the qualities of the evidence the scores convey and apply that evidence effectively for the licensure decisions.

Some aspects of students' competency in writing CIRs are captured in these tasks, such as the inclusion of information, clarity, and mechanics, but unlike the live simulation, other aspects are not directly evidenced. The experience is not situated in context and not experienced in the pressing flow of actual care. We learn less about how well-integrated the students' conceptualizations of CIRs are with nursing knowledge, skill, identity, and values. Feedback on the more finely grained dimensions is not available. We have a degree of validity and fairness as needed for the licensure decision, perhaps as well as can be achieved with lack of context and limited resources, with the video presentation increasing authenticity over static, text-based tasks, and the statistical modeling improving the quality of the available information.

Scenario 3: A Generic Writing Task for Placement into a Critical Incident Report Writing Module

This scenario resembles some writing placement practices in professional schools. The decision is whether nursing students should be assigned a module on writing CIRs. The administrators use a general writing test much like GRE writing, with students producing timed essays on an assigned social topic. The essays are rated holistically, and students who score above a cutoff are exempted.

This use of assessment is cast in trait psychology, assuming writing is writing. It is poorly matched to the targeted claim: whether or not a student has sufficient capabilities in writing CIRs. It is bereft of the CIR context, professional knowledge, and genre-specific conventions, so many alternative explanations arise. A high-scoring student may be proficient with the writing mechanics that many contexts and genres call on, and a well-formed essay does suggest metacognitive skills, but only as displayed in the timed-essay genre. There is no evidence about whether or not the student can recognize CIR situations, follow CIR conventions, or integrate knowledge across aspects of care required to communicate the essential information to its special users—exactly the capabilities the module training addresses. Conversely, a student who scores lower may have had difficulty with mechanics instead of with recognizing relevant situations and structuring CIRs. The mismatch leads to placement that steers away some students who would benefit from the module and assigns it to others who would profit from different instruction.

The Overarching Role of Values

Writing assessment in the professions requires understanding the deep interconnections among skills, knowledge, identities, values, and the very epistemology of the domain. One must think like a nurse to write in the genres through which nurses communicate across the network of people, institutions, activities, and identities that constitute the profession (Poe, this volume). This contextualization is an overarching concern for assessing writing in the disciplines and applies to all assessment uses therein. A sociocognitive perspective on capabilities and an argument framework help us tackle the challenges of assessment design and use. I say "tackle the challenges" rather than "solve the problems," for these are not technical problems with objective solutions. They are engineering problems of inevitable tradeoffs among design choices and stakeholders' needs. As the CIR scenarios suggest, optimal assessments can take different forms for different contexts and purposes. Assessment is inherently situated reasoning, which we can support through the rhetorical structure of evidentiary argument, whether or not measurement tools are used.

Some assessment problems do have technical aspects, and we can use machinery from measurement modeling to illuminate issues of evidence and inference, of comparability and generalizability, of usefulness and fairness. As Samuel J. Messick reminded us, these are not just measurement issues, they are "*social values* that have meaning and force outside of measurement wherever evaluative judgments and decisions are made" ("Interplay" 13). Validity and fairness originate in conception and design, before the first data point appears. Validity comes from matching the information to be obtained to the appropriate purpose, as best one can under the given constraints, and mitigating alternative explanations. Fairness is providing information that reflects individuals' capabilities in the intended ways. Opportunity to learn is a critical aspect of fairness. Both fairness and opportunity are easy to miss when viewing assessment mainly through a measurement lens but impossible to ignore through a sociocognitive lens (see Elliot, "Theory"; Mislevy and Elliot; and Moss et al.).

Access, Outcomes, and Diversity: Opportunities and Challenges in Basic Writing

Ruth Benander and Brenda Refaei

Perspective

In this essay we focus on the significance of agency within writing processes and products for basic writers as a means to promote equity at Blue Ash College, an open admission two-year college. We share challenges faced in basic writing courses, and we propose that thoughtful e-portfolio use—accompanied by attention to self-regulation and self-efficacy—can help students enrolled in these courses forge new identities as college writers. Basic writing courses need outcomes that are fairly assessed through shared rubrics tailored to the interests of each student. We present evidence from various sources, including early and end-of-course portfolio scores and analyses of both students' perceptions of personal agency and their values of equity in the final reflective writing of the course. Each source of evidence illustrates that our respect for students' agency, integrated into the curriculum, may properly be considered an issue of equity.

Basic Writing and Basic Writers: From Deficiency to Student Agency

Historically, students who were identified as incapable of the writing expected in college-level courses have been labeled *basic writers*. Mina Shaughnessy first mapped the issues facing basic writers in *Errors and Expectations*, identifying challenges they had with editing issues, such as spelling, grammar, punctuation, and vocabulary. Programs, curricula, and pedagogies were developed to help students acquire basic literacy skills needed for success in college. In the early 1990s, Min-Zhan Lu critiqued this positioning of basic writers as "deficient" (889). Lu advocated for alignment of basic writing curriculum with theories of language that recognized situated identities created by discourses. Later, critics such as Brian Street argued that this bottom-up approach is based on an "autonomous" view of literacy, suggesting that writing is a neutral construct (417). Drawing on Street's work, Linda Adler-Kassner and Susanmarie Harrington argued for a basic writing curriculum that "enables students to understand how definitions of literacy are shaped by communities; how literacy, power, and language are linked; and how their myriad experiences with language (in and out of school) are connected to writing" (98). This focus on students' experiences with languages and literacies honors their complex identities as writers and members of multiple discourse communities instead of viewing them in a deficit model. Judith Scott-Clayton and Olga Rodriguez note that their research sample of students in community colleges included a significantly higher minority population than in four-year colleges. Similarly, Xianglei Chen and Sean Simone note that women and students of color place into basic writing courses in high numbers. This larger population of students who come from greatly varying discourse traditions highlights the importance of offering a path to success for students unfamiliar with the discourse expectations of college. It is not that they can't or won't do academic English; they just need to learn how to do it.

In a research project funded by the Institute of Educational Sciences, United States, Department of Education, Michelle F. Blake and colleagues describe a basic writing curriculum incorporating several self-regulated strategies: reiteration of writing processes as students work through new genres, modeling writing processes, and integrating such academic success strategies as "goal setting, task management, progress monitoring, and reflection" (162). Angela Rasmussen and Andrea Reid, in their essay in this volume, also describe a protocol for designing a first-year composition curriculum that meets the needs of their two-year college students. Like Rasmussen and Reid, we redesigned the basic course to address the diversity of our students. At Blue Ash College, we incorporated elements of self-regulated strategy instruction as we redesigned our lowest-level basic writing course. Blake and colleagues suggest their curriculum works because students learn "the degree of control they have over their writing," which leads "to increased confidence" (171). We refer to this "control" and "increased confidence" as agency that emerges as students realize their voices matter.

We believe, like KerryAnn O'Meara, that basic writers have agency: they perceive they have control over their actions, and they deliberately act to achieve their own goals. This agency is best cultivated through robust construct representation in e-portfolios and concepts of self-regulation and self-efficacy within the curriculum. O'Meara observes, "[T]his view of agency asserts that individuals are embedded in social contexts that deeply shape the range of agency they may experience at any given time" (2). Through self-regulation strategies, students perceive they have control of their learning, and by using e-portfolios for competency-based assessment and reflective practice, we create a social context in the course where students have control to curate and assess their own work. If basic writers are afforded agency and a voice in postsecondary settings, they get a fair chance at succeeding in college and bringing their diverse experiences and creative problem-solving as a result of their varied experiences in academic discourse. The academy becomes richer with the addition of these voices.

Opportunities and Challenges at Open Admissions Two-Year Colleges: Blue Ash College

University of Cincinnati Blue Ash Regional College aims to provide access and opportunities to pursue higher education and is classified by the Carnegie Commission on Higher Education as associate's dominant, exclusively undergraduate, and primarily nonresidential (*Carnegie*). This regional college is situated among the northeastern suburbs of Cincinnati and draws from local suburban and urban high schools. Students are mostly local, employed at least part-time, and are career oriented. These students are furthering their educations so they can find careers that will allow them to achieve the financial security their families may not have been able to provide. Many are Pell Grant eligible and more than half are first-generation students. These students, who live close to poverty and have little college support from their families, require instructors to make academic expectations clear, since instructors and students do not have a shared cultural experience. About a third of the approximately 1,400 entering students place into basic writing courses. Students placed into the lowest level of two basic writing courses that precede college-level English are overwhelmingly students of color and nonnative speakers of English, often traditional college age, but equally often in their mid- to late twenties.

The most common difficulty basic writing students have, and which often marks them out for basic writing courses, is their use of nonstandard varieties of English. They also are unfamiliar with essay and paragraph structures used in English composition, and they have difficulty developing content. In the "TYCA White Paper on Placement Reform," the executive committee of the Two-Year College English Association notes that these institutions must accommodate the needs of students who may not be familiar with college expectations and structures. With emphasis on the role of critical reform, a 2019 special issue of the *Journal of Writing Assessment* has been devoted to pedagogical, disciplinary, political, social, and ethical implications of writing placement (Kelly-Riley and Whithaus, *Two-Year College*). The very profile of our basic writers—forty-seven percent of whom are first-generation college students, with twenty percent identified as Black, non-Hispanic—highlights issues of equity and inclusion in English courses as gateways to college participation.

Faculty members have a responsibility for providing more than just access to the academy. English faculty members must construct writing classrooms that support all students' development and inclusion in the academy since academic English is crucial for success in other disciplines. We redesigned our lowest basic writing course, one of two basic writing courses, to enable students to become ready for first-year composition in just one semester instead of two by helping them express their writing skills with guidance that explicitly uncovers the implied values of academic writing.

A basic writing course is often the front gate to participation in the academy, and we are responsible for helping our students push the gate open. In *Literacy in American Lives*, Deborah Brandt discusses how "the cultural and social organization of a particular economy creates reservoirs of opportunity and constraint from which individuals take their literacy" (34). We need to ensure that basic writing courses are a reservoir of opportunity and not a vehicle for constraint. In *Digital Griots*, Adam Banks argues that students are often disconnected from their home literacy when they attend postsecondary study, and to be successful in college means adopting the language of the academy, a seeming rejection of their home community. Recognizing this difficult position, the 2005 National Council of Teachers of English Position Statement recommends that "[a]ll students need to be taught mainstream power codes/discourses and become critical users of language while also having their home and street codes honored" ("Supporting").

At Blue Ash College, we attend to the complex demands of basic writers. We see fairness as a form of equity achieved by exposing students to various genres of writing and by advancing the opportunity to learn through instructional and assessment practices that are formative. Following Alicia C. Dowd and her work on moving beyond access in two-year colleges, the teaching and assessment strategies we use may be considered a form of outcome equity. As Dowd argues, "[T]he provision of equal resources is not equitable when educational achievement gaps are so strongly correlated with family wealth and race/ethnicity" (410). As we show, students with greater educational needs require not only more but also different resources in order to achieve rates of course success equal to those with fewer needs. To avoid reproduction of what have been described as unfair writing processes (Inoue, *Labor-Based Grading Contracts*), we redesigned our course to integrate self-regulation strategies within an e-portfolio to foster student agency. Emphasis on both academic literacy practices and home literacies guide students' selection of topics for their writing projects, their representation of themselves in their e-portfolios, and their reflections on their literacy development.

Supporting Fairness through E-Portfolios

The e-portfolio is a critical element in facilitating equity and fairness in basic writing since it helps students demonstrate their progress achieving learning outcomes appropriate to their goals. Katherine V. Wills and Richard Aaron Rice note that "traditionally, portfolios have been considered valuable tools because in addition to embracing principles of validity and reliability as assessment measurements, they enable students to continue to learn as they construct their portfolios" (3). Since the 2000s, the use of e-portfolios for teaching and assessment has increased, and in 2016, the Association of American Colleges and Universities (AAC&U) designated e-portfolios as one of its research based "high-impact practices" (Watson et al. 1). In her introduction to *Electronic Portfolios 2.0*, Barbara Cambridge emphasizes that e-portfolios help researchers and instructors recognize "the breadth of learning that contributes to what students know and do and who they are" (xiii). Although e-portfolios are widely used in post-secondary settings, there is not much published about their use in basic writing programs at open-access, two-year colleges.

In a discussion of e-portfolios and fairness, Diane Kelly-Riley, Norbert Elliot, and Alex Rudniy observe that "ePortfolios have been touted for their flexibility across learning environments, and our study suggests that they are also flexible in their accommodation of learning demonstrated by diverse learners" (18). They found no difference among the white, Asian, and Hispanic students being assessed in two different e-portfolio programs. Since 2011, the *International Journal of E-Portfolio* documented the effectiveness of e-portfolios, and the AAC&U provides a searchable database of peer-reviewed research on e-portfolios going back to 2004 ("E-Portfolios"). Thus, as a high-impact practice that supports diverse student populations, e-portfolios are a logical choice for assessment of basic writers, since our students have little preparation for college writing and can benefit from the self-regulation skills required to build e-portfolios. They are potentially marginalized by not placing into first-year composition, and e-portfolios allow them to construct their identities as college writers. Tilisa Thibodeaux, Cynthia Cummings, and Dwayne Harapnuik assert, "ePortfolio learning has the potential to dynamically shift from knowledge-bearing repositories and assessment options to an interactive learning tool that promotes learner-centered principles, collaboration, and social constructivism" (9). Thus, using e-portfolios with a publicly shared set of rubrics created a fairer process for students. With Eric D. Turley and Chris Gallagher, we agree rubrics might lead to excessive standardization, false claims of objectivity, and formulaic responses from students and instructors alike. The key is to focus on aim, context, inclusion, and values. When tailored to the curriculum and its unique tasks, rubrics can be valuable to both instruction and assessment. Informed rubric design and use is especially important to the aim of fairness in basic writing courses at Blue Ash College. In our unique context, students need a realized sense of belonging as they explore their ability to control their own learning and use that personal agency to succeed in their future courses. The promise of e-portfolios for fair assessment of basic writers is, of course, not without challenges. Stefani Relles and William Tierney point out that not only do these students need to learn college English expectations but they also must learn e-portfolio technology. In "Helping Faculty in Two-Year Colleges Use E-Portfolios for Promoting Student Writing," we document how this is a problem of unfamiliarity with portfolio processes and technologies rather than one of ability. Increasing ability is integral to the values of our program.

Innovation at Blue Ash: E-Portfolios Emphasizing Self-Regulation and Self-Efficacy

Charles MacArthur and Steve Graham describe self-regulation strategies as goal setting, planning, seeking information, organizing, transforming, self-evaluating and revising, among other strategies (33). In our application, we operationalized our intervention to explicitly cultivate these strategies. Students followed the same process through four essays: writing their personal goals for the essay, planning what they needed to research, finding articles that would support and inform their ideas in the essay, writing reading logs that summarized and analyzed the information in the readings that related to their essay idea, turning the research into an outline and then an essay, peer reviewing and revising, and, finally, reflecting on the process and the outcome of the essay in their e-portfolios.

Whereas self-regulation strategies are addressed in the curricular innovation, issues of self-efficacy are addressed by the e-portfolio. MacArthur and Graham note, "unless these efforts [to cultivate self-efficacy] lead to successful independent writing experience, they may not enhance self-efficacy" (35). In the e-portfolio, students curate their process work, drafts, and reflections of each essay. Curating their work in one place where they can easily see and review it facilitates students' abilities to see the progress of their writing over the course of the semester.

Student Responses to the Redesigned Course

We redesigned our basic writing course to help unprepared students become ready to participate in an entirely new learning experience. Problems of time, money, and family make it hard for these students to prioritize their college work, and often attending class or doing homework is sacrificed for more pressing demands or emergencies. Many students come to us with undiagnosed learning disabilities or medical issues that make it hard to meet the normative cultural expectations of academic participation. In one basic writing class we can't address all these concerns. Nevertheless, we can support students as they begin to make their own plans for coping with the complexities of their lives and offer classroom experiences that support learning how to make those choices. Occasionally, faculty members with little experience teaching unprepared students may not be familiar with the challenges these students face and may attribute attendance and homework difficulties to laziness or lack of motivation, which could not be further from the truth.

The redesign of our basic writing course incorporated self-regulation activities, process work, and e-portfolio pedagogy. During spring 2015 through spring 2017, 134 students enrolled in this course in an Institutional Review Board–approved study. Twenty-nine went directly to the credit-bearing, first-year composition course, and eighty-four successfully completed the basic writing course and had the opportunity to progress to the next level of basic writing. This was different from our previous structure, where students often did not advance into the next basic writing course, and it was rare for any student to move directly into first-year composition.

We explored the students' reception of e-portfolios as a means to foster self-agency and self-regulation. We examined the work of sixty-one students from eight classes, spring semester of 2015 through spring semester of 2017. We analyzed a sample of students' final course portfolios ($N = 17$) and institutional data of students' persistence and retention in their subsequent English courses to examine if the course redesign led to more fair and equitable outcomes for students. We collected final course reflections ($N = 61$) and institutional end-of-course surveys ($N = 75$) to explore the role agency played in forging new identities as college writers and how e-portfolios supported student learning. Students were asked to write a final reflection in their e-portfolio about their experiences in the course. We coded sixty-one students' end-of-course reflective writing to measure their perceptions of personal agency and equity as they looked back on the course. We followed the constant comparative analysis of grounded theory (Strauss and Corbin) as we sought to create categories, based on student word choice, capturing the constructs of agency and equity. Two themes emerged from the analysis of reflections: a realization of their ability to control their education and the acquisition of skills that would allow them to participate in their studies as equals with their peers. Our analysis consisted of e-portfolio scores, course reflections, and end-of-course evaluations.

We used a rubric based on writing outcomes for the course to assess the effect of student agency on writing abilities. We assessed the four major essays of eleven students to analyze the progression of writing skills on a three-point scale (1 = not proficient, 2 = developing, and 3 = proficient). We resolved differences in scores through discussion to arrive at a consensus score. Results are given in table 1.

We found students demonstrated statistically significant progress in our rubric areas that measured maintaining a central idea, incorporating ideas from other texts, and executing MLA format. Students progressed in their ability to

Table 1. Early and End-of-Course Portfolio Scores (N = 47)

Maintaining a central idea			
Essay 1 = 2.41 (M) and 0.68 (SD)	Essay 4 = 2.72 (M) and 0.46 (SD)	$t = 2.58$ $p < 0.01$	Finding: Scores improved at statistically significant levels
Incorporating ideas from other texts			
Essay 1 = 1.91 (M) and 0.66 (SD)	Essay 4 = 2.27 (M) and 0.78 (SD)	$t = 2.4$ $p < 0.01$	Finding: Scores improved at statistically significant levels
Executing MLA formatting			
Essay 1 = 1.19 (M) and 0.79 (SD)	Essay 4 = 2.36 (M) and 0.67 (SD)	$t = 7.7$ $p < 0.01$	Finding: Scores improved at statistically significant levels
Developing paragraphs with examples			
Essay 1 = 2.45 (M) and 0.71 (SD)	Essay 4 = 2.63 (M) and 0.5 (SD)	$t = 1.4$ $p > 0.01$	Finding: Scores did not improve at statistically significant levels
Generating and evaluating one's own writing			
Essay 1 = 2.16 (M) and 0.83 (SD)	Essay 4 = 2.36 (M) and 0.67 (SD)	$t = 1.2$ $p > 0.01$	Finding: Scores did not improve at statistically significant levels
Summarizing sources			
Essay 1 = 2.33 (M) and 1.07 (SD)	Essay 4 = 2.54 (M) and 0.52 (SD)	$t = 1.2$ $p > 0.01$	Finding: Scores did not improve at statistically significant levels
Using academic English syntax and vocabulary			
Essay 1 = 2.00 (M) and 0.85 (SD)	Essay 4 = 2.27 (M) and 0.64 (SD)	$t = 1.2$ $p > 0.01$	Finding: Scores did not improve at statistically significant levels

M = Mean; SD = Standard Deviation; t = Difference in means; p = Measure of probability.

develop paragraphs with examples, generate and evaluate their own writing, summarize sources, and use academic English syntax and vocabulary, although not to levels of statistical significance. Scores from essay 1 to essay 4 were higher in all categories, and the range of the spread of their scores (standard deviation) decreased. These outcomes areas are skills that serve students well throughout their college careers in other disciplinarily situated writing tasks. As students perceive their own growth in these skills and realize their agency over their learning, they find success in other courses.

In course reflections, students often described how the course design supported personal agency. Personal agency refers to students' perception that they guided their own work in the course, including developing skills and processes that supported their writing goals. They also identified helpful processes, such as peer review. One student described how she used the feedback to improve her writing: "I have taken my mistakes and used them to further my knowledge in writing." Students also cited technology as something that helped them achieve their writing goals. Weekly quizzes helped improve their vocabulary; the use of collaborative documents helped identify editing issues and how they revised their work for their e-portfolios. Students reported that the course enabled them to learn what they needed to learn. They cited being able to choose which course they would go to next as empowering. One student in particular described how the course empowered her:

> I was so nervous. I thought I would not know what I was doing at all. This semester I just know it was going to be hard until the point that I was going to fail or would want to drop out. I thought that the professor was going to not care about if we fail. I was thinking that the professor was just going to act mean. I thought that the professor was going to criticize me for being pregnant. I came in thinking the students wouldn't want to start a study group with me. I just thought it was going to just be a disaster. Gladly I was wrong about the whole thing.

This student expresses the anxiety many students have when they are placed in this course. They worry they won't belong in the classroom or at the college. This student expected negative judgment from faculty and students that did not transpire. Course design that allows students to work at their own pace and on topics of their choice provides a welcoming environment where students can build on what they know.

End-of-course surveys demonstrated that the course gave students the skills needed to be successful in college, a process for writing essays that helped them write well, and a sense of confidence as capable writers. These basic writers come to the course feeling insecure about their ability to write, and because of their personalized study, they feel more confident about their writing, as figure 1 shows. Students felt a sense of agency in achieving the skills to write more confidently and valued the level of personal choice afforded by the course. They also appreciated the personal attention to choice in the design of the course, as figure 2 shows.

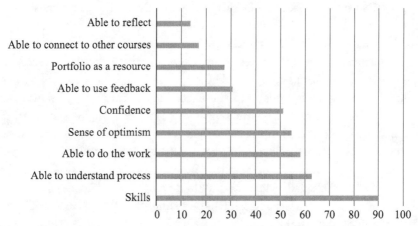

Figure 1. Analysis of Student Perceptions of Personal Agency in Final Course Reflective Writing ($N = 61$).

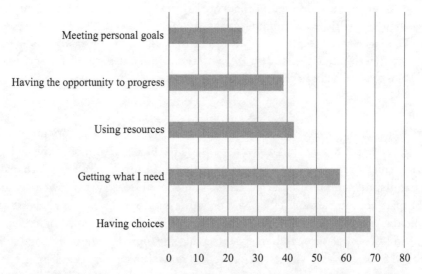

Figure 2. Analysis of Student Perceptions of Equity in Final Course Reflective Writing ($N = 61$).

Finally, we looked at external end-of-course measures. The college distributes an online survey titled "Student Perceptions of Teaching and Learning." From these, seventy-seven students from 2015 (n = 36), 2016 (n = 30), and fall semester of 2017 (n = 11) strongly agreed with the statement "I understood the rationale for the activities/assignments." Indeed, the vast majority reported that they strongly agreed with the statement "I learned a lot in this course." In these surveys, students consistently reported that they perceived the design and facilitation of the course to be effective.

The Future of Basic Writing at Blue Ash College

Institutions of higher education must meet the needs of students who might require support in meeting the cultural and academic expectations of college. Prior to our course redesign, our basic writing course did not respect students' agency as college writers. This previous course did not give them the opportunity to have control over their own writing and goals and may have discouraged them from continuing their education. The former curriculum focused on students as deficient and therefore did not meet their needs. Thus, the first part of our innovation was to give students agency by allowing them to choose their own topics, readings, and personal goals for the course. By structuring the process for each essay, we helped students practice the self-regulation strategies that would give them the tools to exercise agency, such as setting personal goals before writing, researching, summarizing, outlining, drafting, peer reviewing, revising, and reflecting. We addressed the issue of helping students increase their perceptions of self-efficacy through the use of e-portfolios that allowed them to see and reflect on their progress in the course in a tangible way.

Student essays showed improvement over time, particularly in formatting, focus, and incorporating ideas from their research. In their reflections, students commented on how comfortable the course was and how proud they were of their progress. Students also reported in surveys that they valued the skills they learned in the course and that they were able to make choices about what they wrote and what course they would take next.

In a study focused on self-regulation strategies in a basic writing course, Blake and colleagues reported that students who learned strategies such as setting goals, planning, and reflecting reported feeling more control over their writing (agency) and more confidence in what they needed to do (self-efficacy) (169). This positive attitude can be a great support in being able to succeed in other courses. One of our students wrote:

> In this essay the strengths I got was to be able to overcome my weaknesses
> in critical thinking that I had and I was able to look deeper into my personal

capabilities. For example, my personal capabilities are to get good topics, reading to understand what other people wrote, but my weaknesses were not wanting to stress myself to think deep when writing my own essays to give an explanation in the way I love to read to others, but with the deep research process I have learned, it has really helped me to be more productive in my writing. Over this course my emotions changed towards a better attitude for learning. I feel great right now knowing that I was able to challenge myself to improve in my writing, which I could not do in the past, and to be patient to follow the steps given to us by our professor.

This student demonstrates an awareness of critical thinking, audience, and process. He was able to publish his work. Like Blake and colleagues, we view this ownership of one's writing as a sense of personal control that leads to more confidence and will open doors for these students to remain in postsecondary study.

E-portfolios contribute to fostering a sense of agency and confidence by providing a way for students to keep track of the self-regulation skills they learn in the course. The progress from the first essay through the last, with all the process and reflection involved, gives a clear picture of that evolution for students to reflect on. The e-portfolio contributes to the fairness of the course assessment by giving the full picture of the student learning process in the context of all the different kinds of work the students does—emotional and cognitive—instead of just a final essay. The flexibility of the e-portfolio accommodates a wide range of learning and writing abilities in our classes.

Through our emphasis on student agency, we create a social environment that empowers students' choices. These choices and the agency they make possible are integral to the facilitation of equity and the pursuit of fairness. As Chen and Simone point out, placement in a basic writing course for students with weak preparation means they are often less likely to complete college-level courses. Allowing these students to choose how they demonstrate their writing abilities in a supportive environment gives them respect as thinking, mindful, agentic individuals. They are able to create writing, documented in an e-portfolio, that speaks to their capabilities, not their putative deficits. This structure emphasizes fairness for basic writers, because the course addresses external factors reflected in the e-portfolio, such as self-regulation and self-efficacy. The e-portfolio presents a student's pieces of writing in interaction with each other, creating an individual portrait of writing development.

Feedback Analytics for Peer Learning: Indicators of Writing Improvement in Digital Environments

William Hart-Davidson and Melissa Graham Meeks

Perspective

In this essay we explore Web-based peer review platforms embedded within writing classrooms and ways these platforms promote fairness. We begin with the concept of *giver's gain* as inherently useful in a commons-based view of peer production. We then introduce our view that revision is a deliberative practice in decision-making. We turn to a five-factor model to illustrate patterns in peer review among cohorts of students and track its use in the percentage of comments actually added to revision plans. We close with a longitudinal portrait of peer review performance of one student over the course of a semester. As part of the emerging field of writing analytics, such reporting provides a real-time description of individual student and group learning efforts, allowing instructors to identify and respond to those conditions of isolation that threaten a fair, reciprocal learning environment in which conversation about written drafts matters most.

Seeing Writing Practice: Indicators of Improvement

We begin with a narrative. In figure 1, each bar represents the number of words a student wrote in one first-year writing class at a community college in the southeastern United States. Student labels are represented with two types of information: first, a description of the student's performance on the first writing sample (strong, struggling, solid, and a student receiving grades of D, F, or W); and second, the student's ranking within their group based on their contributions in peer learning. For example, the student labeled Struggling01 ranked highest for peer contributions compared with other students whose first writing samples suggested that they would struggle to meet course outcomes. The dark

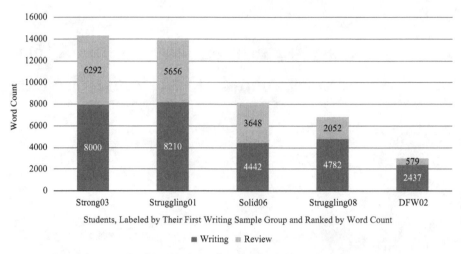

Figure 1. Word Count in Student Drafts and Reviewer Comments.

gray column shows the number of words a student wrote during the process of drafting four one-thousand-word essays. The light gray column shows the number of words the student gave in comments during peer review. Which students do you expect improved in terms of course grades?

You might have guessed that the student labeled Strong03 earned an A average on final drafts. Struggling01 and Solid06 students both showed improvement too, earning a B average on final drafts. The student labeled Struggling08 earned a D, and DFW02 earned an F—and missed out on the chance to practice revision decisions at a similar level to their peers. Strong03, Struggling01, and Solid06 experienced a phenomenon we call *giver's gain*.

In this essay we examine giver's gain as a phenomenon associated with a commons-based view of peer production. Coined by Yochai Benkler and Helen Nissenbaum, "commons-based peer production" is a situated phenomenon of digitally networked environments (394). Building on this concept, Quentin D. Vieregge and colleagues note, "If peer production is to assume its own age, then it must be more about values than about tools, which are replaceable and easily outdated" (3). Teaching and assessing writing in digital environments—especially in the case of peer review, the subject of this essay—has the potential of building community and ending isolation. As writing is taught and assessed in digital environments, opportunities increase for virtuous behavior as students help each other become better writers. Over time, such virtuous practice may transfer not only for individual students but also for those who witness such practice, leading to more and more students adopting peer review practices as their own. If we define virtue as "the full gamut of moral predications" (Wiggins 83), then we may, by extension, define the reciprocity of peer review as contributing to virtuous behavior. Pedagogically, as Kwangsu Cho and Christian D. Schunn have noted, the implementation of peer review into the writing process allows students to take the role of both reviewer and writer (412). This dual role allows students to detect barriers to effective writing that they may not identify on their own (Markman) and to consider effective rhetorical choices related to audience (Bitzer). In science, technology, engineering, and mathematics classes, peer feedback allows students to provide detailed, conceptually focused comments on the work of other students—irrespective of the content under review (Finkenstaedt-Quinn et al. 235).

As we demonstrate in this essay, broad concepts of virtuous practice may be pedagogically instantiated in digital environments by attending to indicators of effective peer review and reporting these indicators in terms of group and individual performance. Before proceeding to qualitative and quantitative analyses of peer review processes, we begin with the concept of giver's gain and the empirical evidence that supports its value.

Giver's Gain and Peer Review: Connections

Giver's gain aligns with E. Shelley Reid's argument in "Peer Review for Peer Review's Sake: Resituating Peer Review Pedagogy." She "reimagine[s] peer review as a core assignment in our classes" (217) because "it is the assignment that best encapsulates what we want writers to do after they leave our class" (219). Giving feedback, Reid explains, asks students to read and talk back to writers about drafts in progress with an eye for meeting criteria. It's where they learn to revise, weighing options for best meeting readers' needs. She argues that reviewers' benefits from giving less-than-expert feedback exceed the costs of writers receiving it. The gains appear across learning groups. English as a second language research, for example, offers clear support for giver's gain (218–21). Notably, in Kristi Lundstrom and Wendy Baker's study of an intensive English institute, low- and high-proficiency second-language writers either gave feedback or received it for the whole semester. Givers made more gains than receivers. Givers from the low proficiency group made the most gains as writers (38).

The most robust evidence from giver's gain is from peer-grading research. Kwangsu Cho and Charles MacArthur propose a "learning by reviewing hypothesis" (74). Their study used *SWoRD*, a peer grading system developed by Schunn, now marketed as *Peerceptiv*. Cho and MacArthur found that among peer reviewers, those who detected the most problems in the sample texts as reviewers went on to produce the highest-rated drafts. Reviewers' solution suggestions and problem detection were positively correlated with writing quality, and problem detection accounted for most of the variance in the quality of their lab report introductions.

Building on Cho and MacArthur's research, in a study of first-year engineering students using *Turnitin*'s *PeerMark*, David Nicol and colleagues found that

> [r]eceiving reviews is seen by students as beneficial primarily because it alerts them to deficiencies or gaps in their work, or because it sensitizes them to the different ways in which readers might interpret what they have written. Providing reviews, instead, is viewed as beneficial because it engages students actively in critical thinking, in applying criteria, in reflection and, through this, in learning transfer. (116)

Mario Gielen and Bram DeWever found that giving criterion-referenced feedback matters in a study that explored how different peer feedback methods used in a wiki improved writers' ability to summarize a professional journal article in educational psychology. After three rounds of practice, peer reviewers who were taught to provide elaborated feedback on ten specific criteria were rated highest as reviewers and writers. Reviewers in the basic structure condition were asked only to name something good and something that needs to change. Reviewers in the basic structure group did improve their own drafts slightly but not as much as those in the criterion-referenced feedback condition. By contrast, reviewers in the no-structure group had no measurable improvement as writers.

Zoi A. Philippakos and MacArthur studied writing skill transfer in persuasive writing of fourth and fifth graders. Like Cho and MacArthur's results, this study compared reviewers, readers of model essays, and readers of age-level-appropriate narrative books. After three days of practice, students revised their arguments. Students immediately wrote another argument (near transfer test) and a third argument followed a few days later (delayed transfer test). On all final drafts, the reviewer group produced drafts with more persuasive elements related to counterarguments, including opposing positions and rebuttal, and more final thoughts for the reader in the conclusion. Reviewers' revised essays were of significantly higher quality than both other groups in immediate post tests and the transfer test. In the delayed transfer test, reviewers' revised drafts were significantly better than the reader group. Melissa M. Patchan and Schunn offer a helpful summary of the giver's gain phenomenon: "in both writing tasks and while constructing feedback, students must detect problems and diagnose those problems or select appropriate solutions. This practice of revision skills while constructing feedback may be an important contributor to why students learn from the process of providing feedback to peers" (607).

The theory and evidence are clear that giving helpful feedback improves writing. In writing classrooms, the opportunity to learn to give helpful feedback is an issue of fairness. Evidence puts a premium on equal opportunity to give rather than receive feedback as a key to writer improvement. As is the case with James G. Greeno and Melissa S. Gresalfi, our approach "[considers] the trajectories of individuals' participation as they become members of a group" (170). The classroom is conceived as an activity system where "learners participate more proficiently in practices that have structure" (171). In our view, reviewers who learn and have adequate opportunity to give helpful feedback are on

> trajectories toward stronger valued capabilities and dispositions [as writers] . . . , [where] high levels of cognitive demand involving meaningful social interaction and significant contact with concepts and principles of subject-matter domains [by offering] participation structures that involve exercising significant conceptual agency; and adequate skills and knowledge for routine procedures and information. (193)

Simply put, peer review that is fair to learners must create the conditions for giver's gain. Instructors should engage students in the deliberate practice of giving helpful feedback. To practice fair pedagogy, instructors should teach helpful feedback methods and assign enough reviews that the weakest reviewers can improve. Within this feedback practice schedule, to be fair, students should contribute at roughly the same rate as their peers.

Comments: Deliberate Practice for Making Revision Decisions

Evidence for the value of criterion-referenced review and revision as a driver of learning in writing led us, more than ten years ago, to create *Eli Review*, a software service that allows instructors to do two critical things in support of a pedagogy that emphasizes review and revision. One is to more easily coordinate reviews. The other is to harvest indicators of learning from the many-to-many interactions in peer learning. *Eli*'s focus on what writers, reviewers, and instructors need to do and see in order to improve makes it a construct-specific digital ecology focused on peer feedback and revision. It is similar to systems like *MyReviewers, Peerceptiv, Peergrade.io,* and others that encode pedagogies of writing assessment rather than merely deliver grading efficiency like peer review tools in LMS platforms such as *Blackboard, Canvas,* or *D2L.* Although *Eli*'s focus is on formative feedback (hence our focus in this essay), our discussion of the research is far from an advertisement for our platform. Indeed, we believe the development of new digital writing ecologies will substantially advance our ability to teach and assess writing. The work we present is based on the belief that rapid, actionable feedback of the kind we report has the capability of substantially advancing the body of knowledge in writing studies.

The mounting evidence for giver's gain led us to investigate how best to foster the deliberate practice of revision. R. T. Kellogg and A. P. Whiteford define "deliberate practice" as a focus on the individual components of a task in order to improve performance and self-regulation (251; see also Ericsson et al.; Zimmerman). Without deliberate practice of revision, writers will not improve. But practicing revision can be difficult because revision typically refers to the changes between drafts. In a typical writing course, instructors can assign only two or three revised drafts per project at most. The result is that the amount of revision practice students get is limited.

We address this problem by focusing on revision decisions instead of on drafts. A revision decision involves detecting a problem and identifying a solution. *Eli* facilitates two types of revision decisions: feedback students give and feedback students use in revision plans. In this essay we limit our discussion to the first of these: the feedback students give. Consider the comments offered by Reviewer A and Reviewer B:

REVIEWER A

I would use the word "until" in replace of till
Failure [an edit]
Although excel is a good word choice in this case, i believe exceed would work
   better.
eliminate this word and the sentence will sound better.

REVIEWER B

During the explain and context portion of this paragraph, I can see where you're coming from. It is good, however to make it better you can try relating more to the quote of the author more. Instead of explaining how scared you are of the class, explain that you are facing your fears and will hit them head on.

   After reading this paragraph, I'm not sure where the rest of this essay will go. It's hard to predict because I'm not aware of the main idea within this single paragraph. However, the main ideas may include the fear of failure, and how anxiety can help or not help one get over this fear of it.

Reviewer A's comments correct diction, and attention is paid solely to knowledge of conventions. Reviewer B's comments refer to various criteria and explain fully how the draft has/lacks those criteria; the suggestions are related to rhetorical knowledge. The differences in these two reviewers' work goes beyond *what* they were commenting on. It's also about *how* reviewers' engagement with the draft affects their own learning. By giving feedback, Reviewer B is practicing revision based on a situated view of language. Reviewer A is practicing something else: editing.

A Heuristic for Helpful Comments that Models Revision Decision-Making: Describe, Evaluate, Suggest

Our materials for instructors and students encourage comments for revision that follow a describe-evaluate-suggest heuristic pattern:

Describing means saying back to the writer what you understand as a reader.

Evaluating is explaining how a part meets or doesn't meet the criteria.

Suggesting is offering concrete advice for improvement.   (McLeod et al.)

This pattern for helpful comments offers three benefits. First, the pattern scaffolds students' thinking and offers a repeatable set of actions: closely read the draft, apply criteria, and consider a change. Once reviewers have the basic moves for giving feedback in their repertoire, the range of criteria they mention in their feedback usually expands. Second, comments that fulfill the heuristic pattern are more likely to convince writers that revision is needed and to help them know how to do it. Third and most important for our purposes here, comments that follow the heuristic pattern allow revision practice for the reviewers who give them. Reviewers who describe-evaluate-suggest are mentally going through the revision process. Such pedagogical heuristics allow instructors to broaden student knowledge of composing processes.

When reviewers **describe** the draft in their own words, they build ethos, proving themselves fair and thoughtful readers of the writer's work.

When they **evaluate** the draft according to criteria, they detect a problem and note its impact.

When they **suggest** a strategy or question or even an edit, they pose a solution.

A comment based on this heuristic pattern makes a clear argument for revision. It has enough information for writers to make a good decision about whether and how they will revise.

A Simple Measure for Giver's Gain: Feedback Fitness

There is big challenge for teachers seeking to use the evidence from the studies cited earlier supporting giver's gain: how do we see and react in real time to the practice routines of our students? To do this, teachers must tangle with the complexities of coordinating multiple reviews, ensuring that each student has an opportunity to give and receive adequate feedback. This means circulating multiple drafts between multiple individuals and groups. In addition, there is the challenge of identifying whose engagement as a reviewer is too minimal for writers to get the feedback needed both to be convinced revision is required and to know how to revise, as well as for reviewers to practice their own feedback skills.

Harvesting data using methods from published giver's gain research is not terribly helpful for teachers because the information arrives too late. The analysis process involves human coding of drafts and comments. Most instructors could never replicate these studies as part of their routine pedagogical practice. In order to use giver's gain as a just-in-time intervention, we have developed a simple measure to alert classroom instructors to which students are doing too little to expect improvement. Our approach uses statistical methods to create data tables and visualizations that help instructors intervene to create better peer-learning experiences for individuals as well as the whole class.

Our method is a very narrow one. It is meant to help instructors identify struggling students quickly. And that is all it does. It is not a grade. It is not a robust evaluation of students' writing ability. It is designed to detect when too little practice is happening by identifying reviewers whose feedback to peers is below the threshold needed to expect improvement.

In the next section of the essay, we present a study of forty-eight students in a first-year writing course at a community college. The data presented have been de-identified, and the full study was reviewed and declared exempt by the campus's Human Subjects Review Board. We have replicated this analysis in more than sixty other courses at a variety of institution types and levels.

Components of Feedback Fitness

We use the metaphor of a fitness tracker in order to emphasize that learning to give helpful feedback requires deliberate practice. We propose that, like athletes, musicians, or dancers, writers improve only with enough frequency, intensity, and quality in their practice.

> **Frequency.** Students should practice giving helpful feedback often (many times a term) and in close proximity (many times in a row).
>
> **Intensity.** Students should practice giving feedback deliberately at or above the level of contribution consistent with peer norms in their class.
>
> **Quality.** Student feedback is criterion-referenced and becomes more helpful (using the describe-evaluate-suggest heuristic pattern) over time.

The way a fitness tracker counts steps or miles, we aim to count students' contributions to peer learning. In our calculations, *frequency* is the number of reviews in which students contribute comments. *Intensity* is word count in the comments exchanged. We use word count as an intensity measure for several reasons. First, recall that the describe-evaluate-suggest comment pattern encourages students to write at least three sentences. Second, although we are not sure more words are better, we do know too few words mean a comment is likely to be unhelpful for revision. Third, word count is reliably measured, but it is important to be conservative in interpreting its validity. Since the goal is to find students who are not on track to succeed, we look for word counts that are too low.

Our indicators for the *quality* of feedback are based on downstream user actions. Writers rate how helpful comments are to them and add the best comments to revision plans. Instructors can also endorse comments. It is important to be cautious about these measures too. We especially want to check that users reliably engage in those actions as a group for the measures to be meaningful. To perform this check, we use intensity indicators and quality indicators.

Intensity Indicators: Peer Norms of Feedback Fitness

To build our real-time picture of practice frequency, intensity, and quality, we establish peer norms across all the indicators. After sorting the roster of reviewers from most to fewest words given in feedback, we group the top thirty percent, middle forty percent, and bottom thirty percent, as shown in table 1. Then, within each group, we calculate the harmonic mean for each indicator. The harmonic mean adjusts for outliers, so it increases the resolution in the distribution. In terms of performance, the top thirty percent of reviewers missed between zero and two reviews and wrote over one hundred comments, producing more than five thousand words in feedback and missing only ninety-four words. Around seven percent of their comments were shorter than twenty words, the common length for praise and edits; sixty-four percent of their comments were

Table 1. Intensity Indicators

Indicators	Top 30% of Reviewers	Middle 40% of Reviewers	Bottom 30% of Reviewers
Number of comments	103	86	37
Total word count in comments	5314	2944	1035
Number of missed words (~average of bottom 30% when no comment given)	-94	-266	-1218
Percentage of too-short comments (fewer than twenty words)	7	13	37
Percentage of long-enough comments (more than forty-one words)	64	36	12

longer than forty-one words, indicating they were long enough to include all three moves of helpful feedback. This trend is confirmed, because these reviewers had the highest helpfulness average, the most endorsements, and the most comments added to revision plans. The middle forty percent of reviewers practiced with similar frequency to the top group, missing between zero and two reviews. But they practiced with less intensity, producing only eighty-six comments and just under three thousand words in feedback. They wrote twice as many short comments and half as many long-enough comments. All three quality indicators for this group indicate that they were, as expected, middle-of-the-road. The bottom thirty percent is distinctive. They practiced less frequently, missing four to six reviews, and they engaged very little when they participated. They wrote fewer than half the number of comments as the middle forty percent and one-third the words of the top thirty percent. Almost forty percent of their comments were too short to be helpful, and just over ten percent were long enough to include describe-evaluate-suggest. This group, unsurprisingly, had the lowest helpfulness ratings, the fewest endorsements, and the smallest number of comments added to writers' revision plans.

Following classification, we use the five indicators of intensity to gauge reviewers' contributions shown in table 1.

Indicator 1: Comment Count

The first intensity indicator is the total number of comments made. As noted above, the top thirty percent of reviewers by contribution composed just over one hundred comments in thirteen reviews, and the middle forty percent almost ninety. By comparison, the bottom thirty percent of reviewers composed fewer than forty. The difference in comment count for the bottom thirty percent is related to missed reviews, but that group also wrote fewer comments in the reviews in which they participated. These data highlight the effects of low intensity and skipped practice.

Indicator 2: Word Count

The second intensity indicator is our strongest, and it is the basis for the groups: the total number of words in comments. There's a two-thousand-word difference between groups when they are sorted by their intensity in peer learning. The top thirty percent wrote five times more words than the bottom thirty percent, and the middle forty percent wrote three times more words than the bottom. This five-three-one pattern in word count is a pattern we've seen repeated across many courses that are highly asymmetrical.

Indicator 3: Missing Words

The third intensity indicator represents a technique we borrow from intent-to-treat clinical trials as a way of addressing missed doses. The clearest picture of reviewer intensity is not only what practice they did but also what practice they missed. To estimate missed practice, we worked from the assumption that a student who had participated in the review would have written at least as many words as the bottom thirty percent. We replace a zero word count for a review with the negative value of the average word count among the bottom thirty percent for that review. For example, in review 3, the bottom thirty percent averaged 106 words. Students who missed that review are shown as having written –106 words. The top group missed so rarely that the harmonic mean of the group is ninety-four words—a paragraph. The middle group missed writing 266 words in feedback—about a page. The bottom group missed more than twelve-hundred words or nearly five pages of feedback. Missing practice is missing learning, and this approach reveals the costs.

Indicator 4: Percentage of Too-Short Comments

The next two intensity indicators relate to comment length. We look at the percentage of comments with fewer than twenty and more than forty-one words. We use twenty words as the floor because in the research we have done comments written by first-year reviewers at that length are very unlikely to have the information writers need to revise. That is, most twenty-word comments cannot contain all the describe-evaluate-suggest moves; many are rather praise or edits. In the bottom group, nearly forty percent of comments were too short to be helpful. The other groups are near ten percent for too-short comments. This pattern suggests low intensity reviewers did not learn to elaborate their feedback using describe-evaluate-suggest like the other groups did.

Indicator 5: Percentage of Long-Enough Comments

For the final indicator, we look at comments longer than forty-one words, because that is the length at which editing and simple praise comments disappear and we are more likely to see describe-evaluate-suggest. We use average instead of harmonic mean for this indicator. (Harmonic mean excludes zeroes.) A reviewer with zero comments longer than forty-one words is meaningful, so an average is used for this indicator. Again, the groups are quite different. The top group has five times more long-enough comments than the bottom one, and the middle group has three times the number of long-enough comments than the bottom one. It's the five-three-one pattern again.

Quality Indicators: Helpfulness, Endorsements, Revision Plans

Quality indicators depend on users to take an action, and they require some interpretation. Adding a comment to a plan is the clearest signal that a peer's comment is helpful for revision. Many otherwise high-quality comments are not added to plans because they are praise, because the writer rejects them, or because the writer never read them. In addition, some unhelpful comments are added to the revision plan. To provide some sense of how reliable these measures are, we also show the percentage of comments rated, endorsed, and added to revision plans. Quality indicators are shown in table 2.

In terms of helpfulness rating by writers, the top thirty percent of reviewers by contribution averaged a 3.06 on a five-star scale. The middle forty percent and bottom thirty percent averaged between 2.7 and 2.5, respectively. Because of the likelihood of skew in the ratings, we find this data worth noting, but it is the least powerful indicator of the set. In terms of endorsements by instructors, only four percent of comments were endorsed by the instructor, but the top thirty percent got twice the number of endorsements as the other two groups. Because of the low overall percentage of endorsements, the strong contrast between the top thirty percent and the remaining two groups indicates that those highly engaged reviewers were also giving high-quality comments based on the instructor's expectations. As the third quality indicator, the number of comments added to writers' revision plans has proven to be the strongest of the three. Even though some helpful comments are not added and some unhelpful comments are added, there is a pronounced contrast among the groups. The top thirty percent of reviewers had thirty-six comments added to writers' revision plans; the middle forty percent had twenty-one added; and the bottom thirty percent only seven.

Table 2. Quality Indicators

Type	Indicators	Top 30% of Reviewers	Middle 40% of Reviewers	Bottom 30% of Reviewers
Quality	Helpfulness rating by writers	3.06	2.69	2.52
Reliability	Percentage of comments rated for helpfulness	75	67	62
Quality	Number of endorsements by instructor	3.83	1.91	1.25
Reliability	Percentage of comments endorsed by instructor	3	2	2
Quality	Number of comments added to writers' revision plans	36	21	7
Reliability	Percentage of comments added to revision plans	34	25	21

What is the value of this kind of report? In real time, a teacher can see these groups forming and help students adjust their practice routines early in the semester. Without this information, teachers may not realize they have a reciprocity gap threatening their goal to create an equitable learning space until it is too late.

Snapshots of Giver's Gain

We close our discussion with an example of how a teacher might detect and respond to an individual student's practice routine in order to help the student improve. Using additional information about incoming skill and final-draft grades, we visualize giver's gain for an individual student.

Figure 2 shows thirteen reviews across the x axis. Over time, we see how a single student's engagement in peer learning varied. The bars are word count. The first bar indicates feedback the student gave. The second bar records feedback the student received. The bottom line plots the average of the word count among the bottom thirty percent of participating reviewers in that specific review. The top line shows average among the top thirty percent of participating reviewers. In this class, note that there is at least a 250-word difference for every single review between the top and bottom thirty percent. This student struggled in the beginning but never missed a review. We also see that the student gave an

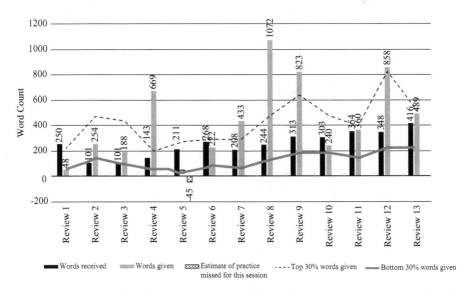

Figure 2. Words in Feedback Received, Given, and Missed Practice Sessions Compared with Peer Norms.

extraordinary amount of feedback about every fourth week. This feedback pattern corresponds to when projects are completed in final drafts. At the beginning of the process, this student did not know what to say about the criteria or the drafts. But after a few weeks of practice and class discussion, the student gains enough confidence and skill to be a helpful reviewer. The (inconsistent) pattern of the practice intensity indicates improvement because this is a reviewer who is figuring out how to say more to other writers. The message here for teachers is this: We need to stay patient because this student is working hard and learning. Working in a complex environment, the student may need help linking the criteria for a project to words in the text. Additionally, the student may also benefit from being paired with a strong reviewer whose comments she can learn from.

Measuring Practice to Enhance Fairness

After analyzing the practice routines of students in various institutions and levels, we see consistent evidence that practicing helpful feedback counts as good writing practice. This data can also help teachers increase fairness, facilitating an equitable, reciprocal learning environment in their classrooms. With foci on both group and individual performance, digital ecologies designed for teaching and assessing writing provide actionable information for students and teachers alike. Although little is known about how these systems will function over time, the emerging field of writing analytics holds promise for the study of writing in digital environments (Moxley et al.). Centering on multidisciplinary research, the intersection of educational measurement, massive data analysis, digital learning ecologies, and philosophical ethics, writing analytics of the kind presented in this essay appears promising in the study of commons-based peer production—and the virtue found within it.

Developing Culturally Responsive Assessment Practices across Postsecondary Institutions

Erick Montenegro

Perspective

In order to understand the learning gains made by all our students, assessment efforts must become culturally responsive. With acknowledgement of the many ways demographic differences influence performance, culturally responsive assessment is a movement arising from the field of program evaluation. This essay explores culturally responsive assessment praxis implemented at institutional, program, and course levels. First, I use a culturally responsive adaptation of the "Transparency Framework" developed by the National Institute for Learning Outcomes Assessment (NILOA) to illustrate an articulated conceptual approach applied to an institutional level. Next, I turn to the program-level outcomes statement for first-year composition developed by the Council of Writing Program Administrators as a framework responsive to situated practice. I conclude with classroom practices described by Cathy N. Davidson and Asao B. Inoue (*Labor-Based Grading Contracts*), respectively, to illustrate pedagogies that promote culturally responsive practice.

Introduction

The significant demographic changes occurring in the United States challenge colleges and universities to properly and fairly assess the learning gains of diverse students. The proportion of non-traditional-age college students between twenty-five and thirty-four years old increased by forty-one percent between 2000 and 2017, and that proportion is projected to be only six percent lower in 2028 than in 2017 (Hussar and Bailey). Between 2017 and 2028, the college enrollment rates of students of color are projected to increase by two percent for Asian and Pacific Islander students, fourteen percent for Hispanic students, and eight percent for Black students (Hussar and Bailey). The increasing diversity in our college classrooms means that student needs, expectations, level of preparation, and other factors of intersectionality will continue to impact campus educational environments.

Learning outcomes assessment is changing to meet the needs of a diversifying student population. Assessment practices look very different in minority-serving institutions (MSI) compared to predominantly white institutions (Montenegro and Jankowski, *Focused*). The Higher Education Act of 1965 established MSIs. There are approximately eight hundred total MSIs divided into seven subcategories, each devoted to serving a specific demographic: historically black colleges and universities (HBCU), Hispanic-serving institutions (HSI), tribal colleges and universities (TCU), Alaska Native– or Native Hawaiian–serving institutions, predominantly Black institutions, Asian American– and Native American Pacific Islander–serving institutions, and Native American–serving nontribal institutions. Of the seven MSI subcategories, only HBCUs and TCUs are founded with a mission specifically purposed to educate, uplift, and matriculate their communities. The remaining MSI types attain their minority-serving status through enrolling a specified proportion of students of color and meeting a financial need component (Higher Education Act). For example, HSIs must enroll at least twenty-five percent undergraduate full-time-equivalent Latinx students, of which at least fifty percent must be Pell Grant eligible (Higher Education Act). Thus, MSIs educate not only students of color but also students from low socioeconomic backgrounds, two populations largely disenfranchised by both higher education and society overall.

Minority-serving institutions have long recognized the importance of fairness in assessing student learning in order to gauge what students know and can do through differential assessment practices based on particular student populations. As my work with Natasha A. Jankowski demonstrates, MSIs have tailored their assessment practices to better fit the needs of their specific student populations (Montenegro and Jankowski, *Focused*). This is not to say that no predominantly white institution does this, too, but such practices are more likely at MSIs. The communities that MSIs enroll are underserved in society, meaning that these students walk through the college gates with differing levels of preparation, needs, and challenges that are not readily captured by standardized assessment practices. As such, MSIs tend to be more attentive to their institutional and student contexts in order to utilize assessment methods that are truly appropriate for all students. Norbert Elliot asserts this need for alignment, claiming that "fairness demands score disaggregation by group to identify those who are least advantaged so that positive action may be taken to minimize those differences" ("Theory"). In other words, to adopt this perspective educational leaders would hold that practices used to assess student knowledge take a threefold approach. First, assessment practices must be appropriate for every student and free of complex language, clear in its goals, and absent of assumptions and bias. Second, they should be applicable to every student in accounting for students' previous learning opportunities—based on demographic, cultural, and intersectional experiences—and must be directly linked to topics explicitly covered in the learning experience. Third, assessments must be disaggregated to illuminate specific impacts for all student groups involved and thus allow instructors to take stock of and improve on the varied ways that students from different backgrounds have historically performed on a given assessment.

Given the changing demographic profiles of campuses and students' diverse attributes, it makes sense to use assessment practices aligned with the varied needs of diverse learners. Culturally responsive assessment provides a scholarly framework to advance what many faculty and administrators have practiced at MSIs. As Natasha Jankowski and I have argued elsewhere:

> Defining "culture" and explaining what is meant by culturally responsive assessment is complicated. . . . Culturally responsive assessment is . . . thought of as assessment that is mindful of the student populations the institution serves, using language that is appropriate for all students when developing learning outcomes, acknowledging students' differences in the planning phases of an assessment effort, developing and/or using assessment tools that are appropriate for different students, and being intentional in using assessment results to improve learning for all students. Culturally responsive assessment involves being student-focused, which does not simply mean being mindful of students. Instead, being student-focused calls for student involvement throughout the entire assessment process including the development of learning outcome statements, assessment tool selection/development process, data collection and interpretation, and use of results. An essential aspect of maintaining focus on students is truly understanding the student population at the institution and/or level at which the assessment is being conducted.
>
> (Montenegro and Jankowski, "Equity" 10)

In the early 2000s, the field of program evaluation articulated approaches that were culturally competent. Melva Thompson-Robinson, Rodney Hopson, and Saumitra SenGupta detailed approaches in their edited collection, *In Search of Cultural Competence in Evaluation: Toward Principles and Practices*, that demonstrated a variety of private- and public-sector contexts in which diversity and differences presented complexities, challenges, and political issues in evaluation. These considerations and approaches moved into the fields of education. In education, culturally responsive assessment has been influenced by Gloria Ladson-Billings's concept of culturally relevant pedagogy, viewing student differences as a strength of the classroom experience to provide equitable learning outcomes for all students. Barry MacDonald's conceptualization of democratic evaluation acknowledges that evaluation processes and results can benefit some stakeholders at the expense of others. Of equal benefit to all, democratic evaluation is mindful of equity, recognizes power distributions, and involves those affected by the assessment process. As part of democratized evaluation, culturally responsive assessment requires attention to the actual learning outcomes—not just the intended outcomes—that occur as a result of learning experiences; this approach also considers the needs, requirements, and value perspectives of stakeholders (Stake 12). Equally related to democratized education, responsiveness challenges stakeholders to explore all preconceived notions of success and of what should happen in the classroom, increasing institutions' concern toward the needs of students and involving students in the assessment process. There are ways that culturally responsive assessment can be implemented at a variety of levels in postsecondary settings, and we turn now to some of those implementations.

Culturally Responsive Assessment at the Institutional Level

The National Institute for Learning Outcomes Assessment's "Transparency Framework" provides an articulated model to build upon for culturally responsive assessment at the institutional level. Founded by the universities of Illinois and Indiana under the leadership of George Kuh and Stanley Ikenberry, NILOA's primary objective has been to discover and disseminate ways that academic programs and institutions can productively use assessment data: internally to inform and strengthen undergraduate education and externally to communicate with policy makers, families, and other stakeholders. The "Transparency Framework" is a national effort by colleges and universities to obtain, use, and openly share evidence of student learning to strengthen student attainment and improve undergraduate education ("About Us"). The framework can also be used to inform culturally responsive assessment practices by helping institutions become increasingly transparent about their overall assessment processes through publicly sharing assessment plans, resources, data, and related elements of assessment design through institutional Web sites. Each section of the "Transparency Framework" suggests different resources that may interest institutions' stakeholders and elements that may help ensure the success of the assessment process. To be intentional in how resources are presented and organized, institutions must first consider their stakeholders and the purpose(s) of the assessment.

The "Transparency Framework" relies on institutional context in order to be effective. The description below details the six main components of NILOA's "Transparency Framework." Each component prompts explicit and clear language use, updated resources, and continuous feedback on quality and utility sought and incorporated as an ongoing activity.

The components below illustrate ways the framework may enact cultural responsiveness through added emphasis on the context where the assessments take place before, during, and after the assessment process; also, the framework elicits consideration of the impact of assessment results on stakeholders within that context. Making assessment-related materials available on institutional Web sites invites feedback regarding quality and usefulness. To this end, assessment efforts that aim to be culturally responsive must be highly transparent and open to feedback, specifically feedback from those who are directly impacted by assessment efforts and subsequent evidence-based changes. Formative feedback from stakeholders—especially students—is actively sought and used to inform the assessment process. Too often, students are bystanders in the assessment process. Listening to whether students feel the assessment process adequately captures their learning gains and whether faculty members believe that conclusions can be appropriately drawn between students' performance on an assessment and their actual ability can help improve the overall fairness of the assessment. In addition, the description below provides a combination of the six components of the assessment process articulated by NILOA and culturally responsive considerations incorporated at different stages of the assessment process.

CULTURALLY RESPONSIVE FRAMEWORK: THE NILOA TRANSPARENCY FRAMEWORK

Student Learning Outcomes Statements

Component Description: Outcomes statements articulate what students should know and be able to do upon graduation.

Markers of Transparent Resources: Specific to the institutional context

Culturally Responsive Questions to Consider:

Are learning outcomes statements devoid of vagueness and written clearly so every stakeholder understands them?

Are outcomes statements measurable?

Are outcomes statements verified with faculty members, students, employers, etc., to ensure they align with their values, needs, and goals?

Are outcomes intentionally and repeatedly communicated with students through-out their academic journey?

Are outcomes statements aligned across the institution and curriculum?

How will institutional, program, and classroom contexts including student com-position and needs be understood?

Will there be multiple points where stakeholder groups are involved and their feedback sought and incorporated in the assessment process?

Assessment Plans

Component Description: Assessment plans encompass the entire assessment process, including expected timelines, what evidence of student learning will be gathered, what methods will be used, and how often data will be collected.

Markers of Transparent Resources:

Descriptive representations of the assessment process

Detailed articulation of individual assessment measures used, including frequency of use, intended purpose, and ways both are applied

Culturally Responsive Questions to Consider:

How will institutional, program, and classroom contexts—including student com-position and needs—be understood?

Will there be multiple points where stakeholder groups are involved and their feedback sought and incorporated in the assessment process?

How are you being intentional in which assessment methods are used and how have such methods fared in the past with specific student populations?

What are the intended uses for assessment results, and how will they be verified by and shared with stakeholders?

Are the intended assessment tools a true representation of the learning gains of all students?

Are students involved in the assessment process, or are they merely the objects of assessment?

Are you collecting data that can be disaggregated by student demographics in meaningful ways that can lead to action?

Assessment Resources

Component Description: This component focuses on the resources, training, and guid-ance offered to those at the institution who participate in the assessment process to help them better understand how to gather, use, and communicate assess-ment data.

Markers of Transparent Resources: Written and presented so everyone, from experienced assessment professionals to novice-level practitioners, can understand

Culturally Responsive Questions to Consider:

> Is assessment data being collected as planned or should changes be made to increase both fairness for all students and the usefulness of results?

> Are enough different sources of evidence of student learning being incorporated into the assessment process?

> How are you mindful of biases and assumptions?

Current Assessment Activities

Component Description: Assessment activities are real-world, institution-specific examples of completed assessment activities or current ongoing assessment projects that attempt to gauge and improve student learning.

Markers of Transparent Resources: Clear about where the assessment activity fits into the overall assessment process, how it relates to the institution's mission, and how it will be used to improve learning

Culturally Responsive Questions to Consider:

> Is assessment data being disaggregated by student demographics?

> Is assessment data being compared to past data to see if there are changes or continuing trends both generally and disaggregated?

> Are results being shared with stakeholders to offer their interpretation, perceived accuracy, usefulness, and potential implications?

> How are you mindful of biases and assumptions?

Evidence of Student Learning

Component Description: Evidence can be direct or indirect examples of student learning, including institutional performance indicators, classroom assignments, pre- and post-surveys, etc.

Markers of Transparent Resources:

> Specific to what each piece of evidence of student learning means at the institution and/or program level context(s)

> Written and presented so everyone, from experienced assessment professionals to novice-level practitioners, can understand

> Presented using multiple media, such as reports, graphics, results snapshot briefs, etc., as appropriate for stakeholders

> Are the changes being made truly informed by evidence?

Culturally Responsive Questions to Consider:

> Are there changes being made in areas that will directly impact the student populations, programs, and activities that were assessed?

> Will intended uses of evidence be checked with stakeholders first to see how they align with stakeholders' perceived needs and data interpretations?

What are the potential intended and unintended consequences?

Is evidence simply graduation, retention, and/or participation statistics or is it more in-depth (e.g., classroom tasks, reflections, e-portfolios, and cocurricular experiences)?

Use of Student Learning Evidence

Component Description: The extent to which assessment results and data used to make changes in policy, practice, decision-making, and pedagogy to improve student learning, including how assessment data is used for accreditation purposes, faculty development, institutional and program goal setting, etc.

Markers of Transparent Resources:

Presented in various ways, each targeted to fit the needs of a specific audience

Supported by specific examples of use of assessment data

Forward-thinking regarding the next steps in the assessment process

Aware of how use of evidence has had an impact on student learning and practices at the institution

Culturally Responsive Questions to Consider:

What are the actual impacts of the changes made (intended and unintended, disaggregated impacts by student demographics, short- and long-term)?

How do stakeholders feel about the results?

What improvements can be made to future assessment processes and uses of evidence to improve teaching and learning for all students?

What changes need to be made to learning outcomes statements and sources of evidence to better capture student learning?

To document the ways culturally responsive approaches can enhance assessment efforts at the institutional level, I want to highlight a NILOA case study of North Carolina Agricultural and Technical State University (NCA&T), an institution that moved from a culture of compliance toward a culture of inquiry and assessment using the "Transparency Framework" and asking questions similar to those posed in the description above. North Carolina A&T, a historically Black university, has been a leader in producing Black engineers ("N.C. A&T"). The institution has campus-wide learning outcomes statements to which programs and courses align. In addition, NCA&T uses a mixture of classroom assessment, local surveys, and national instruments to collect assessment data. Their initial efforts, though, were largely done out of compliance mandates. Now NCA&T is more intentional in involving stakeholders in the assessment process, and the culture at the institution has begun to change toward a culture of inquiry and assessment (Baker 3).

In particular, the institution developed a deeper understanding of their institutional context by investigating their students' demographic profiles, ascertaining students' needs, and encouraging student involvement throughout the assessment process. Thus, institutional stakeholders avoided making false assumptions about teaching, learning, student needs, and student preparation for their local context. Faculty members at NCA&T believed that the majority of their students were first-generation college students due to the high enrollment of students of color. After taking stock, however, the university discovered that only one quarter were first-generation students (Baker 6). These kinds of potentially incorrect assumptions about students can negatively affect both how assessments are conducted and how data are interpreted and subsequently used to inform changes. To avoid these pitfalls, NCA&T asked stakeholders—including students—to interpret assessment results (Baker 3). This practice guarded against harmful, unintended consequences for specific student populations.

In addition, students at NCA&T were given increased agency through student-led focus groups. This process uncovered students' interests, feelings toward faculty members, needs, opinions about campus, academic issues, and other factors related to assessment activities. Perhaps more important, their involvement in assessment equipped students with experiences that might be useful in the workforce. Students gained deeper understanding of how learning experiences and outcomes throughout college connect to one another (Baker 5–6). One NCA&T faculty member expressed the opinion that students who participate in the assessment effort are more likely to succeed because they can make the connection between what they are learning across courses (Baker 6). Also, by creating real feedback opportunities for all stakeholders, the assessment process became more transparent, valid, and impactful, as changes occurred that were informed by assessment data and based on what stakeholders indicated as being problematic, important, and meaningful.

Culturally Responsive Assessment at the Program Level

The NILOA "Transparency Framework" is one proven strategy that can help develop culturally responsive assessment if coupled with the right equity-focused approach. Yet another is to focus on the situated nature of a construct—how it is taught and assessed. In this work, members of the Council of Writing Program Administrators (WPA) have developed and continued to evolve the "WPA Outcomes Statement for First-Year Composition" for program-level assessment, and it has been used to identify issues for culturally responsive assessment. In a strategy similar to the component approach of NILOA, council members have identified four central competencies outlined in the 2014 version of the outcomes statement: rhetorical knowledge; critical thinking, reading, and composing; knowledge of writing processes; and knowledge of conventions. Each competency has respective traits that delineate what students should know and be able to do after their first-year composition course. Included with each competency are recommendations for faculty members to better help students achieve these outcomes. Kathleen Blake Yancey observes that a unique feature of the "WPA Outcomes Statement" was its focus on outcomes and not levels of performance: "While outcomes articulate the curriculum, they do not specify how well students should know or understand or do what the curriculum intends. . . . Because outcomes are not benchmarked against levels of performance, individual programs or institutions can have the same curricular outcomes but have different ideas about when and how well they want students to perform" (Yancey, "Standards" 22). Emphasizing equally contextualization and the situated nature of writing, Diane Kelly-Riley and Norbert Elliot note that

> the focus on outcomes was a way to recognize the unique local situation of first-year composition programs while providing curricular stability that resonated on a national level. . . . As a result of the focus on outcomes and the absence of levels of performance, a first-year writing program at a two-year, rural community college focused on retraining adult, displaced factory workers in the state of Michigan could have the same outcomes as undergraduates enrolled in the highly-selective first-year writing program at Harvard University.   (90)

Thus, the "WPA Outcomes Statement" is set up to support culturally responsive assessment practices if intentionally prompted.

The WPA outcomes areas do not specifically prompt culturally responsive assessment practices, and so programmatic applications must be intentional. For example, competency in rhetorical knowledge calls for students to "learn and use key rhetorical concepts through analyzing and composing a variety of texts" as well as "develop facility in responding to a variety of situations and contexts." ("WPA"). In this outcome statement, the phrases "key rhetorical concepts" and "develop facility" are deliberately general. To enact culturally responsive assessment, site-based institutional stakeholders would explicitly name which concepts might be aligned with the student populations at hand. This specificity would allow students to identify the knowledge, skills, and attitudes they are expected to acquire or develop further, as well as clearly inform them about what specific aspects of rhetorical knowledge will be assessed. In addition, the meaning behind "develop facility" may be confusing for some learners and difficult to assess. How much is enough "facility"? Which demonstrations of it are acceptable? Although some of the intended interpretation of this outcome can be discerned through contextual cues, learning outcome statements are best rendered campus- and culturally specific when explicit, action-oriented, and measurable (Adelman). It seems appropriate to ask how the questions of cultural responsibility raised in the framework described above would benefit students if applied to the outcomes statement.

Through the development of explicit, clear, and measurable outcomes statements that are appropriate for learners at specific institutional sites, we ready the assessment process to become more culturally responsive. There is no assessment practice, it appears, that is exempt from result disaggregation in order to more clearly understand the consequences of our practices. In "An Empirical Framework for E-Portfolio Assessment," for example, Kelly-Riley, Elliot, and Alex Rudniy demonstrate the disparate impact effect through consideration of the WPA outcomes assessed through e-portfolios. E-portfolios are "authentic assessment that draws on the work students do in regular course activities and assignments" and "reconnect assessment to the ongoing work of teaching and learning and to the work of faculty, raising the prospects for productive use" (Kuh et al. 36). E-portfolios can be tools of culturally responsive assessment by giving students agency to include projects they believe truly showcase their abilities. E-portfolios can be useful in programmatic assessment too, because they can draw student learning artifacts from across multiple sections of a program. In a study of e-portfolios across writing courses, Kelly-Riley, Elliot, and Rudniy nevertheless demonstrate that when scores are disaggregated by gender, race, and socioeconomic status, a more complex picture of student performance emerges. In terms of fairness,

> our analysis . . . highlights that students may concurrently occupy demographic spaces that place them in positions of both advantage and disadvantage . . . [which] encourages us to think about such complexities in our assessment reporting and to move beyond categorization of our students in isolated, demographic silos. Once we can begin to understand how student characteristics interact with domains of writing, we can then begin to chart an equitable and just way forward.   (112)

Because no genre of assessment is fair in and of itself, the use of such programmatic assessments provides key data that allows us to consider ways to promote culturally responsive practices more widely.

Culturally Responsive Assessment at the Classroom Level

In moving from writing outcomes to classroom practices, I find especially useful Davidson's and Inoue's documentation of two culturally responsive assessment practices situated in the classroom. In *The New Education*, Davidson describes how she cocreates her course's learning outcomes statements with her students. This practice serves to ensure both the clarity of outcomes and the involvement of stakeholders in the assessment process. Davidson begins each course with blank learning outcomes, and challenges her students with the task of creating learning goals for the class. Of course, she already has outcomes in mind, but this process helps negotiate the goals of the course with those of her various students. The process, which she has tried in seminars as large as six thousand students, involves teamwork, feedback, and consensus on a final set of learning outcomes, and the course is altered accordingly. This coconstruction also allows for the language and applicability of learning outcomes statements to be clear of assumptions that may not bode well for students from diverse cultural backgrounds. This process allows for learning outcomes to be collaborative and familiar to her students, as opposed to prescriptive. It is a process that helps increase students' understanding of the knowledge they gain and how it ties into students' overall college experiences. Students benefit from reflective and introspective activities such as these that allow them to make connections between various learning experiences; these are practices that help students transition from learning about lessons from experts in the discipline toward becoming experts themselves.

In *Labor-Based Grading Contracts: Building Equity and Inclusion in the Compassionate Writing Classroom*, Inoue describes the ways he has radically changed the grading practices in his postsecondary composition classrooms to ones that account for student differences. In his view, traditional grading practices "[engage] idiosyncratically with structured language systems that confine and pressure us in uneven power relations, relations that are mediated by our varied racialized, gendered, and linguistic embodiments" (21). Inoue uses grading contracts that are

> a set of social agreements with the entire class about how final course grades will be determined for everyone. These agreements are articulated in a contract, a document, that is negotiated at the beginning of the term or semester, then reexamined at midpoint to make sure it is still fair enough for everyone. It is a social, corporate agreement, which means it may not be a product of full consensus, but instead hard agreements.   (129)

In doing so, Inoue accounts for the different starting points of students in his courses and provides them the agency to achieve a desired grade based on their labor rather than on a certain standard of performance. Inoue sees this practice as a way to do social justice work with students through the determination of their course grades.

Conclusion

Assessment practices that bring fairness to the forefront and are culturally responsive can better position students to take charge of what they know and can do, properly apply and grow from feedback, and be better positioned to understand and lead in an ever-changing society that fashions social inequities. These are all impacts that are also deemed important by Davidson (9). Culturally responsive assessment works best with course-embedded assessments that are more authentic and direct. As Kuh and colleagues note, effective assessment is embedded within the natural, ongoing work in the classroom, such as presentations, course assignments, papers, and other performance genres (34) that instructors already use to gauge student learning. Embedded assessments directly align with measurable learning outcomes. In the instance that instructors need help achieving this alignment, NILOA offers guidance on how instructors can design assignments that are more transparent, accessible, and relevant for students and align to desired outcomes ("Assignment"). Mary-Ann Winkelmes and colleagues find that these practices in assignment design increase students' persistence, retention, academic confidence, sense of belonging, and skills; however, the impacts were more significant for students of color, first-generation students, and those with low socioeconomic status. As Davidson reminds us, assessment that organically moves classroom activities beyond "teaching to the test" and more toward embedded assessment can help promote pedagogical practices that can better prepare students to take lessons from the classroom and apply them in real-world contexts (8). Culturally responsive assessment is the first step in this process.

Using Transdisciplinary Assessment to Create Fairness through Conversation

Jeremy Schnieder and Valerie M. Hennings

Perspective

In this essay we present a transdisciplinary approach to assessment and fairness as a way of engaging meaningful communication among faculty members. At Morningside College, faculty members learn about the unique disciplinary perspectives of others and work to create a shared institutional vision of both the learning outcomes and learning experiences needed for this vision. Through these conversations, faculty members can reflect on the value from institutional assessment processes—sustained faculty development, curriculum development, and faculty-member-driven assessment—and adopt those lessons to their unique disciplinary settings. This essay therefore serves as a case study demonstrating that fairness may be promoted in meaningful ways in individual departments and across the wider institution.

Introduction

For some campuses, institutional assessment is done by solitary figures tucked away in an inaccessible corner office or relies on tests written and scored by external companies. Morningside College, a private, four-year college affiliated with the United Methodist Church, was one of those institutions. Morningside is categorized as a master's college and university, medium program institution by *The Carnegie Classification of Institutions of Higher Education*. In 2018–19, the school enrolled 2,697 students, with 1,212 full-time undergraduate students. The student body comprises predominantly white, non-Hispanic students; fourteen percent of students identify as students of color, fifty percent are women, and seventy-nine percent are from Iowa, Nebraska, and South Dakota.

At Morningside, a distributed, purchased test to assess student learning was a staple, but with it came questions regarding the validity of scores, since students weren't motivated to do well because the test was not part of a class and did not receive a grade. Initial efforts to develop homegrown tests met with similar concerns. As Ou Lydia Liu, Brent Bridgeman, and Rachel M. Alder note, student investment to perform well on assessments is a relevant issue, since motivation in testing situations affects scores, particularly essays (359). At Morningside, these questions led the faculty to desire a more authentic assessment, which transformed our assessment practices so that we use actual assignments generated in our classes. In this essay we present a transdisciplinary approach to assessment as a way of engaging communication among faculty members who work from disciplinary-specific expertise and contribute this perspective to create a shared institutional understanding. This understanding includes attention to both learning outcomes and learning experiences supporting assessment reform at the classroom and institutional levels.

Framing Transdisciplinary Assessment as an Opportunity to Learn

Patricia L. Rosenfield notes that in multidisciplinary approaches scholars from different disciplines work in parallel settings to eventually bring thoughts together; and in interdisciplinary approaches scholars from different disciplines work together but still from distinct disciplinary perspectives (1351). Only transdisciplinary approaches, we have found, result in something new, because scholars from different disciplines come together using a shared approach and framework that transcends pure disciplinary perspectives for a common goal.

Besides lack of student motivation, Morningside had other concerns with its assessment practices. Assessment sometimes generated data brought back to faculty members, but the data available were at best murky, and it was difficult to envision their use in individual classrooms. National surveys showed students felt like they were writing and speaking often, but faculty members wondered if the students were doing those tasks well and what performing well meant. Like many institutions, Morningside wrestled with how to define communication, critical thinking, and ethical reasoning—both within disciplinary contexts and more widely at the institutional level. For some faculty members, there was a clear disconnect between assessment practices, curriculum, and student learning.

Faculty members were concerned whether students had the same access to learning experiences or types of learning that the boxed assessments purported to measure. Faculty members were focused on the opportunities students were given to learn. The concept of opportunity to learn dates back to the 1960s and means that all students need to have access to the types of knowledge and skills being assessed and the same opportunity to do well on the test. Scholars Pamela A. Moss, Diana C. Pullin, James Paul Gee, Edward H. Haertel, and Lauren Jones Young reasserted the importance of this concept in their 2008 edited collection, *Assessment Equity and the Opportunity to Learn*. These concerns were situated in the context of writing studies in 2018 by Mya Poe, Asao B. Inoue, and Norbert Elliot for the potential for opportunity to learn to enhance fairness and social justice ("End" 4). As Gee discusses, in a traditional view of knowledge acquisition, equal opportunity means all students are exposed to the information; in a sociocultural perspective, however, the context of learning is also significant ("Sociocultural Perspective" 82). Transdisciplinary work allows investigation of situated learning and thus leverages fairness. In our view, social connection is integral to establishing fairness. As Iris Marion Young observes in *Responsibility for Justice*, "People act within institutions where they know the rules, that is, understand that others have certain expectations of how things are done, or that certain patterns of speech and behavior have certain meanings, and that individuals will react with sanction or in other, less predictable ways if the implicitly formulated or formal rules are violated" (61). As Poe and her colleagues conclude, for the purposes of justice, establishing these patterns as they are uniquely formed within specific contexts is as important as categorizing the patterns themselves ("Legal" 591). By extension, we take a transdisciplinary framework for assessment, as aligned with our institution's responsibility for creating fair assessments that, in fact, capture the situated learning important to our institutional mission.

At Morningside, faculty members asked where students were actually provided with opportunities to learn and which outcomes supported those experiences. Instructors accepted responsibility for outcomes and assessment, which resulted in a shift in traditional views of disciplinarity. This shift required viewing students in a more inclusive manner, valuing more similarities and differences in perspectives, and the creation of institutional structures supporting conservation and fairness. Faculty members questioned issues of fairness related to opportunity to learn since many of the outcomes are embedded in capstone work. If the outcomes represent the values of the institution and instructors with regard to what is important for students' success after college, then all students should have the same opportunity to achieve those values. Unfortunately, many faculty members assumed such opportunities were taking place in someone else's class.

To respond to this organic assessment movement by our faculty members, we were influenced by Christine M. Tardy's call for transdisciplinary and translingual perspectives in writing studies; as well as by Poe and Inoue's special issue on writing assessment and social justice in *College English*; and Diane Kelly-Riley and Carl Whithaus's special issue on ethics and writing assessment in the *Journal of Writing Assessment*. Finally, our campus work required that we attend to issues of context and localization common in writing assessment, articulated by Marie C. Paretti and Katrina M. Powell ("Bringing").

The concerns of Morningside faculty members are not uncommon. Chris W. Gallagher notes that corporatized "out of the box" assessments remove agency from instructors; as a result, collaboration is reduced to something focused on the needs of other stakeholders rather than on those of teachers and students, even though "teaching and learning, which include assessment, are acts of engagement, and they succeed or fail on the strength of the relationships" ("Being" 463). Frank Serafini describes the three paradigms of assessment: measurement, protocol, and inquiry. He notes that a focus on measurement places students in the role of test taker for comparison, and protocol focuses on the assessment method, whereas assessment as inquiry enables a research process that addresses meaningful questions (387). Measurement or protocol approaches potentially miss the opportunity to positively shape learning environments and empower teachers and students.

The view of assessment *for*, *as*, and *of* learning seeks to change the perception of assessment. The Western and Northern Canadian Protocol for Collaboration in Education asserts that assessment *for* learning provides information needed to make meaningful changes to classroom practices for the sake of learning; assessment *as* learning enables students to take on the role of assessor, and assessment *of* learning then assesses the learning that has taken place (13). Harry Torrance, like Serafini, warns of placing too much emphasis on assessment protocols. He also calls for awareness that "local communities of practice are the context in which all meaningful judgements are made and thus should be the level of the system at which most efforts at capacity building are directed" ("Assessment" 292–93). Like Serafini and Gallagher, Torrance highlights assessment as a means of enhancing learning, particularly by valuing teachers' and students' participation, as well as through the use of assessment information in classroom settings. Perspectives like these shift views from assessment as the end of a conversation to assessment as a conversation starter. Such perspectives can create practices that are more meaningful and localized and generate opportunities for faculty members to learn from other disciplines. Spurred by disciplinary and epistemological perspectives, instructors can tease out and illuminate different approaches. Through these spaces, questions can and should be asked across boundaries and understanding sought for the benefit of student learning; this is what transdisciplinary work looks like.

Morningside College has revamped its assessment practices, uniting them with the core curriculum to localize and apply theories with a focus on opportunities to learn. This revamped practice and its implications for fostering fairness in student learning are highlighted in figure 1. As a case study, Morningside College demonstrates the possibility of moving toward a more transdisciplinary discussion and an evidence-based model attuned to opportunities to learn while also making space for unique disciplinary contexts. At the institutional level, a transdisciplinary process provided an alternative to the use of purchased tests. Although we recognize these tests are valuable in allowing standardized inferences, we also note that individual instructors know little about how to use the scores such tests yield. Conversely, at the level of the classroom instructor and the disciplinary body of knowledge that instructors use (which in the Morningside case spanned disciplines across such fields as computer science, journalism, nursing, and political science), our framework allowed us to observe the situated use of reasoning and the language used to convey that reasoning. A transdisciplinary approach enhances the desire to build and equalize students' educational experiences within specific contexts while creating spaces for instructors to learn as well. Accomplishing this required that we first address the way disciplinary perspectives of assessment were viewed, find an appropriate way to work with those views to achieve a common understanding and to make institutional changes, and then create a sustainable structure that incorporates the gains and implications.

To work toward the common goal of enhanced opportunity to learn in student learning within a complex system, Morningside went beyond distinct disciplinary perspectives and adopted a transdisciplinary approach. Every institution has organizational structures and departments that shape the ways discipline is perceived on campus that are really administrative necessities rather than disciplinary identifiers. Anne Ruggles Gere and colleagues discuss localized definitions of disciplines within writing across the curriculum and writing in the disciplines (247). They argue that there are multiple ways to draw disciplinary lines. Determining what *disciplinary* means can help establish transdisciplinarity itself. At Morningside, these primary discussions regarding disciplinary bound-

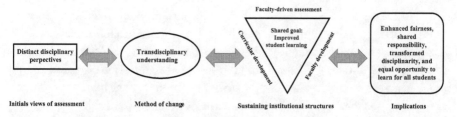

Figure 1. Fairness Achieved through a Transdisciplinary Approach to Assessment.

aries opened pathways for a new communication and writing-in-the-disciplines requirement for students. These discussions fed into the first transdisciplinary assessment group looking at writing situated across campus and seeded fruitful discussions about what it meant to write and think in the discipline. Once again, some faculty members were already teaching one another about their lines of thought, as they began finding ways of translating what they did in their classrooms for instructors in other disciplines.

Components and Benefits

The transdisciplinary approach became the method of change that provided Morningside with multiple benefits. These components and benefits are described in table 1. We understand these elements of our work as a demonstrable articulation of Iris Marion Young's call for understanding situatedness as prerequisite to structuring opportunity. Morningside entered into the design and discussions, particularly early on, with a sense of cooperative innovation and negotiation. Acknowledging that it is easy for disciplines to take ownership of certain outcomes or to clash over definitions, Morningside used a problem-centered approach to student learning around faculty-supported outcomes through collaboration and open discussion grounded in practices devised among the faculty members taking part in the assessment.

The challenges of this model lie in the connections and communication necessary for negotiated boundary crossing. Gee observes that shared experience

Table 1. Transdisciplinary Components and Benefits

Transdisciplinary Component	Benefit
Collaborative, boundary-crossing, and negotiated	Keeps faculty members talking with each other about learning goals, pedagogy, and assessment in open ways
Complex, problem-centered, and surrounding a common goal	Keeps faculty members focused on inquiry around a complex problem (e.g., student learning) that transcends disciplinary perspectives, encouraging fairness
Reframing discussion	Encourages faculty members to determine why the outcomes are relevant; understand how the artifacts illustrate the desired learning; and document who was involved, why and how the assessment was done, and what would be done with the findings
Shared language/understanding based on conceptual clusters	Creates a shared understanding of the concepts to be integrated and places of student learning across disciplines
Reflexivity	Pushes faculty members to understand their role in teaching and outcome development, which addresses equal opportunity to learn, universal design, and fairness

is important for actual communication ("Reflections" 305), and understanding someone else's perspective to avoid conflict as "not confronting genuine differences in values, epistemology, perspectives, and taken-for-granted assumptions. In this respect 'alignment' can become evasion and a way of, ironically perpetuating the lack of alignment, respect, and understanding among Discourses" (308). We take this observation to be one of the most important challenges to the view we advocate in this essay. Put simply, emphasis on aligning the perspectives shown in figure 1 is as dangerous as making decisions from purchased tests: both seek to obviate difference. Important to work such as ours, therefore, is recognition of actual difference among types of student learning, diverse pedagogical perspectives, and assessment strategies. The faculty members involved in the process welcomed the opportunity to talk about how their disciplines approached outcomes such as writing, critical reasoning, and ethical thinking differently. We consistently saw faculty members wanting to discuss the distinct ways their disciplines approached knowledge and valued unique approaches. Transdisciplinary assessment is, like the pursuit of fairness itself, a process. It should be noted that the changes to the assessment process accompanied changes to the general education curriculum. Faculty members did worry about ways the curricular changes would affect disciplinary offerings, which illustrates that even with an openness to difference and even as positive changes are being made in disciplinary offerings, there can still be resistance to equal opportunity to learn.

A transdisciplinary approach requires an examination of assumptions about expertise. How much does someone need to know about the practices of another discipline to assess the work coming from students in that discipline? Harry Collins and Robert Evans discuss levels of expertise and specialization in relation to the possession of tacit knowledge: "contributory expertise" and "interactional expertise," where contributory expertise "enables those who have acquired it to contribute to the domain" (24) and "interactional expertise" facilitates "expertise in the language of specialism in the absence of expertise in its practice" (28). They note that "the transition to interactional expertise is accomplished, crucially, by engaging in conversations with experts" (32). They also note that through this conversation, the person gaining the interactional expertise can sometimes articulate the values more clearly than the expert, in part because conversations are slowed down and there isn't as much assumed agreement or knowledge about what is being discussed. Observing varied levels of articulate expertise is an important way to note and recognize challenges—and to avoid obviated difference, just as Gee warns about in his caution about dangers of alignment.

Implementation Cycle: Challenges and Processes

Transdisciplinary conversations and collaboration are not necessarily easy to foster. There is a level of honesty and humility necessary to enter into this space and to admit at times that there is a lack of understanding in how other scholars and disciplines approach communication and ethics. There is also a need for a genuine desire to learn in order to communicate and collaborate in the ways necessary for a transdisciplinary approach to work. In this space, fairness is vital to developing a deeper understanding of assessment. Faculty members, who are experts and nonexperts simultaneously, all have the same opportunity to analyze and interrogate their own disciplinary practices through meaningful interaction.

As an institution, we had to create sustainable institutional structures that supported our vision of a campus assessment that enhanced fairness of educational opportunities and assessment. That responsibility fell to the vice president for institutional assessment, whose expertise is in organizational psychology, and the faculty assessment coordinator, whose field is rhetoric and writing. These specialists had to reframe their definitions and values regarding assessment and what it should accomplish. In other words, they both valued assessment for its ability to enhance student learning but had different thoughts about how assessment worked. This process took some time, as they didn't realize just how ingrained their own perspectives were until they had to explain the relative differences, particularly in terms of quantitative, qualitative, and different approaches to learning. As they worked, they brought up the merits of and problems with their respective perspectives, realizing that sometimes a merit for one person was a problem for the other. From their conversation emerged a model that pulled together multiple approaches, because the goal was enhanced student learning.

Together they fleshed out a possible structure built on collaboration and faculty involvement for the sake of enhanced student learning. They approached the process in three components, through a blended relation among curricular development, faculty-driven assessment, and faculty development. With a plan in hand, they approached Morningside's Curriculum Policies and Assessment Committee (CPAC), and the chair of the Faculty Development Committee (FDC). There was significant discussion and more surfacing of assumptions, primarily among CPAC members with support from FDC members. Then CPAC mapped out ways and places the outcomes would be addressed for all students, and FDC began strategizing ways to foster conversations about the outcomes using assessment data. In time, a teaching and learning coordinator position was created. Departments also started mapping where and how they would teach the outcomes in the discipline to all students in their programs, as well as how they would know when outcomes were developed in other disciplines. Also tracked were the types of department-level efforts focused to enhance student learning. Departments and programs addressed the context by identifying and mapping places where each institutional and programmatic outcome would be taught in the disciplinary curriculum as part of a developmental process.

Summer groups of paid faculty members from across disciplines working with a single outcome now meet every three years to assess student work. The assessment of the institution's ethical reasoning and application outcome serves as a typical example of how this approach is grounded in the greater discussions that occur among faculty members engaged in the assessment process. In this case, faculty members gathered on the first day of the workshop to examine how the concept of ethical reasoning could be defined. Before any application of rubrics and review of artifacts, they spent time learning about and defining for themselves what the learning outcome of ethical reasoning could be and the components of what this means. They also spent time reflecting on a case study that dealt with an ethical dilemma. In discussing this case study, faculty members experienced what they would eventually be teaching and assessing—the process of reasoning through various ethical contexts. A reframing negotiation devoted to understanding and developing a definition of ethical reasoning was a critical part of the learning process for this group of faculty members. The process provided an opportunity to address fears about assessing student work outside of one's discipline while crafting an assessment process that was not premanufactured but, rather, understood through the transdisciplinary understanding of the learning outcome that was agreed upon by the group.

Following the negotiation of learning outcomes, the faculty members turn to generating the assessment tool using student work. Most groups have generated a version of graphic scale rubrics. After that, groups read, watch, or listen to, depending on the outcome, each student-generated piece; the goal is not consensus but rather discussion of what each team sees within the piece. Although the teams do choose a place on the rubric, they note key characteristics of their discussion—both where they agree and where they do not—in a group document. This process can ultimately change the rubric that is then used for the duration of the summer session.

After two to three days of looking, reading, watching, or listening to work from various classes and levels, the entire group discusses what they have experienced. Group members review both the rubric scores and the qualitative notes. The groups come together at the beginning and end of each session to talk about what they have seen. They note trends, places where there was a lot of agreement, and points where they disagreed. All this information is captured for the final discussion and reported back to the faculty. They also discuss the assessment process and the work itself. On the final day, they then coauthor a report discussing the process, findings, and recommendations. Their findings formally go back to the faculty through faculty meetings, but they are also delivered to the Institutional Student Learning Committee (ISLC), CPAC, and to departmental meetings.

The ISLC prioritizes how institutional resources should be allocated based on the work of the summer or previous years, follows up on goals from the previous year(s), and establishes student-learning goals for the year. Based on the assessment results, the committee may request funding for faculty members to attend conferences, invite the faculty development committee to devise programming, propose that faculty and staff members to work on a student life issue together, explore infrastructure investment in certain types of technology, and so on. Then ISLC meets again in January to discuss progress on goals, request information for the spring meeting, convene summer groups, and discuss ways to ensure the greatest faculty member participation possible (e.g., ensuring that a faculty member is not on all summer groups). At the end of the year, ISLC meets again to discuss goals and formulate a report to the faculty about the progress on student learning goals. In true collaborative fashion, the faculty and administration work together to decide student-learning goals and encourage responsibility for what was or was not achieved.

As an example of this commitment to collaboration and shared responsibility, ISLC supported a series of "closing the loop" luncheons based on the summer assessment results of the ethical reasoning learning outcome. This decision by ISLC was based on one of the recommendations by the faculty of the summer assessment work group and is supported by scholarship suggesting that faculty member engagement is crucial to closing the loop and implementing change informed by assessment data (Banta and Blaich). These luncheons were reflective in nature and grounded in the assessment results that suggested students' ethical reasoning abilities seemed to decline as they progressed through their four years of undergraduate education. Through this process, faculty members became more reflexive, through sustained deliberation on their personal approach and delivery of the outcomes and on how each faculty member was contributing to the learning of all students, which further reinforced equal opportunity to learn for all Morningside students. The members of the assessment summer group, as well as ISLC, agreed that these results called for campus-wide faculty development sessions, where all faculty members teaching ethical-reasoning-designated courses in the curriculum would have a chance to come together as a group to focus on the following: discussion of the core components of ethical reasoning, review and practice using the ethical reasoning rubric developed by the summer work group on genuine student artifacts, and development of potential assignments and activities that could enhance ethical reasoning instruction in the classroom. These luncheons, although voluntary, were highly attended by faculty members teaching ethical reasoning courses and were coled by the chair of ISLC, the Teaching and Learning Coordinator, and the faculty member chair of the summer work group.

Even disciplinary practices go through layered conversations leading to transformed disciplinarity. The disciplinary processes exemplify the value of transdisciplinary conversation as a key practice in a collaborative environment through which student learning and equal opportunity, not assessment for the sake of assessment, is the goal. Student work is assessed in faculty groups, and what is learned is valued equally with institutional assessment findings. For this project, programs devise a disciplinary assessment tool. Some choose to start with the institutional tool, whereas others determine what they need to use on their own. Their plans and tools are submitted to CPAC's Assessment Subcommittee. The subcommittee, which comprises faculty members from across the disciplines, reviews all assessment plans and provides feedback to the programs and departments. Each program identifies one outcome to assess each year and submits a report of what they find and what they intend to do with those findings. The CPAC Assessment Subcommittee reviews each assessment report and provides feedback on what they have observed qualitatively and quantitatively. Each department receives feedback, such as whether the findings are mostly based on the assessment process (e.g., teaching to the test), the relevance of the process to the outcome (e.g., using a content test to assess critical thinking), or other meaningful results. The CPAC Assessment Subcommittee then updates the "Assessment Almanac," available online, which presents the findings of institutional assessment processes, ad hoc assessment groups, and various programmatic assessment reports. The almanac is also used as part of the institution's evidence for its culture of assessment criterion in its report to the Higher Learning Commission, the college's regional accrediting body.

Based on collaboration, everyone involved created a system of assessment with enhanced fairness through shared responsibility, transformed disciplinarity, and fairness through equal opportunity to learn for all students at the core. Institutionally, the assessment structure makes use of faculty-member-driven groups that discuss student work, valuing both the consensus and dissensus that stem from disciplinary and personal views. Likewise, the practices seek to balance institutional and disciplinary perspectives on student work. This process encourages faculty members to talk about the contexts in which student work was created. The attention to context also enabled discussions among teachers

regarding ways skills are grounded in practices and disciplines, which can enhance agility for students and teachers to avoid what Torrance terms "conformative assessment" that reinforces a singular perspective or teaching to the assessment ("Formative Assessment" 332). Torrance also speaks to the importance
of contextualizing the assessment itself and opening it up for discussion (338).
These processes can further reinforce equal opportunities to learn and fairness,
as they emphasize the importance of context over a one-size-fits-all approach to
learning sometimes stressed through distributed assessment.

Conclusions

Morningside's concern about the usefulness of pre-packaged assessments and
their meaningfulness are common. Lack of student investment in the assessment process is problematic; unequal access to quality learning environments
is also a concern. Although fairness starts with using data from assessment in
ways that are intended, honest, and authentic, it also involves issues of universal
design and instruction, as everyone needs the same access to learning opportunities and success. When assessment focuses on student learning, not protocols
that are one-size-fits-all, it can attend to equity as well as to context and learning environments.

A transdisciplinary approach makes contextualized assessment possible
and, as we have argued, leverages fairness. Transdisciplinarity encourages connections across disciplinary boundaries, allowing for deeper understanding in
support of a shared goal and group effort to enhance opportunity to learn for
all students through stronger assessment. Transdisciplinary approaches rely on
conversations among faculty members that reframe distinct disciplinary perspectives to create a shared institutional vision. They can foster collaborative
environments in which everyone seeks authentic responsibility, shared among
multiple actors. When everyone is working toward a single goal of enhanced
learning, it creates an environment where faculty members want to do the best
they can. They want to be a part of the assessment work and reflect on the experience and take that back into their classrooms instead of wanting to simply tell
someone else to do it. Most significant, people want to understand one another's
approaches guided by a sense of cooperation, not competition or judgment. The
process takes time, as evidenced by the case of Morningside College, but can be
achieved across various contexts. It requires a commitment to fairness through
meaningful conversations and transdisciplinarity.

Part Three

Disciplinary Writing

Reclaiming English's Disciplinary Responsibility in the Transition from High School to College

Christine Farris

Perspective

Using collaboration between secondary and postsecondary educators as a case study, this essay argues for the use of multigenre text sets as the basis for writing tasks that anticipate intellectually rigorous college expectations and reflect how English contributes more broadly to general education, liberal arts, and a more just world. Based on this collaboration, I advocate for a strengthened bridge between high school and college literacies, instead of forfeiting that responsibility to test companies. Currently in the K–12 system, students' learning in English is bifurcated between reading and writing and between literary and informational texts. This split, which occurred in response to national college and career readiness initiatives, delimits the English curricula. For many reformers, access to college and job skills equates to fairness, and the pedagogy demanded by such initiatives minimizes the ways the discipline of English works. Texts are more than vehicles to foster practical skills. They provide intellectual and rhetorical opportunities for students.

The Effect of National Educational Reform Efforts on English Curricula

In the last decade, a radical shift occurred in the K–12 curriculum for English language arts. The practices of both composition and literature—writing, close reading, textual complexity—figure prominently in the assessment of college and career readiness, particularly by way of the Common Core State Standards (CCSS) for English language arts (see *Common Core*), originally adopted by forty-five states and several territories of the United States. Joanne Addison observes:

> [T]he CCSS are self-described as 'a set of high-quality academic standards . . . [that] outline what a student should know and be able to do at the end of each

grade'. . . while the Standards do not dictate use of any specific curriculum or
pedagogy, they do aim to standardize what is taught in all of our public schools.
. . . [A]nd with the Standards come new high-stakes standardized tests, such
as the one developed through the Partnership for Assessment of Readiness for
College and Career (PARCC) and the one developed through the Smarter Balanced Assessment Consortium.

Addison details the Common Core's dramatic reshaping of the elementary and
secondary English language arts curriculum. Reading and writing are now
taught and emphasized throughout the entire K–12 curriculum. Beginning in
sixth grade, writing is also taught outside of English situated within other disciplines like science and history. Now, however, the types of reading and writing
have changed, largely because of college and career readiness initiatives and the
standardized tests developed to assess the Common Core. Assessments aligned
with the Common Core feature evidence-based reading—identifying the main
point and the sentences that support it—and the inclusion of more informational texts. The Common Core does not assess for interpretive reading or text
production beyond standard genres of academic papers or workplace documents.
Creative production of text is not included.

Arthur N. Applebee points out that the Common Core quickly came to reflect not the K–12 curriculum but the assessments designed by two independent test-development consortia: the Partnership for Assessment of Readiness
for College and Careers (PARCC) and Smarter Balanced Assessment Consortium
(30). Both tests utilize automated writing evaluation of student work and so defined reading and writing in ways that could be scored by computer programs.
The pedagogy presumed and demanded by a test-driven take on proficiency may,
in fact, impede rather than facilitate fair access to college by obscuring the ways
English and other disciplines now approach textual analysis and production as
situated social activities. Test-driven pedagogy oversimplifies English's responsibilities within the liberal arts and its role in a broader vision of how a university
experience prepares students to contribute to a better world. Such pedagogy has
taken a new direction with the 2016 revisions of the SAT test, newly aligned
with the Common Core, under the leadership of College Board president David
Coleman, one of the original CCSS designers. Use of the SAT as not just a predic-
tor of college success but a measure of secondary school achievement raises new
issues of fair access for those students in non–Common Core states, as well as
for students in states that have been exposed to the limited views of language
incorporated in the Common Core.

This essay advocates for a greater role for postsecondary specialists in
strengthening the bridge between high school and college reading and writing,

instead of forfeiting much of that responsibility to other stakeholders, particularly private consortia and test companies with strong legislative support. Working from a goal we share with those in the corporate and legislative sectors—equitable access to education—academics in English can play a greater role in college readiness by doing more locally with elementary and secondary teachers to model not just test-taking strategies but textual work within, as Applebee says, "the social and disciplinary contexts that give them meaning and importance" (30). This essay describes one such initiative for professional and curricular collaboration across the divide between high school and college English that aims to avoid value dualisms that break up the wide-ranging work of English as a discipline. For several years I served as a disciplinary expert from my state working with one of the test-development consortia on Common Core assessment and implementation. Like Applebee (28), I was struck by the separation of standards—reading from writing and literature from informational texts. I have found that students' success in college is often a matter of how well they can write in terms of the ideas in what they read in college-level texts. How closely and critically they engage with not just one but a number of multigenre texts in conversation can determine the quality of their writing in English and other courses. My growing awareness of how assessment of the standards determines rather than reflects curricula aimed at readiness and fair access led me to consider alternative ways of promoting a more connected high school and college English curriculum.

Reformers, from corporate funders, like the Bill and Melinda Gates Foundation, to state officials, have redefined the role of education at all levels as greater, faster, and cheaper access to jobs. They form an alliance that Linda Adler-Kassner referred to in her 2017 Conference on College Composition and Communication chair's address as an "Educational Intelligence Complex" that connects the future of the American economy to the failure of K–16 to prepare the workforce ("Because"). The result is a conflation of college and career readiness that embeds the academic within the utilitarian. This change presents serious implications for English curricula. As Addison argues, "understanding this shift is crucial to reasserting teacher agency at all levels of the curriculum and reinforcing assessment as primarily a teaching and learning practice, not a system of accountability and control." The changes that have occurred at the K–12 level will likely reshape postsecondary English studies unless intentional steps are taken to reclaim the combined roles of reading and writing and promote the widest array of experiences for students.

Concomitantly, the Common Core State Standards for English language arts (or the state equivalent) have precipitated adjustments in the relation of literary to informational texts across the K–12 curriculum, ostensibly to improve preparation for first-year college English courses and, one might hope, the demands of coursework in other disciplines, but primarily in anticipation of the needs of the workplace. There is a common perception among some reformers and policymakers that literacy instruction should focus on the sort of informational texts that jobs demand. Tied to a general dismissal of the importance of the liberal arts, literature especially becomes the antagonist. The CCSS does not mandate curricula but suggests exemplar (and test-friendly) informational texts, particularly what they refer to as "America's founding documents," such as the Gettysburg Address ("Myths vs. Facts"). State officials charged with greater access to education for the workplace often conceive of informational texts as reports or manuals. The CCSS are understandably interested in the ability to repurpose evidence and conclusions into coherent arguments and explanations; they are less interested, however, in students' access to ideas, in the connections students make among both concepts and the sorts of texts they encounter in general education courses—not just in English, but in history, psychology, and sociology. It is shortsighted to think of imaginative literature as enabling only personal connections, and it is unfair to dismiss the importance of personal connection making and engaging topics in students' learning and acclimation to college. It is also shortsighted to think of so-called informational texts as fostering only practical skills. The readings students encounter in courses present personal, intellectual, and rhetorical opportunities for all students that are central to the ways they adjust to college and change as thinkers, writers, and citizens.

Two of the Common Core key components, close reading and textual complexity ("Ensuring"), are generally considered by English faculty members to mean attention not only to word choice, tone, structure, and reasoning, as emphasized on standardized tests, but also to representation: that is, the interpretation of patterns in the language and evidence that tell us something about history, culture, race and gender relations, and ourselves. Faculty members hope that students are engaging closely with texts as part of compelling inquiry in their courses, not because a test timer is ticking or a cut score and classification as college and career ready depends on it.

English teachers at all levels are concerned that, increasingly, students merely skim and scan or fail to read assigned texts altogether; this may be because standardized tests measure students' close reading primarily through multiple-choice tests focused on attention to evidence in passages, often excerpted from longer works. Writing prompts and implementation guides include scripted lessons that create test-like simulacra: "cold readings" without the background, supporting context, or connection making that provide a fair and accessible bridge between what students know and the new questions college instructors hope they are able to ask of texts. Although not replacing teacher-supported reading, cold reading without scaffolding is defended as a skill useful in both test taking and the workplace.

That said, whereas nearly all writing assignments in college call for students to write about what they have read, composition pedagogy at the postsecondary level has, until recently, paid relatively little attention to reading (Carillo; Sullivan et al.). With the exception of a few scholars whose work has long focused on reading and intertextuality (Bartholomae and Petrosky; Harris; Salvatori and Donahue; Scholes; Scholes et al.), the field has largely circumvented reading, often conflating it with literature, which, historically, many compositionists have argued should take a back seat to an emphasis on students' texts and the stages of their writing process (Lindemann, "Freshman Composition" and "Three").

At the same time, recent criticism of state standards among secondary English teachers has often focused on the perceived rebuff of literature in favor of informational texts. Many high school teachers, in particular, faced with new curricula and test preparation incorporating informational texts, are anxious about leaving the comfort zones of their literary expertise. Although literature may be getting the brush-off from reformers, in fact, many college courses, in both English and other fields, juxtapose fiction, nonfiction, and visual texts to broaden historical and cultural contexts for inquiry. Instead of extolling the ability to cold read a text independently, college faculty members use facts, concepts, and personal accounts in other texts to help students ask new, more complicated questions of what they read, of themselves, and of the world in which they live (Anderson and Farris; Farris). Such intertextual work is vital to affording students fairer access to the discourse of the academy and the professions to which they aspire and to strengthening the resources of the secondary teachers who prepare them.

It is not only literature specialists who encounter challenges connecting their expertise and production of knowledge to education reforms. In the face of data-driven assessment with regard to the bridge between secondary and postsecondary levels, composition programs have also found it necessary to defend their raison d'être and central focus in required writing courses. Equitable access and economic incentives for multiple stakeholders have driven the explosive growth of alternative ways to earn college credit for writing, including more AP and International Baccalaureate (IB) courses, and test score exemption. Dual-credit and concurrent-enrollment courses, originally intended to provide increased rigor and greater college access for underserved populations, are being folded into the "readiness" and "taking care of" narratives, often to make more room in students' college schedules for job preparation (Hansen and Farris). Not only is readiness for college work (and the standards and testing that accompany it) the focus of policymakers, it is also the mission of testing enterprises that, in aligning with the CCSS and other readiness initiatives, have been able to expand their markets for diagnostic, implementation, and professional development products and services. At the same time, policymakers are enabling the expansion of test makers' authority, not just to predict college admission and success but also to function as an "advisory and implementation partner in states' efforts at improvement . . ." (*Reach*). In short, they are playing a greater role in determining what college and career literacy is. In other words, policy makers, testing companies, and textbook publishers are largely determining what counts. Instead, we would do well to consider teacher-centered, discipline-informed approaches such as that advocated by Chris W. Gallagher in *Reclaiming Assessment: A Better Alternative to the Accountability Agenda*. Such approaches foster engagement, emphasize relationships between teachers and students, and encourage teachers to make sure the accountability systems work for students by placing them at the center of assessment efforts.

Reclaiming English's Disciplinary Responsibility

In response to internal scholarly skepticism and to external challenges of higher education's utilitarian turn, the field of English studies has doubled down on approaches that demonstrate composition's contribution to what is believed to be a more complex process of literacy acquisition than what Adler-Kassner's "Educational Intelligence Complex" imagines ("Because"). One might wonder if our actual English hermeneutical and rhetorical expertise—what we do with texts—might be taking a back seat to an aspirational sense of what we know, or would like to claim we know, about learning to write. In staking out a body of knowledge about composition (discourse about writing) that students must, through reflection, locate themselves within, are we still allowing them to make valuable connections to the ideas in texts as the basis for what they write?

If we do indeed view writing as situated and genre as a social and disciplinary activity, not just a function in the service of readiness, it would be wise for us to pay more attention to reading and writing as relational and to the critical reading practices that give students' writing more interesting work to do in the present. Clearly, the role readiness—prior to, across, and beyond the college curriculum—plays in a larger dynamic that includes fairness, school reform, and education politics cuts across the divide between secondary and postsecondary education. Scholars and teachers are under pressure to adapt to or resist elaborate sets of standards and outcomes in ways that may build or disrupt a sound, seamless English curriculum. How might we redirect the field's attention from doubling down on what we may (or may not) be able to guarantee will transfer out toward what is transferring in? Instead of just fearing the elimination of first-year writing courses by means of standardized test scores or disapproving of exemption through dual-credit courses because they supposedly lack rigor, how might we encourage a more effective and meaningful pedagogy in the courses high school already offers, one that grows from English's longstanding strengths as a discipline and what instructors at both levels do with texts to enhance understanding, tolerance, and pleasure in their complexity?

Many current efforts articulate the value of the disciplinary knowledge of English composition and disrupt the "Educational Intelligence Complex" culture. These include writing about writing (Downs and Wardle; Wardle), teaching for transfer (Yancey et al.), and threshold concepts (Adler-Kassner and Wardle). External pressure for accountability has forced a reckoning with the longstanding assumption that the habits and skills students acquire in first-year English transfer easily to other courses and real-world situations. This sense of demand comes at a time when the field is finally adjusting in practice to its own scholarly acknowledgment that there is no such thing as universal academic writing and that students' repurposing of prior knowledge from first-year composition may be limited. Although the Council of Writing Program Administrators' "WPA Outcomes Statement" contends that faculty members in disciplines other than English can "build on" what students learn in first-year composition by helping them learn the habits and conventions of writing and expectations of readers in their fields, the scholarship and research in composition, particularly writing across the curriculum, has called attention to the extent to which rhetorical and genre knowledge are domain-specific, rather than universal or transferable (Beaufort, *College Writing*; Smit).

In response to these pressures, both external and internal to the field, composition scholarship, textbooks, and programs have pivoted to an emphasis not on learning to write but on learning about writing (Wardle 783). Drawing from principles of rhetoric, educational psychology, and genre theory (Bawarshi and Reiff; Miller), writing about writing (WAW) views the purpose of first-year courses to be the development of students' awareness of language, genre, and conventions as situated. Instead of adopting belletristic essays or essays from a sampling of disciplines, WAW courses typically include readings from composition theory and literacy scholarship that reinforce the concept of genre. Bolstered, and, at times, challenged, by the findings in a number of empirical studies of students' reflection on and repurposing of prior genre knowledge to new contexts for writing (Beaufort, *College Writing*; Yancey et al.), WAW attempts to justify first-year writing as disciplinary, not a-disciplinary, and yet still necessary for students' development of a metacognitive awareness that will transfer to other disciplines, the workplace, and public life. More recently, the interest among some composition scholars (Adler-Kassner and Wardle) in the articulation of what Jan H. F. Meyer and Ray Land identify as threshold concepts—transformative thinking central to the mastery of a subject—is another attempt to identify a disciplinary core at the center of what the field of composition knows and, subsequently, should more consciously build into curricula and impart to students.

A Collective Sense of Textuality

We need to be closing, not widening, the gap between high school and college reading and writing and between secondary and postsecondary teachers by not abdicating professional development to the test makers. English faculties in universities, not for-profit test companies, should be the ones "partnering in the state's efforts to help students get on the right track to success" (*Reach*). We should be collaborating with secondary teachers on a connected 9–16 curriculum, not just approving them to teach concurrent-enrollment versions of our courses. The missing piece in school reform and fair access to college is the postsecondary presence in teacher professionalization. Some of the capital changing hands in assessment initiatives, bound up in testing, could be going toward collaboration across the divide between high school and college—framed by a sense of writing as a discipline and a social activity—not just as a function in the service of readiness. College faculty members are in the best position to share with secondary teachers their best practices for integrating reading and writing and what moves they would like to see when students interpret and produce texts. Teachers, in turn, are quite capable of identifying what their stronger readers and writers can do that their struggling readers and writers cannot yet do. Many disparage the unfair tracking of those considered (or not) to be on AP, dual-credit, or college-ready trajectories. In that space, there is room to expand a collective sense of textuality in English language arts, so that more students can become better prepared for thinking, reading, and writing across and beyond the college curriculum.

In the transition from high school to college, many writing problems are, at the root, reading problems. Students struggle with understanding the texts they encounter in both English and other courses, and they struggle with using those texts in their writing to frame and support their ideas in complex ways. Whereas college faculty members expect papers that reflect active engagement with authors' arguments, concepts, and rhetorical strategies, many students arrive dependent on plug-in formulas for papers characteristic of timed writing and on what Rebecca Moore Howard calls "patchwriting": "copying from a source text" with few alterations (233). Although new state standards mandating more work with informational texts are being implemented, students still bring more experience writing in response to literature. Most students come to college not yet knowing what it is professionals in various fields actually do with texts. Rather than just skim and scan for the gist or retrieve evidence for a test, professionals reread, often with one text providing a frame for understanding another more deeply.

Perhaps the best way to contend with skepticism about disciplinary expertise, transfer anxiety, and the relation of secondary to postsecondary literacies is to focus not just on genre awareness, but on the earlier development of students' deeper, more complex reading abilities as the basis for more nuanced and successful analytical writing. In "Symposium: Standardization, Democratization, and Writing Programs," Gallagher calls this type of partnership "articulation . . . a pragmatic method through which administrators, teachers, and students both *express* their learning goals and *place them in relation* to other such expression . . . learning goals are treated, not as standards to be imposed upon teachers and students, but rather as starting and check-in points for shared work" (495).

A Model Partnership: The Writing and Reading Alignment Project

After bearing witness to my state's plans for Common Core implementation, I launched, along with my colleague Ray Smith from the Indiana University School of Education, the Writing and Reading Alignment Project (WRAP), with funding from an Improving Teacher Quality Grant, a federal program of the Department of Education in the United States (Farris and Smith). In my reflection on this program, I provide the conceptual framework rather than emphasize data drawn from that program. Although both are needed as forms of evidence, my approach here is to link expanded views of language arts to a case study demonstrating their implementation. For two years, in both summer seminars and an online professional learning community, we worked with fifty English and history teachers and administrators from ninth through twelfth grades in what the state of Indiana had identified as underperforming high schools. Framed by the need to provide greater and fairer access to college for more Hoosiers and an alternative to the Common Core exemplars, we wanted to help teachers develop new strategies to promote skills in critical reading and evidence-based writing. The weeklong seminars were devoted to curricular redesign that juxtaposed fiction, nonfiction, and visual texts as the basis for a sequence of increasingly complex low-stakes writing assignments, building toward longer papers.

We wanted to complicate the binary between literature and informational texts by having the teachers develop multigenre text sets of the sort student will encounter across the curriculum, not just in the first credit-bearing English course. We sought to expand teachers' repertoire for text-dependent writing beyond structural elements and personal response. Although we both have teaching, research, and administrative experience in composition, writing across the curriculum, and concurrent enrollment, the focus of the WRAP project was to revise aspects of the regular high school curriculum, not institute the college course in high school.

We began by sharing with the high school teachers some of the skills and habits of mind considered to be critical for success in what lies ahead for their students. We looked at the *Framework for Success in Postsecondary Writing* developed by the Council of Writing Program Administrators, National Council of Teachers of English, and the National Writing Project, calling attention to where there was overlap with the Indiana Statewide Written Communication Competency Outcomes, placing them alongside the newly revised state English language arts standards, formerly known as the state's Common Core. We called particular attention to how reading in a variety of media and genres and from multiple perspectives is an important part of constructing strong, nuanced claims in writing. The best way to demonstrate this was to model how at the college level we might broaden the context for understanding an iconic figure, book, or film, taking into consideration not just genre and conventions but also historical conditions of production and reception. As our focus for the weeklong seminar, we chose representations of racial justice and injustice.

Smith worked first with the iconicity of Abraham Lincoln, having teachers compare how Lincoln is represented in folksy Hollywood films from the 1930s with the recent 2012 depiction by Daniel Day-Lewis of Lincoln as a shrewd politician. We also examined how, in his various writings, Lincoln, the Great Emancipator, makes very clear distinctions between arguments regarding the abolition of slavery and racial equality. I chose to defamiliarize a book the teachers know well: Harper Lee's *To Kill a Mockingbird*, a work of fiction second only to Harriet Beecher Stowe's *Uncle Tom's Cabin* in impact on American attitudes to racial injustice, and one they had all taught, though primarily as a coming-of-age story emphasizing empathy and tolerance ("You never really understand a person," says Atticus Finch, "until you consider things from his point of view . . . until you climb into his skin and walk around in it" [33]).

For several days, our focus became not just *Mockingbird* as a discrete text but also a larger historical moment: the civil rights struggle from the time Harper Lee wrote the book (set in the 1930s but published in 1960) up to 1964. The additional informational texts I juxtaposed it with included the 1964 Civil Rights

Act; several iconic civil rights photographs; civil rights worker Anne Moody's *Coming of Age in Mississippi*; Malcolm Gladwell's 2009 prescient critique of *To Kill a Mockingbird* in *The New Yorker*; and excerpts from and reactions to Harper Lee's *Go Set a Watchman*, a first draft of her 1960 classic that was published in 2015, which significantly complicates the iconicity of the white savior Atticus Finch. We were able to reread the Atticus Finch in *Mockingbird* more closely in light of the *Watchman* version. In *Watchman*, Atticus, by the mid-1950s, is a state's rights advocate and member of the White Citizens' Council fighting the NAACP, at loggerheads with Scout, the now-grown daughter who once idolized him. What new questions could we put to these two texts, particularly juxtaposed with Gladwell's 2009 argument that even the 1930s *Mockingbird* Atticus was an accommodationist, not the civil rights reformer of American lore?

The seminar group considered how to help students examine the conditions that contributed to Lee's publisher's decision that the reading audience was not ready for grown-up Scout's disillusionment with Atticus's white supremacist views, or for the truth she told about racism among not just the lower-class Ewell family but also the respectable Alabama white middle class. In what ways was the six-year-old Scout's perspective on racial prejudice less threatening to a 1960s audience? Our seminar's pedagogical activities encouraged beginning more often, as college courses do, with questions, not answers: How does a text, fiction or nonfiction, relate to its historical situation? To what extent is it factual? How do authors support their claims? Whose interests are served? How is each work received and critiqued and when, and by whom? Why tell the story this way at this time? How does a text raise questions that it doesn't always answer?

Teachers then worked in groups to construct multigenre text sets (fiction, poetry, songs, articles, films, photographs, government documents), grouping new texts with ones they already taught. They designed a sequence of low-stakes writing tasks (Bean) that included summary, passage explication, and use of a source as a lens—tasks that ask students to do something in writing with the readings so as to ease them in to college-level analysis. One 250-word assignment might be devoted to a close reading of a significant or puzzling passage or film scene. Another might ask what specifically in Gladwell's argument (a lens) would help readers better understand the contradictions in the character Atticus. Or what in *To Kill a Mockingbird* or in *Go Set a Watchman* is not accounted for in Gladwell's argument?

We also asked teachers to write some of these assignments themselves and respond to sample student papers, in part to point out differences between a five-paragraph format or a just matching comparison, and a stronger comparative analysis that strives for more significant connections across texts.

Each teacher prepared a final portfolio describing a set of literary and informational texts and an assignment sequence in which low-stakes writings functioned as scaffolding for one longer writing assignment. The portfolios included a reflective statement on the cognitive, rhetorical, and disciplinary aims behind their text set and assignment sequence and how they imagined this unit would prepare students for college-level work. These were later posted to an online forum, along with follow-up statements about the success, plans for revision, and any new materials. On the last day of the seminar, we invited all the school principals to hear the teachers' portfolio presentations. The group also let the administrators know what conditions would be necessary back at their home school to implement this sort of curricular change, e.g., more collaboration among teachers of English and history and the school librarian.

Toward Afterwardness

Both our teaching and research practices in English seem to suggest that curricula and assessment cannot always predict or determine the degree of transfer, the level of engagement with what students read, or the success and significance of what they write. We generally think of college writing as a continuous sequence, with first-year composition as preparation for later writing tied to knowledge making in a chosen field. Anne Ruggles Gere, reporting in *PMLA* on a recent longitudinal study of writing development at the University of Michigan, however, found that many students "selected a multidisciplinary path, instead of concentrating on a single discipline, as they traveled toward greater expertise in writing" (141). Often taking upper-level writing courses outside their major and developing their own systems for classifying genres, many students in the study made their own connections between thinking and writing across four years (142). Similarly, with reading there can be, as critic Rita Felski points out, an "afterwardness"—a making of connections to texts across moments of schooling, disciplines, and courses—that comes later in one's development and is unique to each learner (119). Hope for meaningful connections that should buttress any college readiness initiatives lies in collaborative efforts to teach reading and writing as linked critical rhetorical processes. In these contentious times, such collaborations are a means by which both secondary and postsecondary teachers can help students connect language and image to history, own the pedagogical changes they choose to make, and take back local control of educational policy and praxis.

Opening an Assessment Dialogue: Formative Evaluation of a Writing Studies Program

Beth Buyserie, Tialitha Macklin, Matt Frye, and Patricia Freitag Ericsson

Perspective

At our large, public research institution, we use a formative, evidence-based assessment of our local first-year composition (FYC) program to inform an ongoing faculty development effort enacted in the program to promote fairness. Our project builds a culture of evidence through an assessment-focused framework that promotes formative pedagogical dialogues and situates the conversations about fairness within the context of our ongoing program assessment. We use an adapted version of the Council of Writing Program Administrators' "WPA Outcomes Statement for First-Year Composition" to frame this work.

Formative Assessment to Influence Pedagogy

As evidenced in this collection, multiple disciplines outside of rhetoric and composition now consider writing as central to student learning and disciplinary knowledge. Writing studies remains unique, however, in that writing is, and has been, the focus of our disciplinary scholarship, expertise, and pedagogy (Adler-Kassner and Wardle). Because of this historical focus, writing studies can contribute considerable expertise to productive multidisciplinary conversations about assessing writing and writing programs, formation of educational writing outcomes, fairness in applying established outcomes, and evidence-based assessment of these outcomes. We add that fairness must also foreground language as it connects to the assessment of writing, formatively examining how the language of our outcomes can be reinforced in teacher pedagogy. Although we recognize the importance of defining *fairness* in terms of teacher assessment of student writing, for this essay we explore the ways faculty members define and assess fairness within our first-year composition program, and we detail the ways our program used those results to inform our ongoing professional development for our instructional faculty, which includes graduate students, instructors, and tenured faculty members. We define fairness programmatically as a way instructors define outcomes broadly and then develop pedagogical responses to assessment results. This supports our goal of enhancing pedagogy, not merely collecting data (Shepard, "Classroom Assessment" 627). We examined student performance to ground programmatic discussions about pedagogy and shared outcomes, so teachers could consciously respond to assessment results. In other words, we more explicitly teach the outcomes by which students will be assessed and ensure the program undergoes an active review that looks for unintentional bias.

Assessment Foundations

This portfolio outcomes project builds on a foundation that encourages local contexts to respond to the results of their own programmatic assessment (Witte and Faigley; White et al., *Very*). In designing this study, we were careful to emphasize program assessment, not the assessment of particular teachers or students. Because a culture of fairness is integral to assessment practices, we consider community members—including teachers, program administrators, and outside stakeholders—in this project to be sufficiently positioned to "achiev[e] equality of opportunity in our [local] society" (*Standards* 49). Teachers are an integral part of this assessment, but this project does not evaluate the quality of their teaching, either individually or collectively. As for students, formative assessment of their writing in FYC courses is frequent and embedded within a larger university culture of writing assessment (Haswell, *Beyond*). Experienced teachers of writing, including teachers outside of writing studies, routinely assess student writing to determine how students are progressing and, ideally, to make revisions to individual pedagogies. This process happens so frequently that teachers might not consider it assessment, and some might prefer if assessment stayed on this individual level. Indeed, given research and assessment's connection to projects of structural injustices and institutional inequities (Inoue and Poe; Poe et al., "Legal"; L. Smith), there are good reasons for programs to question the means and local purposes of research-based assessment projects. As data collection moves beyond an individual classroom, programs need to consider both what they are attempting to assess and what structural inequities they might simultaneously be reinforcing through that assessment.

Although programs must acknowledge the complexity of assessment, well-defined and purposeful assessment can also be a way of affirming and challenging what we know about our own teaching and programs. If we needed to communicate only with the internal audience of teachers in our program, perhaps assessing individual students would suffice. But as Edward M. White and colleagues (*Very*) and Linda Adler-Kassner (*Activist WPA*) remind us, our community includes stakeholders external to writing program assessment, such as university administrators and accreditors, with whom we need to communicate. Conversations with multiple audiences are crucial because, as with many postsecondary institutions, FYC is a required course at our institution. Our position at times feels conflicted as we balance competing needs: establishing that we have the disciplinary knowledge and expertise to provide a required writing course that serves all majors while simultaneously contributing to multidisciplinary conversations around writing and writing assessment. But if writing studies and disciplinary faculty members committed to writing cannot engage in evidence-based multidisciplinary dialogue on writing assessment—and use the results of our assessment—our professional expertise is of little value to a broader audience and potentially to ourselves.

Below we describe our programmatic assessment, an empirical case study that centered on our FYC portfolio, a cumulative, end-of-semester assessment used by all FYC courses at Washington State University (WSU), the institution we were all affiliated with when this research began. This project allowed us to assess how well the program addresses our outcomes as demonstrated by our students' writing; this process also provided us with a common language to discuss program development, which is of key importance to our operational definition of fairness. These discussions took place during our weekly, pedagogy-based Professional Development in Composition (PDC) sessions attended by all FYC faculty members. In PDC, program faculty members analyzed the results of this project, reflected on patterns in the data collected, and discussed enhancements to pedagogy (Shepard, "Classroom Assessment" 634). Specifically, we collected data to assess which outcomes were met less consistently and with less proficiency in portfolios. We used those data to provide the framework for discussions among faculty members on how and why those outcomes were not as strongly represented as others, and we worked together as a program to develop pedagogical solutions for addressing outcomes that needed attention.

Our programmatic approach to fairness aims to involve as many stakeholders of classroom and programmatic assessment as possible. This approach ultimately allows us to foreground the needs of students going forward. Our local definition of fairness emphasizes instructor engagement in pedagogical responses to assessment. We combine the theoretical underpinnings, research design, and methods described below to support program-level assessment that addresses the needs of our local program and engages in multidisciplinary conversations with outside stakeholders. The resulting programmatic assessment dialogue is discussed in more detail in the section below on applying the lessons.

Research Design and Methods

Our study began with three research questions designed for our local FYC community. These questions were also designed for external audiences and stakeholders, including institutional administrators and accreditors. Therefore, the guiding questions below allowed us to gather data useful for continual conversations on the teaching of our outcomes—both ongoing internal programmatic dialogue and external conversations with community stakeholders—all while emphasizing the language of our outcomes as the bridge between these audiences.

> Which FYC Portfolio Outcomes are most successfully demonstrated (as defined by the faculty member reading the portfolio) in student portfolios?
>
> Which outcomes can and must be addressed in our classroom pedagogies more fully?
>
> In what ways can teachers and administrators collaboratively design PDC sessions for FYC to enhance the teaching of the outcomes?

Our research questions are designed for our local context, but developing similar research questions is possible for courses in all disciplines.

As we began this assessment project, we relied on our local FYC portfolio outcomes shown in figure 1, which are adapted from the Council of Writing Program Administrators' "WPA Outcomes Statement for FYC (3.0)" (refer to Dryer et al.), and the *Framework for Success for Postsecondary Writing*; both documents contribute to a body of knowledge for writing studies (Adler-Kassner and Wardle). These consensus documents have been developed with a significant amount of faculty expertise and articulate nationally recognized common outcomes. In localizing these two documents, certain standards of performance are intentionally not articulated. As well, although we have divided the outcomes into rated and unrated categories for this assessment project, the version that students are given contains all the outcomes listed in figure 1 so that the variables of language, not their assessment, are emphasized.

Therefore, our local FYC outcomes provide an assessment framework familiar to our faculty-member raters because it is used regularly in teaching and evaluation, thus supporting uniformity among raters. The "WPA Outcomes Statement" and the *Framework* simultaneously promote and reinforce multidisciplinary dialogues on writing and writing assessment, as well as shape the day-to-day interactions of WSU's FYC program and pedagogies. Localization is crucial.

WSU English Department Composition Program
English 101 Portfolio Outcomes

All English 101 classes are portfolio-based. A portfolio-based course develops and challenges students' skills as reflective authors and researchers. All portfolios are graded holistically based on the Outcomes below. The ENGLISH 101 Portfolio Outcomes are based on the Outcomes for First-Year Composition from the Council of Writing Program Administrators and the Information Literacy Competency Standards for Higher Education from the Association of College and Research Libraries.

Critical Thinking

Writers think critically when they analyze, synthesize, interpret, and evaluate ideas, information, situations, and texts.

RATED
_ Identify problems or questions
_ Develop positions or arguments concerning problems or questions
_ Use reading and composing for inquiry, as well as evaluating and reevaluating perspectives
_ Integrate personal ideas with those of others
_ Recognize and critique the relationships among language, knowledge, and power

UNRATED
None

Information Literacy

Writers use information literacy to understand when information is needed and to locate, evaluate, and effectively use that information.

RATED
_ Determine the extent and relevance of information needed
_ Find, evaluate, summarize, analyze, and synthesize appropriate sources
_ Use information effectively to accomplish a specific purpose
_ Use information ethically

UNRATED
_ Explore the concepts of intellectual property that motivate documentation conventions

Rhetorical Awareness

Writers develop rhetorical awareness by negotiating purpose, audience, context, and conventions as they compose a variety of texts for different situations.

RATED
_ Focus on a purpose
_ Respond to the needs of different audiences and cultures
_ Respond appropriately to different rhetorical situations
_ Adopt and use appropriate voice, tone, style, and level of formality
_ Employ the available and appropriate composing modalities to address a variety of rhetorical situations

UNRATED
_ Address and satisfy requirements of an assignment

Composing Processes

Writers use multiple strategies and composing processes to conceptualize, develop, and finalize projects. Composing processes are flexible and seldom linear.

RATED
_ Demonstrate awareness of the need for multiple drafts and revision to create and complete successful projects
_ Reflect on the composing process
_ Use composing processes and tools as a means to discover and reconsider ideas

UNRATED
_ Develop flexible strategies for reading, drafting, revising, designing, and editing
_ Engage in the collaborative and social aspects of composing
_ Learn to provide and make use of productive feedback

Conventions

Conventions are the formal rules and informal guidelines that shape readers' and writers' perceptions of correctness or appropriateness. Conventions arise from a history of use and are not universal.

RATED
_ Apply conventions of format, design, and structure appropriate to the rhetorical situation
_ Practice appropriate means of systematically documenting sources
_ Negotiate and control grammar, punctuation, and mechanics

UNRATED
_ Understand why conventions of structure, paragraphing, tone, and usage vary

Figure 1. Washington State University's First-Year Composition Outcomes.

Although we support broad philosophical treatments of fairness and have been influenced by them, figure 1 stands as our demonstrable commitment to fairness. Lorrie Shepard ("Role") has proposed a practical concept of fairness: "Having access to evaluation criteria satisfies a basic fairness principle (we should know the rules for how our work will be judged)" (11). As Shepard proposes, by publicizing the concepts that will be assessed, along with their evaluative criteria, we allow students to improve that which is required (11–12). There is no external, purchased test to stand in the way of these shared outcomes, and there is little chance that an instructor's voice will be silenced. Figure 1 represents our shared assessment values. In reality, the opportunity structures discussed so often in this edited collection are created by widely disseminating outcomes as we have done in figure 1.

Institutional Context

Washington State University is a multicampus, land grant, R1 university. The Pullman campus, where this research was conducted, is located on the traditional and ceded homelands of the Nez Percé and enrolls an average of 2,500 FYC students per year. The student population is approximately seventy percent white and thirty percent students of color ("Quick Facts"); about forty percent are first-generation students ("Define").

Sample

The sample FYC portfolios were collected from portfolios with passing grades completed within the previous year. Each FYC portfolio comprises several drafts of at least three major projects, including at least two source-based essays. In addition, our portfolio allows up to one multimodal project. Three portfolios were collected (using a randomized process) from each of twenty sections, for a total of sixty portfolios. Because we were evaluating the program formatively rather than assessing student writing summatively, this deliberately small sample is not necessarily representative of the student population. Rather, this set of portfolios indicated where our heuristic discussion might begin. The portfolios were redacted to remove any student or instructor identifying information. Although this assessment method can accommodate multimodal work, the initial sample drew from sections that used text-primary projects in their portfolios (e.g., research essays, analytical essays).

Data Collection

We collected and analyzed the data through software designed in-house by Matt Frye. This user-friendly software was designed to distribute electronic copies of portfolios, allow readers to rate each outcome, and compile the data with minimal labor from readers and the assessment team. Although this tool did not automatically calculate reliability or other metrics, it reduced the labor involved in the assessment process and enabled us to quickly tabulate and view results. Those without such a resource could collect and analyze their data in *Excel* or another program familiar to them. Although entering data into programs like *Excel* would be more time consuming, the goal is to identify patterns in assessment data and encourage programmatic dialogue; technological apparatus is incidental.

Measures

In our pilot test, a small group of FYC faculty members assessed several portfolios using our full set of FYC portfolio outcomes through analytic scoring. Because our weekly PDC sessions reinforce FYC portfolio outcomes, the readers in our project were already normed in the assessment criteria. Additionally, we designed this project to collect more concrete data beyond individual anecdotes. Moving beyond anecdotes of performance in individual classrooms allowed more meaningful dialogue regarding equity and fairness in student assessment and classroom practices. As such, this group noted several outcomes that could not be reliably observed in final projects alone, thus narrowing the list of observable outcomes to those presented in table 1. After adjusting the process slightly, a full assessment began with a team of thirteen raters. Each sample portfolio from the most recent academic year was evaluated by four FYC faculty members. Raters then assessed the outcomes observed in each portfolio using the scale in table 2. This primary-trait analysis (i.e., focusing on individual portfolio outcomes) differs distinctly from our program's requirement that teachers grade their students' portfolios holistically; when teachers grade student portfolios, they evaluate all outcomes holistically and assign one grade. In contrast, this formative programmatic assessment used trait scoring to assess each outcome separately (Hamp-Lyons). This process identified specific outcomes that were most consistently rated satisfactorily or better and other outcomes that were less successfully met. Focusing on individual outcomes also helped us emphasize the relations between outcomes, supporting the design of specialized PDC sessions to improve student learning in those outcomes.

Table 1. Summarized Ratings across All Washington State University First-Year Composition Portfolios (percentages indicate the proportion of ratings in that category per outcome)

Outcome (refer to table 2 for complete language)	Percentage satisfactory or above	Percentage not satisfactory
Rhetorical Awareness (Overall)	**78.5**	**21.6**
Focus on a purpose	87.2	12.8
Respond to the needs of different audiences and cultures	72.0	28.1
Respond appropriately to different rhetorical situations	81.8	18.2
Adopt and use appropriate voice, tone, style, and formality	85.8	14.3
Use the available and appropriate composing modalities	65.6	34.5
Critical Thinking (Overall)	**70.5**	**29.5**
Identify problems or questions	86.7	13.3
Develop positions or arguments	73.4	26.7
Use reading and composing for inquiry	69.0	31.1
Integrate personal ideas with with those of others	72.4	27.6
Recognize and critique the relations among language, knowledge, and power	51.3	48.8
Information Literacy (Overall)	**80.3**	**19.6**
Determine extent and relevance of information needed	76.2	23.8
Find, evaluate, analyze, and synthesize appropriate sources	74.7	25.3
Use information effectively	78.7	21.3
Use information ethically	91.6	8.5
Composing Processes (Overall)	**74.4**	**25.6**
Demonstrate awareness of the need for multiple drafts and revision	77.3	22.7
Reflect on the composing process	81.3	18.7
Use composing processes as means to discover	64.6	35.5
Knowledge of Conventions (Overall)	**90.4**	**9.5**
Apply conventions of format, design, and structure	95.5	4.4
Practice appropriate means of systematically documenting sources	84.7	15.3
Negotiate and control grammar, punctuation, and mechanics	91.2	8.9

Table 2. Washington State University First-Year Composition Program's Rating Scale

Option Shown to Rater	Definition
Outcome met at **outstanding** level	Performance exceeded our expectations in FYC
Outcome met at **satisfactory** level	Performance met our expectations for FYC
Outcome met at **minimal** level	Performance fell short of expectations for a student finishing FYC
Outcome **not in evidence**	Performance on this outcome could not be observed (neither positive nor negative)
Use of outcome seriously **diminishes effectiveness**	Performance on this outcome was counterproductive to student's purpose

Results and Discussion: How the Numbers Inform Our Program

Our assessment found that students regularly performed satisfactorily or better in the larger categories of Rhetorical Awareness, Critical Thinking, and Composing Processes, but analysis of individual portfolio outcomes revealed potential areas for improvement. Although the teachers had noticed some of these patterns in their individual assessment of student writing, the results of this study provided concrete data supporting these anecdotal observations. Once the teachers were presented with these results, we opened the assessment dialogue, discussing how this information might formatively influence our program's weekly PDC sessions. This programmatic dialogue began with the results in table 1.

Applying the Lessons

Our assessment results showed us previously unidentified opportunities to improve fairness at a programmatic level. The addition of a data-driven assessment component enabled us to interpret these results with the raters and FYC instructors (which include both full-time instructors and graduate students). In these dialogues, many instructors were surprised by the weaker performance on local outcomes like the ability to "Recognize and critique the relations among language, knowledge, and power," as course themes often overtly focus on political or economic issues and require students to examine the language employed in written, visual, and oral discourse. Behind these numbers, we found that our courses asked students to engage with issues of language, knowledge, and power in class discussion, homework assignments, and other activities, but not in a way that was easily evaluated in final portfolios. Individual instructors noted that they could identify where students were meeting this outcome in portfolios submitted for their own courses due to a central part of our portfolio's deferred grading process—the emphasis on composing processes and revision—but the results were not clear at the programmatic level. This finding was telling to us.

Based on the results presented in table 1, we applied our definition of *fairness*—a programmatic effort to define outcomes broadly and develop pedagogical responses to assessment results—by making changes to our PDC sessions. These pedagogy-based changes were collaboratively made by the then program leaders and graduate students who attended, participated in, and helped lead key sessions. Our community dedicated several of our 2017–18 weekly PDC sessions to specific outcomes associated with Rhetorical Awareness, Critical Thinking, and Composing Processes. As Mya Poe points out in her essay in this volume, "in disciplinary environments, foundational issues surrounding collaboration, access, cultural responsiveness, and justice are related to improving student outcomes." We specifically framed several of our weekly sessions to support the

Critical Thinking outcome on language, knowledge, and power. Though the most recent revision of the "WPA Outcomes for FYC (3.0)" has removed this outcome (Dryer et al.), our program has chosen to maintain it, recognizing its influence on the teaching of rhetoric (Holiday) and critical literacies crucial to both students marginalized by the university and their teachers (Buyserie et al.). Since this outcome received our lowest ratings, with only half of the portfolio ratings at outstanding or satisfactory levels, our commitment to this outcome's focus on language, knowledge, and power obligated us to consider it more fully and find out ways we could better teach it across all course sections.

Therefore, our Fall 2017 PDC series focused on language, knowledge, and power. Teachers explicitly defined these terms and discussed what they meant to students; our discussions were influenced by the respective work of Lisa King and colleagues, Staci Perryman-Clark and colleagues, and Victor Villanueva, who collectively examine the connections between race, language, colonization, and writing studies. Fall semester ended with two workshops focusing on pedagogical approaches to the teaching of language, knowledge, and power: one focusing on readings and assignments, another on syllabus design. In both workshops, teachers examined their current materials through the lens of language and power, considered possible approaches with other teachers, and formed plans of action. The goal of these workshops was for teachers to bring the content of these discussions into the classroom, so students could then apply those concepts in their composing, revising, and final portfolios.

Our results also suggested other outcomes that needed additional attention. In response, FYC instructors designed several PDC sessions focusing on the Rhetorical Awareness outcome associated with multimodal composing. Workshops included in-class multimodal activities: multimodal beyond the digital and designing and assessing multimodal projects (inspired by Arola et al.). All these sessions emphasized the importance of making claims. Throughout the sessions, FYC instructors stressed that so-called individual outcomes must connect to each other, as student portfolios are evaluated holistically.

As mentioned in the section of this essay on measures, evaluators found that not all composing processes could be evaluated. Final portfolios in this study did not include feedback from instructors, peers, or other individuals. Beyond a reflective cover letter, the portfolios collected did not include any reflective writing that might allow students to identify and discuss the ways their writing took shape during the semester. Although raters largely agreed that the work they saw was satisfactory in some aspects of the composing process, raters ascertained that the collected portfolios could not demonstrate whether students had developed flexible strategies for reading and composing, for engaging in collaborative processes of writing and revision, or for effectively providing and using feedback. For colleagues in other programs and disciplines, we present this data to emphasize that not everything that a program values will be assessable via a final portfolio or project. Rather, programs must recognize that much learning happens in class and in students' individual learning processes that simply will not be accounted for in a final project. At the same time, programs should continue to create opportunities for stakeholders, particularly teachers and administrators within a program, to encourage programmatic dialogue about and improved teaching of their outcomes.

Validity, Reliability, and Fairness

As we emphasize throughout this essay, faculty members must be active in establishing evidence of validity, reliability, and fairness at the programmatic level. Ideally, their engagement can be in response to meaningful assessment. When teacher-researchers are involved in programmatic assessment and analysis, teachers themselves drive pedagogical improvements, something that rarely happens in top-down assessment of writing programs. Our assessment provides teachers with opportunities to better understand and participate in the program's writing constructs (reinforcing validity), so that all teachers in the program might more consistently and transparently deliver a curriculum across all sections (encouraging reliability). Within these program-supported dialogues, teachers may reflectively assess the fairness of their own pedagogies stemming from their backgrounds and positionalities for ways they might better incorporate the outcomes into their own writing classes; in this way, we do not seek to eliminate inherent biases, but to identify, challenge, and openly discuss them. Rather than focus on transferability of results (since our assessment results are local), we recommend other programs focus on transferability of the assessment process.

This recommendation is founded on our belief that our project can serve as a model that other programs could adapt to assess their own programs. Given the local focus of our project, we do not expect that future assessments or other programs will replicate our results. Indeed, replication in terms of reproducibility here is not our goal; there is no replication recipe, as Mark J. Brandt and colleagues term this linear system. Rather, our goal is to model assessment design principles so that others may use and tailor them to their unique student populations and institutional missions. As Shepard ("Role") has noted of her own research, "To develop effective practices based on social-constructivist perspectives, it will be important to conduct studies in classrooms where instruction and assessment strategies are consonant with this model. In many cases this will mean 'starting over again' and not assuming that findings from previous research studies can be generalized across paradigms" (104). Needed, then, are not programs of research using standardized methodologies but, instead, commitment to collaboration advancing fundamental understandings of complex, situated learning.

Our approach provides a flexible research framework, not only for writing studies but also for any number of disciplines. The grassroots nature of this project creates a writing assessment system with a focus on community building and local values that develops "writing assessment methods that not only support teaching and learning but also are supported by evidence-based and theoretically-informed arguments" (O'Neill, "Moving"). Teachers assess student writing programmatically, and the findings of the assessment are addressed by teacher-led PDC sessions to improve the results of future classroom teaching practices, thereby improving future outcomes-based assessments. These sessions encourage professional development regarding classroom practices, portfolio projects, and course outcomes.

Expanding Our Assessment Dialogue: Community Engagement

Our assessment conversations eventually expanded into multidisciplinary assessment committees elsewhere on campus, ensuring that our assessment dialogue was not limited to our department. Beth Buyserie represented FYC on a university-wide assessment committee, which consisted of representatives from chemistry, history, human development, physics, psychology, veterinary medicine, and the libraries. After presenting our data to several members of the assessment committee, common themes emerged between discipline-specific assessment projects. For example, our assessment project revealed that two of our areas of concern (our outcomes of "Develop positions or arguments" and "Integrate personal ideas with those of others") were shared in other departments. Both outcomes ask students to make an arguable claim regarding a significant, relevant, and debatable topic. The results for these two outcomes (refer to table 1) particularly interested us as our FYC course emphasizes making and supporting claims. Other programs on this multidisciplinary, general education assessment committee noted similar patterns in their own internal assessments regarding students' use (or absence) of claims, connecting our common observations on assessment of student writing. These conversations open the door to university-wide dialogues regarding fairness across the curriculum.

As this essay was completed, these conversations were still in the beginning stages, but having continual, programmatic conversations about our shared assessments allows us to reinforce and collaborate with multiple disciplines in the teaching of writing. This communication allows for writing studies faculty to support other disciplines' written communication expectations in positive ways. In addition, it supports continued programmatic discussion that allows for the development of common language about writing and writing assessment, supporting definitions of fairness. Our goal of equity-based multidisciplinary conversations about writing and writing assessment also potentially affect disciplinary transfer (Yancey et al.) and student retention (Reichert Powell). Ultimately, dialogue on programmatic outcomes benefits students, teachers, and administrators.

Conclusion

This programmatic approach allowed our faculty members to participate in an assessment process that valued their expertise and judgments about writing studies. We believe that even the most assessment-wary faculty member can engage in program assessment, and we urge that such assessment be grounded in commitments to fairness and opportunity. In addition to performing an important self-assessment function (Inoue, "Self-Assessment"), the approach we provide is transferable to multiple disciplinary contexts. Regardless of the discipline, such assessment can help teachers within a program learn more about program outcomes—and in turn, more intentionally address those outcomes with their students. As one of the final steps in our assessment process, we asked our thirteen raters (by way of an informal anonymous survey) several open-response questions that connect program assessment and teacher pedagogy. We asked, "Did participation in this project change your understanding of [FYC] portfolio outcomes?" One rater responded that the process "helped me to understand which of the outcomes I can realistically assess in the portfolio, while others, still being crucial to the class, may filter throughout in-class work, teaching, and discussion." Another rater asserted that "this project pushed me to think about *how* students are meeting the outcomes, not just *if* they are meeting the outcomes."

We also asked raters if assessing the portfolios for this project helped them learn more about their teaching. One rater echoed others that the project "gave me a wider exposure to the kinds of assignments given to, and the writing done by, our FYC students. . . . Having this much practice just reading for specific outcomes has made it easier for me to explain them to students." Finally, we asked our raters if this assessment served as a type of professional development opportunity, as we hoped the project was not simply additional (although paid) work for teachers. One rater confirmed that the project both supported their professional development and helped them learn more about their own teaching, reporting that "[p]articipating made me reconsider how I interpreted the outcomes and how students demonstrated them."

As evidenced by the comments above, program assessment can provide programs with language to describe what a program truly values, what its strengths are, and what outcomes it is committed to improving. This assessment project has changed the way our program discusses our own outcomes. We now talk about them more explicitly and consistently. We have adjusted our PDC sessions so that teachers can cultivate models and strategies for teaching these outcomes in their classes. Significantly, this dialogue has emphasized how our outcomes connect and intersect. It is not hard to imagine how interactions, comments, and pedagogies might grow from a similar assessment project in any discipline.

Overall, our assessment project has provided us with empirical data that promote the disciplinary integrity and importance of writing studies to outside audiences (Phelps and Ackerman). Our collection of specific, evidence-based data challenges us to be explicit in how we communicate the language of our outcomes to students. The practice of being explicit in the teaching of our outcomes—outcomes by which we then assess student performance—responds to calls for justice in rhetoric and composition (e.g., Reichert Powell). Ultimately, this formative assessment project provides teachers and administrators from multiple disciplines with the language necessary to evaluate approaches to the teaching of writing—but, more important, to reinforce the concept of fairness in our individual and programmatic writing pedagogies.

Incorporating Self-Relevant Writing in a Social Science General Education Class

Karen Singer-Freeman and Linda Bastone

Perspective

In this essay we describe the use of reflective writing to increase fairness in a general education course on child development. We discuss our use of reflective writing and its utility value in fostering fairness within this social science course. Our findings demonstrate that participation in a single deeply engaging class can have a broad impact on students' experiences in college. We conclude our discussion with recommendations for others who wish to incorporate reflective writing assignments with a high utility value in large general education courses.

Reflective Writing and Utility Value in General Education Classes

A recent survey of chief academic officers conducted by the Association of American Colleges and Universities reported that most colleges have clearly articulated general education learning outcomes (Hart Research Assoc.). Many institutions lack developed means of assessing mastery of these outcomes, however. Frequently, general education outcomes are assessed in ways that fail to measure deep understanding or integrative knowledge. Common assessments, such as multiple-choice questions, prevent students from expressing learning in their own words or contextualizing their learning. Too often, large general-education-designated classes default to didactic lectures paired with multiple-choice or short-answer assessments. Restrictive pedagogical approaches may disproportionately limit underserved students' abilities to demonstrate learning. We propose that reflective writing is uniquely situated to act as a conduit for the acquisition and assessment of general education learning outcomes. We have revised a large general education course in child development to integrate more reflective writing to attend to the diverse needs of student learners. Kathleen Blake Yancey, an early proponent of the use of reflective writing, observes, "Through reflection, we understand curriculum pluralized: as lived, as delivered, as experienced: it is in the intersection of these curricula that identities are formed; students exert the most authority in that intersection since they are the ones who inhabit that place; learning more about that place is a prime goal of reflection used for educational purposes" (*Reflection* 202).

Although Yancey considered the role of reflection primarily in the context of writing instruction, reflective writing assignments in other contexts have the potential to encourage integration across cognitive, intrapersonal, and interpersonal domains. Cognitive work is required to demonstrate mastery of an academic area; intrapersonal work occurs when students reflectively apply conceptual knowledge to the self; and interpersonal work takes place when the work is shared with faculty members, peers, and family members. According to James W. Pellegrino and Margaret L. Hilton, this sort of conceptual integration is associated with deep learning and improved transfer of knowledge (National Research Council 135).

Reflective writing can also increase students' investment in the production of written content. As Mya Poe observes in this volume, "Written communication is a deeply situated behavior." Often students view writing as a task to be completed rather than as a means of communicating with others. Authentic writing requires an authentic audience. Randy Bass describes this as "social pedagogy," when increased opportunities for learning are present and students engage in intellectual tasks that center around sharing knowledge (65). Social pedagogy enhances and encourages reflection and can support personal change. We have constructed assignments that have high social pedagogy by encouraging students to either curate their work in e-portfolios or share their body of work with family and friends.

A task is high in utility value when students perceive the resulting work to have relevance, meaning, or worth beyond its value within a specific academic context (Eccles et al. 72). When reflective writing integrates general education concepts with personal experiences, the high utility value of the work can deepen students' engagement. Judith M. Harackiewicz and colleagues found that assignments that require academic content be related to the self are high in utility value. Students at risk for academic difficulties, such as ethnic minority and first-generation college students, learned more in introductory biology classes when a portion of the assignments were high in utility value. The redesigned general education class described in this essay incorporates reflective writing and rubric-guided evaluation to increase fairness, equity, and the quantity of writing students produce. We have integrated opportunities for students to assess and reflect on what they have learned as a key strategy to promote deep learning across disciplines.

As we implemented our course redesign we discovered that opportunities for reflective writing increase assignment utility value. If we define fairness as the advancement of opportunities to learn, as has Carol Lee in her work on culturally robust classrooms, then the genre of reflective writing is aligned with her instructional models, because it allows students to expand prior knowledge and make sense of their learning. Since the relations between genre and fairness have not been fully explored, it is our hope that this discussion contributes to research in this area.

The research described in this essay was conducted at Purchase College, State University of New York. Purchase College is a four-year comprehensive college located thirty miles north of New York City that is classified as arts and science focus, with some graduate coexistence in the Carnegie classification system. Purchase College is the only public four-year institution in Westchester County and plays an essential role in providing access to higher education for low-income and racially and culturally diverse students. The most recent four-year graduation rate was fifty-seven percent and six-year graduation rate was sixty-eight percent. The college serves approximately four thousand matriculated undergraduates, including eighteen percent first-generation college students and students from diverse racial and cultural groups (twenty-four percent Hispanic, twelve percent Black, five percent mixed ethnicity, four percent Asian, and less than one percent American Indian, Alaskan, or Pacific Islander). Many students have economic need, with seventy-six percent receiving federal loans and forty percent eligible for Pell Grants ("Purchase College").

State University of New York students satisfy general education requirements by selecting courses from at least seven of ten content areas (basic communication, mathematics, natural sciences, social sciences, the arts, humanities, American history, Western civilization, foreign language, and other world civilizations). Although it is common for general education classes to constitute a large percentage of undergraduate college curricula, ranging from a third to half of completed credits (Fox 7), in the State University of New York system only twenty-five percent of students' credits must fulfill general education requirements. Child Development fulfills a lower-level elective requirement for psychology majors and the social sciences general education requirement for all students. The course learning outcomes are informed by several Association of American Colleges and Universities' Liberal Education and America's Promise learning outcomes: written communication, inquiry and analysis, quantitative literacy, critical thinking, intercultural knowledge and competence, integrative learning, and applied learning (3).

Child Development seats between sixty and one hundred students when taught in a traditional format and thirty-five when taught online. In each ninety-minute traditional class, approximately seventy minutes are dedicated to lecture and twenty to discussion. In the online class, students view several twenty- to thirty-minute lectures each week, which include slides with animated writing and a video of the professor speaking. The class enrolls primarily first-year students and includes large numbers of students who might be considered at risk academically. In 2017, thirty-six percent of the students enrolled were from underrepresented racial categories and thirty-one percent were first-generation college students. The results reported in this chapter are drawn from four semesters of the course offered by the first author between 2015 and 2018.

Increasing Fairness through Assignments

We revised the Child Development curriculum with the goals of increasing fairness, providing more substantial opportunities to engage in writing, increasing conceptual retention, and supporting student wellness. The revised curriculum incorporated reflective assignments with high utility value and used culturally responsive instructional and assessment practices. Our class revision was guided by best practices in writing instruction proposed by Steve Graham and colleagues, which include requiring students to write frequently and for different purposes, creating a supportive environment, scaffolding assignments, and teaching students how to self-assess their own work (8–9).

We encourage students to connect class material to broader issues in two types of assignments that have high utility value: reflective-writing and chapter reflections. We assign eleven to thirteen reflective writing assignments in which students summarize an area of research, apply the material autobiographically or to a contemporary problem, consider ways the material informs their plans for interactions with children, and select the most important things they would like to remember. In different years of instruction, we have included these assignments as part of an e-portfolio or as traditional papers. When the assignments are given as traditional papers, we curate each student's assignments into an attractive document that is returned to the student at the end of the semester. We encourage students to revise their work before submission by providing the grading rubrics as a part of the assignment instructions. This is done to encourage reflection in action. We prompt constructive reflection by asking students to consider contextual influences and to reflect on autobiographical experiences (Yancey, *Reflection*). For example, the instructions for an assignment on language development are as follows:

In your own words describe the major accomplishments of language learning during infancy and early childhood. Describe two ways families or communities can support language development and two ways they can impede language development. Describe the benefits of bilingualism and dangers of language loss. Reflect on your own life and describe your language-learning environment. What languages did you hear? Did you speak or understand a language other than English? Include any information you know about your first words or phrases. Describe your experiences learning a second language in school or at home. Look forward and describe the language environment you would like to create for a child. List three things you would like to remember about language development and bilingualism to be a positive influence on children.

In addition to completing reflective writing assignments, the sixty to eighty students enrolled in the in-person class or thirty-five enrolled in the online class complete thirteen chapter reflections. The instructor describes these assignments as an opportunity for students to select personally relevant information from the textbook. The only requirement for the assignments is that students write about something that was not discussed during lectures and explain why they find the information to be personally relevant. The professor or undergraduate teaching assistants respond individually to each reflection.

Another technique that can increase fairness in classes and encourage authentic writing is the use of brief psychological interventions. These interventions improve individuals' lives by changing the way they think and feel about the world. The primary mechanism of change in brief psychological interventions is hypothesized to be reflection (Walton 81). Students are provided with a different way to view pivotal experiences that supports more resilient responses to future challenges. Brief psychological interventions that target students' sense of belonging, views of intelligence, attention to personal values, and grit have been shown to improve underserved students' grades, persistence, and overall well-being for long periods of time. Many of these interventions help reduce academic achievement gaps by increasing ethnic minority students' performance (Walton 79). One powerful and widely used intervention is designed to change students' belief that intelligence is genetically determined and unchangeable. Carol S. Dweck (*Mindset*) refers to this belief as a fixed mindset and pioneered work in which brief lessons on brain plasticity led to shifts in students' views of intelligence. When students are taught to take a growth view of intelligence, they become more interested in attempting difficult tasks and more likely to persist after an initial failure (Paunesku et al. 787–90). In Child Development, to reduce achievement gaps, four reflective writing assignments that include brief psychological interventions (sense of belonging, mindset, values affirmation, and grit) were included. These interventions were selected because they have been shown to reduce achievement gaps in other settings (Walton 77). Brief psychological interventions are easily adapted into reflective writing assignments because they encourage students to integrate new concepts with personal experiences and evoke high levels of self-reflection.

Evaluating all students fairly is a critical issue in higher education. Accordingly, the assessment of student writing must consider fairness. Because evaluations completed using rubrics provide a lasting record of assessed learning, it is possible to conduct an audit of outcomes across different classes or instructors. Rubrics are likely to increase grading fairness by helping a single evaluator apply the same standards across multiple individuals. Finally, rubrics can focus evaluators' attention on specific concepts and reduce the bias that may occur when evaluators assess nonessential elements of a piece of work. For example, Yancey reported that Oregon State University was able to recruit a more ethnically diverse group of students who were successfully retained at the college when rubrics focused the evaluation of brief reflective writing in admissions materials on critical thinking and reflection rather than on grammar and punctuation ("College").

We take an outcomes-based approach to our Child Development course, emphasizing student learning and authentic assessment of knowledge and skills. Each grading rubric includes five similar learning outcomes that involve conceptual mastery, integration, and application as shown in table 1. Each learning outcome is assessed using a three-point scale of fully present, missing important elements, and absent information. Individual feedback to students explains areas in which learning outcomes were not met and expresses confidence in the student's ability to show evidence of mastery in future assignments. The consistency of rubrics used across assignments allows students to improve in their ability to self-assess as the course progresses and scaffolds a higher level of performance. Yancey suggests the use of rubrics also enhances the reflective nature of the assignments in two ways. Rubrics encourage students to engage in reflection-in-action by providing specific information that encourages revising and reviewing writing as it is being completed. As similar rubrics are used across weekly assignments, they encourage reflection in presentation by encouraging students to create an integrated sense of writing in a specific context for a specific audience.

In Child Development, the course content has the potential to change students' understanding of their own childhood experiences and to change their plans for how they will parent, teach, or interact in other ways with children in the future. Invoking the strengthening effects of social pedagogy has the poten-

Table 1. Sample Reflective Writing Assignment Rubric

Learning Outcome for Reflective Writing	Description
Concepts	Describes language development including sufficient detail for each stage
Integration	Describes two ways the environment can support and two ways the environment can impede language development
Integration	Provides description of benefits of bilingualism and dangers of language loss
Application	Describes own language experience and the future environment writer would like to create for a child
Application	Describes three applications that relate to language development

tial to increase the likelihood that students will enact changes in their future interactions with children. The reflective writing assignments used in Child Development ask students to describe key moments from their lives and their wishes for the future. Some also encourage students to include images from childhood or letters to the students' future selves. These elements of the assignments make both the future self and family members authentic audiences and invoke social pedagogy. In addition to feedback by means of rubrics, the professor and teaching assistants provide students with at least two supportive comments about each assignment. We share common themes from assignments during class. The professor encourages students to save and share their assignments with family members and curates all student work into an attractive document that is returned to the student at the end of the semester. Chapter reflections are submitted and responded to through e-mail to personalize the connection between the student and the professor or teaching assistant.

We create a sense of community in the classroom using culturally responsive pedagogy. Culturally responsive pedagogy invites the best work from traditionally underrepresented students and acknowledges differences as a positive attribute. A critical component of culturally responsive pedagogy is the maintenance of high standards, coupled with the communication that the professor is confident the student can meet the standards (Morrison et al. 435). In Child Development we use rubrics to clarify expected learning outcomes. A rubric aligned with learning outcomes guides instruction and provides students with an understanding of what they must do to succeed on an assignment. In this way, rubrics can limit what Asao B. Inoue refers to as "quality failures" and encourage performance approach behaviors ("Theorizing" 338). We also provide individualized feedback that includes instructions about how to improve and communicates confidence in the student's ability to improve.

A second important feature of culturally responsive pedagogy is the inclusion of material from students' heritage groups (Morrison et al. 437). In Child

Development, autobiographical writing assignments are used as a means of increasing the representation of students' lived experiences. Autobiographical writing empowers underrepresented students by providing them opportunities to increase an instructor's understanding of their life experiences. Reflective writing can also be a powerful tool to empower students with disabilities. As we read the work of students from diverse backgrounds, we expand our understanding of our students, which increases our cultural awareness. As we share what we have learned from student writing with the class, students from the groups being represented are further empowered. When students experience acceptance and respect for their perspectives and cultures, they are well positioned to produce their best work. The impact of autobiographical assignments is increased when we share examples from student writing with the class or when the writing occurs in shared e-portfolios. When students are encouraged to share work with family members and friends, the expanded audience includes heritage groups, which increases both utility value and social pedagogy.

Student Perceptions of Reflective Writing in a Child Development Course

To determine whether our changes to the course fulfilled our desired objectives, we collected information about students' experiences in Child Development. We found that students responded positively to the reflective writing assignments. In exit surveys, over seventy-five percent of students reported they felt the assignments enhanced learning, provided an accurate assessment of learning, encouraged reflection, and should be used in future classes. Students commented on the value of personal reflections as encouragement for authentic learning. Many students included broad concepts in their list of the most important things they learned in the class and reported that reflective writing assignments encouraged conceptual integration.

Responses to the reflective writing assignments included many references that demonstrated the utility value of the assignments. For example, one student's response shows both an awareness of the utility value of the assignment and the presence of the student's heritage culture:

> Similar to what my mom taught me, I hope to teach children that they should respect and be kind to their peers and elders. . . . One way that I will teach this to them is by using positive reinforcement. . . . According to the textbook, this is an effective way of teaching social learning. Another way that I hope to teach these values is by being repetitive, like my mom.

Another student described immigration experiences that caused her to learn and lose languages as a child. This response also shows the inclusion of references to the student's unique experiences and background as well as awareness of the assignment's utility value:

> While Spanish was my primary language as a child, it did not remain this way after we moved back to New York when I was about five or six years old. According to my mother, I had no desire to relearn English when we returned. When people would speak to me in English, I would respond to them in Spanish not really understanding what they had said. . . . My mother decided to stop speaking to me in Spanish in an effort to force me to speak English because she was concerned about me falling behind in school. Needless to say, I eventually regained fluency in English but lost it almost entirely in Spanish. . . . Ideally, I would love to create a balanced bilingual environment for my children. Not just for the cognitive or social benefits of being bilingual but also to embrace our cultural background.

Students showed similar expressions of utility value and descriptions of their own experiences in chapter reflections. For example, in response to a discussion of ways in which culture influences child development, one student wrote:

> Personally, I agree that race and ethnicity are social constructions. However, ethnicity as a social construction is a strong part of American culture. As a young African American woman, I never think too much about my ethnicity when I am around other people of color. As the text says, "ethnic identity becomes more specific and more salient under certain circumstances." Sometimes those "circumstances" may draw more attention to me in settings where people are completely different than me, sometimes I blend in.

Blending of personal experiences with awareness of utility value is evident in another student's chapter reflection in response to a section of the textbook that describes the interaction between environmental and genetic influences on alcoholism:

> My family has an incredibly long (and active) pattern of alcoholism, so this example hit home for me. Thinking of the environment as a factor of whether alcoholism and/or addiction is exhibited made me think a lot about how my family has gotten together frequently (holidays, birthdays, etc.), and at every event there would always be a lot of alcohol consumption. I haven't mapped a personal karyotype, but I imagine that my family's pattern of alcoholism could be purely environmental, purely genetic, or perhaps a combination of both.

Although there were no length requirements for the written assignments, students produced a substantial body of writing over the course of the semester. In the in-person class, in which undergraduate teaching assistants provided some of the feedback to students, students produced an average of 592 words each week (480 words in reflective writing and 112 words in chapter reflections). In the online class, in which all feedback came from the professor, students produced an average of 712 words each week (583 words in reflective writing and 129 words in chapter reflections). Interestingly, ninety percent of students submitted chapter reflections when they were e-mailed directly to the professor or an undergraduate teaching assistant, but only sixty-nine percent of students completed chapter reflections when submission took place through the course management system. In exit surveys, students also rated the assignments as being more valuable and less bothersome when submitted by e-mail than when submitted through the course management system. Students' more positive responses to the e-mailed assignments may reflect the increased presence of an authentic audience when the work was submitted and responded to through e-mail. Thus, we believe the social context in which writing is completed must be considered as part of a broader effort to increase fairness.

Toward Fair Assessment through Reflective Writing

The use of reflective writing appears to reduce the achievement gap in Child Development. Black and Hispanic students received grades similar to those received by white and Asian students. An equitable pattern of grading was observed both in classes where the professor graded all assignments and in classes where undergraduate teaching assistants participated in grading student work. Although the teaching assistants gave higher grades on average (ninety-three percent) than the professor (eighty-nine percent), this difference was not significant. The slightly higher grades given by the teaching assistants likely reflect that the professor carefully reviewed instances in which the teaching assistants did not credit students but was less careful in reviewing instances in which credit was given.

To determine whether more traditional types of assessments might reveal evidence of an achievement gap, we examined students' performance on low-stakes open-book quizzes that were used in two of the course offerings. This analysis revealed that Hispanic and Black students in the traditional class received significantly lower quiz grades (average = seventy-seven percent) than white and Asian students (average = eighty-six percent). Interestingly, there was not a statistically significant difference between the quiz grades in the online class (Black and Hispanic students' average = eighty-four percent, white and

Asian students' average = eighty-eight percent). We hypothesize that the online setting may create a more positive environment for Hispanic and Black students. The fact that in online classes race and ethnicity are less salient may reduce activation of stereotype threat (Steele and Aronson).

We were interested whether completion of the mindset intervention influenced students' views of intelligence. Students completed Dweck's Theory of Intelligence Scale, a measurement of mindset, during the first and final week of the semester as part of a larger online survey (*Self-Theories*; *Mindset*). Students reported the extent to which they believe intelligence is malleable using a six-point Likert-type scale. Higher scores reflected more of a growth view of intelligence. We found that students received significantly higher scores after completing the intervention (mean score = 4.66) than before completing the intervention (mean score = 4.40). Many students also mentioned learning about grit and developing a growth mindset in exit surveys when asked to list the five most important things they learned. These results provide some evidence that students were influenced by the interventions.

Students also completed values affirmation, sense of belonging, and grit interventions. Similar interventions have been found to increase retention on other college campuses (Walton 76). Early retention data comparing participation in Child Development with participation in another large general education class (Introduction to Psychology) revealed that participation in Child Development may increase retention at Purchase College. Whereas eighty percent of liberal arts students who were enrolled in Child Development in fall 2015 were in good academic standing or had graduated by spring 2018, only seventy percent of liberal arts students who were enrolled in Introduction to Psychology had graduated or were in good academic standing. Looking only at first-year students, we also found some evidence of improved retention. For liberal arts students who began their studies in fall 2015, the college retention rate as of spring 2018 is fifty-eight percent. First-year students who completed Introduction to Psychology in fall 2015 have a similar retention rate of sixty-one percent. In contrast, first-year students who completed Child Development in fall 2015 have a retention rate of sixty-nine percent. Although preliminary, these findings may reflect that participation in a single, deeply engaging class can have a broad impact on students' experience in college.

Conclusions

In concluding this discussion, it is important that we acknowledge that no writing genre or accompanying rubric is fair in and of itself. As Poe and colleagues have written in their work on disparate impact, "[W]hile locally developed measures are vital, they are not a proxy for validity" ("Legal," 604). Or, we would add, evidence of fairness. Instead, a thorough rethinking and redesign of course structure and pedagogy must accompany efforts to increase fairness. Those efforts must be guided by research and tailored to the needs of students.

As part of designing for fairness, reflective writing is a useful tool that can encourage students to integrate course material with personal experiences in the context of a large social science general education class. The writing assignments described in this essay can serve as a model for other large general education classes. We conclude with the following recommendations for others who wish to incorporate high utility value reflective writing assignments in large general education courses outside of writing studies.

> Provide rich opportunities to write in different genres for authentic audiences. Infuse assignments with reflective activities to increase utility value, engagement, conceptual integration, and retention.

> Curate a complete set of each student's reflective writing into a document that is formatted with attention to audience or have students curate their own work in an e-portfolio. Encourage students to share this document with family members and friends.

> Increase fairness by creating a sense of community and inclusion. Inform students about experiences that were described in student writing and share examples that demonstrate the diversity of experiences.

> Improve outcomes by providing proactive instructions and conveying confidence in students' ability. Provide individual feedback that details weaknesses and expresses confidence in students' ability to improve on future assignments.

> Use evidence-based assessment. Create rubrics that link success on assignments to clearly articulated learning outcomes and train all evaluators in rubric use.

Too often general education classes default to didactic lectures paired with multiple-choice or short-answer assessments. These pedagogical approaches can limit integrative learning and may disproportionately harm students from traditionally underrepresented groups. We believe providing students in large general education classes with meaningful opportunities to engage in reflective writing may fundamentally alter their experience in college and lead to more authentic learning. We demonstrate that thoughtfully designed general education curricula can support fairness, student wellness, engagement, and cultural inclusiveness while providing students with rich opportunities to engage in self-relevant writing.

Writing in Architecture: Multidimensionality, Language Making, and New Ways of Becoming

Jeffrey Hogrefe and Vladimir Briller

Perspective

This essay provides a model of writing based on concepts of architecture and contemporary critical theory within the Architecture Writing Program at Pratt Institute. In scale and scope, the program is arguably the only curriculum of its kind in a five-year undergraduate professional program in architecture. Based on the concept of a double operative responsive to the power of language and the transformative power of reflection, this innovative program engages the disciplines of humanities and architecture to introduce a writing curriculum applicable to our diverse cohort of students. Because we view instruction and assessment as complementary and mutually beneficial, we present a research program conducted from 2016 to 2018 to evaluate our program. Although challenges remain, our dedication to writing is shaping an approach to architecture that encourages new ways of becoming for our students.

Introduction: Double Operatives

At Pratt Institute, we linked writing courses to the architecture studio and discovered that, metaphorically, the links operated like acupuncture points. Commonalities opened pathways between the disciplines to create a metacognitive orientation to the interpretation of knowledge in both visual and verbal media. Through exercises in rhetorical strategies, literary figuration, situational plays of genre, and expanded concepts of media, students learned how to write into their architecture design and their humanities course in a doubly operative exchange (*Double Operative*). The term *double operative* is used to covey both location and desire. The program is located in the interstitial space between a writing seminar and an architectural studio, and it is our desire that this location enable students to use language making as part of their critical architectural practice. In this way, the student emerges as a unique interpreter of architecture: an interpreter who is able to refer inwardly to architecture itself as an autonomous aesthetic system, even as the built environment overlaps and interacts with language systems informing lived experiences and economic determinants.

In this program, students learned how to write as a performance of becoming. This expanded concept of self is directly related to the aim of fairness that informs our Architecture Writing Program. As Mya Poe observes in this volume, "The identification of outcomes is, in fact, an illustration of an articulation of fairness in the curriculum; the fulfillment of these outcomes is evidence of the creation of opportunity through education." Indeed, it is not just the writing community that benefits from this perspective. Any academic community advancing fairness benefits by expanding the identity of students, especially as that identity grows through encounters with new theories, practices, and communication genres. Once restrictions are lifted and students are treated as colleagues, deepening occurs.

The deepening of experience described in this essay is integral to the mission of Pratt Institute, a highly ranked private, not-for-profit institution classified by the Carnegie Foundation as a special-focus four-and-five-year art, design, and architecture institution (*Carnegie*). We are primarily urban, with campuses in Brooklyn, Manhattan, and Utica, New York. Our architecture student body is significantly female and international in a profession that is still predominately male and white. For us, fairness is promoted through a multi-dimensional method of instruction and assessment that positions the student in the center of the educational process and incorporates formative assessment and learning. In this way, we can define *fairness* in our program as the identification of opportunity structures that are based on our disciplinary knowledge about successful architects who advance the public good while having fulfilling professional lives. Our student is an interpreter who is able to reflect on architecture as a formal aesthetic system while realizing that the built environment incorporates lived experiences and economic demands. The ability to hold these contradictory ideas simultaneously, while refusing hierarchical judgment, informs our educational design. In this way, the curriculum is similar to the program in engineering presented by Julia M. Williams in this volume, which shows the transformative value of language in an established profession with a tradition of being unwelcoming to women and members of underrepresented groups.

As is the case with instruction, the assessment process is flexible, situated, negotiated, and increases opportunities to learn. Both instruction and assessment operate in a double operative framework. We adhere to accreditation requirements from two different external agencies with their own sets of requirements: the National Architectural Accrediting Board (NAAB) and the Middle States Commission on Higher Education (MSCHE). In responding to both program and regional accreditation demands, we have found that the interstitial orientation that informs our curriculum also informs our approach to assessment. We are able to meet external calls for accountability successfully while maintaining our emphasis on local program innovation. In our program of assessment, we view the professional architect as a mediator, providing interpretive skills on many different platforms. Primary to these roles is communication, which is considered essential by the NAAB. Especially important to NAAB is the ability to "build abstract relationships and understand the impact of ideas based on the research and analysis of multiple theoretical, social, political, economic, cultural and environmental contexts" (*Procedures* 8), an ambition that informed the level of instruction in the courses. Among the diverse range of media that graduates must be able to command, NAAB emphasizes the importance of "the ability to write and speak effectively and raise clear and precise questions, use abstract ideas to interpret information, consider diverse points of view, reach well-reasoned conclusions, and test alternative outcomes against relevant criteria and standards" (*Procedures* 110). The prescriptive NAAB requirements guided the outcomes of our courses while the open-ended MSCHE requirements informed them conceptually.

These external accreditation bodies can be viewed as an occasion for performance, a way to showcase the abilities of our students. Here we adopt a perspective similar to that of Robert J. Mislevy in this volume, that is, a sociocognitive perspective—one that is deeply situated in language and experience—allowing us to exhibit to visiting accreditors how disciplines interact, with the familiar assessment issues of validity and reliability as categories of evidence and expanded by fairness, opportunity to learn, and a contemporary view of writing in the disciplines.

Architects: Visionary Utopias and Real Urban Agglomerations

Because it is ever-present in language, history is part of the present. To understand fully the uniqueness of the Architecture Writing Program, a brief history of our discipline is helpful. The first schools of architecture in North America to confer professional degrees were established in the years after the American Civil War to accommodate the boom in building that took place as a result of the Industrial Revolution and the rise of the modern city. Vitruvius, the Roman philosopher and first architectural theorist, proposed that, although context was important for a work of architecture, the primary consideration was to be aesthetics (14). Indeed, a preference for aesthetics dominated early architectural education, along with a preference for Latin-based terms to distinguish architects from builders (Rybczynski). Beginning with MIT in 1866, universities and technical institutes with the resources for a laborious course of instruction were able to grant professional architecture degrees, which led to apprenticeships and testing boards that were—and still are—largely male, white, and middle class. As a contingent aesthetic project, a student design was—and often still is—expected to speak principally through graphic forms of representation. Critics drawn from the profession provided a language for the student, who was passively tested by the experts. Advanced students proceeded to postprofessional terminal degrees that enabled them to speak, write, and teach in the profession. The catastrophic events of the middle of the twentieth century refocused the profession on the design of public amenities in utopian schemes that introduced the language of social science to architecture. The growth of the postwar period of the late twentieth century created a demand for architects in the developing nations where modernity took on a distinctive local quality by architects who were largely educated in the North American academies, adding to the diversity of the student body.

The emergence of the Internet and rise of global cities around the turn of the twenty-first century introduced transnational practitioners working together on projects in distant locations. The speed with which architecture can be designed in the systems and networks of the urban agglomerations led to a discourse that is, in reality, a form of cultural studies on expanded platforms. Instead of proposing utopian futures from the outside, architects entered the gritty real of the city from which "architecture was inextricably linked" (Jameson). The contemporary architecture studio experiments with form and culture in various, diverse landscapes (Allen 226).

Attuned to the span of this history, the Architecture Writing Program developed as an ad hoc experiment in the early years of the millennium in response, in part, to new requirements from NAAB. By aligning the writing courses with the intellectual agenda of the studio (in addition and complementary to the traditional history and theory sequence of writing courses), the curriculum expanded the voice of the student. The challenges of scale and meaning in architecture have been informed by an approach to the humanities that is flexible and open to many different approaches and the value of writing and speaking in the digital age.

The Architecture Writing Program began as a project in writing across the curriculum, an established pedagogy for the teaching of clear, concise writing skills. We were alert, however, to the fact that writing-across-the-curriculum programs may lead disciplinary faculty to default the primary responsibility of teaching writing to the English department (A. Young 1–4.). As it developed, it became clear that *architecture writing* is not writing *about* architecture in the traditional writing-across-the-curriculum model; it is writing *as* architecture—an orientation that is often found in writing in the disciplines. In the Architecture Writing Program, writing was deployed to map and diagram knowledge across the disciplines. The program encouraged collaboration across the disciplines to introduce architecture writing genres that are generative and descriptive of architectural form. The program shifted responsibility to the students, who found that the courses led them to view writing as fundamental to an architecture project.

Architecture Writing: A System of Systems

Within this history, language plays an increasingly central role—and so some background on philosophy of language is also needed. Although indebted to Jacques Derrida's deconstruction of philosophy, which brought writing into architecture, concepts of *architecture writing* are derived from Aristotle's formulations of poetics and techne: making language and making form. Challenged by Immanuel Kant's dictum that the primary purpose of knowledge is synthesis, in the early twentieth century Charles Peirce outlined the three stages by which knowledge could be synthesized, which became known as *percept, affect,* and *concept* (after Deleuze and Guattari; Kant; Peirce), which are essential to our program. In Roman Jakobson's model, language is composed of many different kinds of subsystems, each subsystem being the means to accomplish a particular goal or purpose of communication. Language is viewed as system of systems with crosscutting properties such as paradigmatic and syntagmatic oppositions. Developed to resonate with the architecture courses, the writing courses are based on philosophy of language applied practically in a studio through structuring of the web of meaning between inner speech and written speech (after Jakobson; Kant; and Peirce).

The courses, in turn, provided a metacognitive, reflective orientation to the production of knowledge as a written performance in multiple media. Here, our metacognitive orientation is informed by intersectional instruction in class, race, gender, and sex by such philosophers as Michel Foucault, Judith Butler, Franz Fanon, and bell hooks. These perspectives provided new ways of becoming (that is, expanded ontologies) for students from diverse backgrounds. In this way, students learned to establish the terms by which they want their architectural work to be assessed (their epistemologies) and to develop a critical set of terms to evaluate, understand, and explain their work within the ways in which thought and feeling are mediated by social, symbolic, and political structures (their axiological perspectives). Consistent with constructivist theories of pedagogy informed by Lev S. Vygotsky and Jakobson, respectively, the program fostered highly individualistic expression in professional projects. The constitutive nature of language—for individual students and for the profession of architecture—is always and everywhere emphasized.

The Curriculum: Assignment Design

Concentrated in the conceptual moments in the first and fifth year, when abstract ideas from outside architecture predominate, we focus here on the results of the first-year courses. Because of the recent founding of our program, the students who will have arrived in the fifth-year courses having taken the first-year course were still outside the scope of the study. Appropriating the place of the standard first-year writing course, the first-year curriculum introduced a one-credit studio writing course, Transdisciplinary Writing, and a three-credit course, Introduction to Literary and Critical Studies for Architecture Students. In this way, students acquired critical tools to carve a self-directed path through a genealogy of texts that paralleled the development of an architecture project that was unique for each student.

In the introductory course, we divide writing tasks into four units, each of which requires students to focus on a different medium, including literature, film, and architecture. As the final project of each unit, students produce a written assignment that is expository, persuasive, and reflective. In each unit, students first complete a series of predraft assignments from which the written assignment is developed. At the end of the term, students submit a complete portfolio with all the writing produced during the semester. To provide a more detailed idea of the course, here is a representative assignment from the second week of the class's first unit:

This assignment invites a two-page response to our classroom discussion of four readings: selections from Gertrude Stein's *Tender Buttons*, Maurice Merleau-Ponty's *Phenomenology of Perception*, Virginia Woolf's *A Room of One's Own*, and Gregory Bateson's *Steps to an Ecology of Mind*. In your response, locate the differences in Woolf's thinking from that of her colleagues, as she situates her body in the material world that men had built for hundreds of years at "Oxbridge." Identify the pathways and bridges and the role of gender differences, paying particular attention to the analogy of the fish and the turf to illustrate how differences can become visual analogies that assist us to expand the capacity of thought.

This assignment reveals two important curricular features of the Architecture Writing Program. First, writing instruction is aligned with best practices, as identified by Grover J. Whitehurst. Because these are first-year students, we align writing practices with those proven successful for high school students: Instruction is based on a model, practice, and reflect cycle; explicit writing strategies are integrated into the assignment; a language arts approach is used in which reading and writing are integrated; and timely feedback is used as part of a formative assessment process. Second, because this course is taught by a humanities faculty member who is engaged in the spatial turn in cultural studies that resonates with instruction in architecture, these best practices are demonstrated by someone in the same discourse. As such, students do not perceive a shift between writing studies and architecture. The constitutive nature of language, and its power to transform through reflection, is instantiated in the writing process model.

From a practical standpoint, such assignments delivered in our unique curriculum allowed us to ensure students have an introductory understanding of the ways thought is generated on different scales and the ability to extract a synthetic understanding of a text as it corresponds with their architectural design. Diagramming and mapping played a central role in linking the seminar and studio, in that new information comes into architecture through graphic forms of representation, so operations of diagramming and mapping brought the work of literary figuration, motivational rhetoric, and situational genre directly into the studio as forms of generative writing.

Empowering students to see their design projects as heuristic devices in guided research, the Architecture Writing Program encouraged new ways of thinking for our students. They became participants in an expanding cultural dynamics available through digital tools that impact basic concepts of architectural representation and experience. Students learned that language and architecture exist within systems that are overlapping. Reading and performing the text as a web of influences extended out of the classroom and across the studio in anticipation of the future text of their architecture. As the curriculum evolved, the faculty realized that the form of the architecture project itself generated a language of immanence. By adapting principles from the philosophy of language, students learned to locate a material language that corresponded with their making process and to engage in a play of verbal and visual media on an expanded semantic field. We turn now to two forms of assessment: performance before an external accreditation team (a qualitative measure) and student survey responses (a quantitative measure). Both are necessary for accountability to others—and to us.

Assessment as Performance

The Architecture Writing Program curriculum of required writing courses has already been presented to 523 first-year students. (In the 2017–18 academic year, of the 4,829 matriculating students at Pratt Institute, 627 were enrolled in the undergraduate architecture program.) As reported above, fairness in assessment was achieved through participation from students, external and internal critics, and faculty members across disciplines through rubrics that allow for differences of ability and background to be measured in the achievement of shared goals and outcomes. These, in turn, were incorporated in the curriculum at every level of instruction, which, in turn, provided an expanded public dimension to the teaching of a profession with its own hermetic discourse. For students, language skills became a way of assessing their own work as it developed at many different stages of completion: from the formation of an individual stick model that resides in a neologism to the development of a complete project that resides within a cultural context. Ethical considerations were an important component in the cross-disciplinary curriculum, since architectural designs present public spaces with consequences for large numbers of people.

To develop the program, we identified, implemented, and assessed architecture writing genres as integral to instruction in architecture. This endorsement of the new genre of architecture writing as practice by both the writing and architecture instructors demonstrated the value of the practice of writing in the studio, which was new to most of the faculty. To introduce the program, we formulated discussion strategies that brought the architecture and humanities faculties together regarding the assessment of the courses. Can the language diagrams in the studio writing course be assessed by both faculties on terms that are understandable to students? Can grading rubrics with delineated traits for essential criteria be developed so that the rubrics are meaningful to both faculty members and students? Can assignments be independently scored and yield acceptable levels of interreader agreement? What role do students have in the assessment of their own work? Can recommendations be made for subsequent study?

The writing assignments used in our study included traits that cover a range of rhetorical operations applicable to both humanities and architecture, with a particular emphasis on the NAAB requirements of abstract thinking on different platforms: part-to-whole and whole-to-whole comparisons; interpretive practices with a variety of texts; synthesizing ideas from multiple sources and applying abstract theory in analysis of a text; engaging with, contextualizing, and critically applying differing theoretical understandings of language and its relation to space or architecture; and presentation skills that include text and image compilations and language diagrams. Central to the assessment was the metacognitive skill to stand outside a text (including a student's own architecture) and see its operation at differing levels of interpretation. These traits were dimensions of the assignment itself, rhetorical moves by students to demonstrate proficiency. Students learned to self-assess based on the traits; faculty members arrived at interreader agreement based on the traits; and the external agencies received artifacts that demonstrated the traits in outstanding and average students. Since the text was conceptualized, written, spoken, presented, and figured with equal or more contingency and responsiveness to temporal and corporeal happenings, assessment took place multidimensionally: with the student at the center of the classroom, during public presentations of student work in the design studio with internal and external critics, and in dedicated faculty assessment meetings in both the humanities and architecture departments.

In assessing a first-year student project, the external architecture critics concluded that, owing for limitations in the formal operations, such a project was comparable to a capstone project, due to the confidence with which the student was able to present and engage in the concept for a project in complex scales. The humanities assessment group agreed that, allowing for the inevitable loss in translation, students were able to appropriate a philosophical concept to explain their architecture with a high level of proficiency. Clearly, students demonstrated a viable method for learning philosophy with applications to real-life experience.

Assessment as Response

To learn more about the experiences of our students, we also conducted a series of student surveys with first- and third-year students to provide their perception of the architecture writing courses. The survey respondents indicated that the curriculum improved their overall understanding of architecture design; the third-year students understood the benefits more clearly; their scores for each item were higher than for the first-year students, and the difference was statistically significant. More than half the respondents agreed that, as a result of having taken the course, they were able to present their architectural project in a text-image sequence with photographs and contextualize a project in a broader cultural framework; more than sixty percent of the third-year students agreed that, as a result of the course, they were able to conceptualize and present some of their second- and third-year studio projects. Several of the respondents additionally demonstrated clear understanding of the underlying philosophy of language that informs the program. One student wrote that "thinking about the design process in terms of a language system is useful in order for developing the system and concept by which the design derives." Another student noted that "understanding language is fundamental in the development of a coherent architectural concept."

Overall, the survey showed that students felt more confident in conceptualizing their studio projects as a result of taking the architecture writing classes, and analysis of their grades in studio courses and in those centered on academic writing demonstrated relations between participation in architecture writing classes and overall student achievement. We controlled important input characteristics and found no statistically significant difference between two groups: they had similar gender, race or ethnicity composition, high school GPA, and SAT and ACT scores. Whatever differences we found were due, at least in part, to the curriculum we had designed.

A quasi-experimental approach compared the outcomes of the students who participated in the writing program with those of students in previous years who did not participate in the program. We defined outcomes as student retention rates, cumulative GPAs, and overall satisfaction with academic experience. To evaluate the outcomes of the program, we used three instruments: an assessment of student achievement, a survey of student perception of the program, and interviews with architecture design faculty members.

The survey was distributed electronically to 330 first-year and 320 third-year students in 2016–17 using Pratt *WebAccess* survey software. The survey consisted of five Likert scale questions and one open-ended question. The response rate was eleven percent for the first-year students and fifteen percent for the third-year students. Data analysis showed that all the items had high covariance, with Cronbach's alpha 0.94 for the first-year respondents and 0.88 for the third-year respondents. Practically all items, with a shared covariance, measure the same underlying concept: students' perception of the impact that architecture writing is having on their architectural design. The analysis also showed statistically significant interitem correlation in both surveys shown in tables 1 and 2, although the correlations in table 1 were higher than those in table 2. This high correlation could be related to the intensity of instruction during the first year of the curriculum. In table 3, we see the student GPA and retention rates for first- and third-year students. As table 3 shows, student GPA is little higher than for previous years' students before the writing program, but there

Table 1. Analysis of Responses to the First-Year Students Survey

Year One Variables	N	M	Range	SD	Interitem Correlation Matrix				
					Q1	Q2	Q3	Q4	Q5
Q1. Develop project as a concept.	36	3.17	4	1.64	—	0.58*	0.7*	0.97*	0.96*
Q2. Generate a language diagram.	36	3.17	4	1.70	0.58*	—	0.90*	0.56*	0.60*
Q3. Present a project in a text-image sequence.	36	3.17	4	1.40	0.70*	0.90*	—	0.71*	0.77*
Q4. Contextualize a project in a broader cultural framework.	36	3.17	4	1.70	0.97*	0.56*	0.71*	—	0.96*
Q5. Conceptualize future studio projects.	35	2.92	4	1.62	0.96*	0.60*	0.77*	0.96*	—

Cronbach's alpha based on standardized items = .94
*$p < 0.01$ (two-tailed)

Table 2. Analysis of Responses to the Third-Year Student Survey

Year Three Variables	N	M	Range	SD	Interitem Correlation Matrix				
					Q1	Q2	Q3	Q4	Q5
Q1. Develop project as a concept.	48	3.56	3	0.96	—	0.44*	0.11*	0.77*	0.50*
Q2. Generate a language diagram.	48	3.44	3	0.81	0.44*	—	0.38*	0.22*	0.57*
Q3. Present a project in a text-image sequence.	48	2.75	3	0.93	0.11*	0.38*	—	0.32*	0.54*
Q4. Contextualize a project in a broader cultural framework.	48	2.44	3	1.03	0.77*	0.21*	0.32*	—	0.56*
Q5. Conceptualize first- and second-year studio projects.	42	3.14	4	0.95	0.50*	0.57*	0.54*	0.56*	—

Cronbach's alpha based on standardized items = .80
*$p < 0.01$ (two-tailed)

Table 3. Student GPA and Retention Rates

Group	Nonparticipants (n = 423)	Architecture Writing Participants (n = 330)
First-year GPA	3.32	3.34
Third-year GPA	3.45	3.46
First-year retention	86%	91%*

*$p < 0.01$ (two-tailed)

is no statistically significant difference. First-year retention, however, is higher for the program participants, and the difference is statistically significant, as demonstrated in a two-tailed t-test = $t(330) = 2.10$, $p < 0.01$.

Overall, the survey results and interviews with faculty members indicate students have learned how to incorporate philosophy of language in their architectural designs, and first-year retention rates indicate evidence of fairness. Having to meet the requirements of two different external agencies means that the architecture writing courses have to be assessable to faculty members and students on different levels than the writing courses that are offered to students in other disciplines. As noted above, the program was initially developed in response to criticism from both NAAB and MSCHE and developed to respond specifically to the NAAB requirements. In recent campus visits, both agencies praised the program for its innovation.

Conclusion: What Remains

In this essay we demonstrated how writing was used to fulfill the ultimate aim of the humanities to form all knowledge at the seat of knowledge: language. If the program could be assessed so readily, that fact is due to the authenticity of a curriculum in which students are placed at the center of our efforts and treated as colleagues.

Our work, however, is far from completed. Indicative of the extent to which students and faculty members valued the writing courses was the frequently expressed concern in student surveys and interviews with architecture faculty members that students were not receiving comparable instruction in their sections. Reliability of course instruction remains a challenge. Indeed, a significant challenge for the future coordination of the curriculum is the size of the school. There are currently twelve sections of the first-year courses, each composed of two faculty members from different disciplines whose own training did not include instruction in architecture writing. Therefore, achieving consistency in instruction between sections is an area for concentrated future growth. At the present writing, we have responded to consistency issues by adding a tenth semester capstone, so students will be able to conclude their studies with instruction in writing.

As a result of this study, we are also developing a comprehensive assessment plan for the first- and fifth-year courses that will enable us to document in greater detail how we know what students are able to perform as they move through the architecture and liberal arts curriculum. By introducing writing as metaskills that can be repeated from the first to the fifth year, it has become increasingly clear that we have created far more than a series of writing-intensive courses. Writing is woven through each student's education so that each graduate will see that writing is a way of performing—not merely a way of reporting. In this way, writing is shaping an approach to architecture that encourages new ways of becoming for professionals who are responsive to lived experiences and economic determinants.

Writing to Outcomes:
Genre in Nursing Practice

Rhonda Maneval and Frances Ward

Perspective

Recognition of writing as nursing practice facilitates professionalization in the discipline. The incorporation of nursing-specific writing genre assignments in undergraduate courses immerses students in the language of their profession, thus elevating writing itself as practice. In this essay we discuss the findings of a research study that suggest the design of nursing-specific writing genre assignments with associated grading rubrics provide an evidence base for writing as nursing practice. Exposure to reliably evaluated assignments carefully crafted from knowledge of the discipline promotes fairness in learning and equality of opportunity to succeed.

Introduction

Writing allows nursing students to document the practice of nursing; as such, writing is an essential nursing practice. To explore a shift in nursing from viewing writing as an important function but one external to nursing practice, we posit proficiency in nursing-specific writing genres (NSWGs) as essential practice itself.

Site-specific research within a discipline gives new meaning to the familiar call for localism in writing assessment (Huot) in terms of the significance of genre (Spinuzzi) and interplay of instruction and assessment in expanding opportunity to learn for students (Moss et al.). With attention to such contextualization, nursing's history documents the essentiality of practice, with writing as a supportive function. Put straightforwardly, the student who loves nursing but hates writing was acculturated to this view naturally. Ownership of language interrupts this dominance and elevates writing as nursing practice.

Whether learning documentation on health records or other NSWGs, students advance in nursing through written communication. Writing in NSWGs is a vehicle for explicating nursing practice as well as professionalization; as writing reflects thought, language mirrors a profession. In this essay we demonstrate how NSWGs can be used to improve outcomes in our field. We postulate that NSWGs assessed by reliable and valid grading rubrics provide, as John Rawls advocates, "fair equality of opportunity," with the accompanying premise that all "should have a fair chance to attain" opportunities (*Justice* 43). Our connection between genre and equality of opportunity is of paramount importance. The more exposure students have to the varied ways language is used in nursing practice, the better they will be able to perform as professionals. Conversely, restriction of genre limits attainment. It is prevention of unfair limitations that we examine in our discussion. We first highlight societal changes that have influenced nursing; subsequently, we describe a research program conducted in 2016–17 at a major public research university in the midwestern United States. Designed as part of the present volume, this research aimed to evaluate a writing model in which instruction and assessment are understood as complementary for students enrolled in a Bachelor of Science in Nursing program. We conclude by offering directions for further research.

Nurses: On Duty

It is impossible to understand the significance of genre without knowledge of nursing curricula. As Robert J. Mislevy notes in his contribution to this volume, a sociocognitive psychological perspective connects both with familiar assessment issues such as purpose, design, validity, fairness, and opportunity to learn and a contemporary view of writing in the disciplines. It is precisely this connection we now establish.

As a consequence of the industrial revolution, hospitals replaced city dispensaries and nurse training programs were established with pupil nurses on duty 24-7 (Nelson 11–31). Training programs demanded obedience. A fin de siècle application for the Newark City Hospital Training School for Nurses includes the following questions: Do you promise at all times to obey implicitly the orders of your superior officers? Do you have any uterine complaint? Moving away from the Sairey Gamp image of nurses described by Charles Dickens in *Martin Chuzzlewit*, training schools flourished with textbooks defining nursing's scope of practice. Clara S. Weeks's textbook emphasized documentation of patients' symptoms, and patient wards, such as those pictured in figure 1, were orderly, with physicians the central figures in a hierarchical environment.

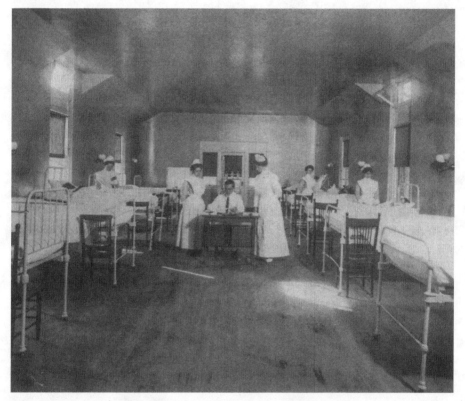

Figure 1. Patient Ward, Englewood Hospital, Late Nineteenth Century (courtesy of the Englewood Hospital and Medical Center School of Nursing Archives).

With the 1893 Chicago World's Fair as context, nurse leaders organized the American Society of Superintendents of Training Schools of Nursing—their foci a standardized curriculum offered by hospitals and a legislative movement to solidify nurse registration (Reverby; Snively 24–25). Hospitals enjoyed a captive workforce (Shannon 1328). The restriction of both educational experiences and professionalized practice embraced by nineteenth-century nurse leaders was a result of power relationships, optimized by the hospital and normalized within a patriarchal culture.

The demand for nurses during World War II culminated in the 1943 Cadet Nurse Corps, reducing nursing program length and facilitating collaboration with colleges (Petry 704–05). The Hill-Burton Act subsequently increased hospital construction and the 1948 Commission on Higher Education created community college nurse-education programs (Brown 13, 77; President's Commission). Post-Sputnik, the United States refocused on science, technology, engineering, and mathematics programs (Conant 59–60, 172). As college enrollment soared, hospitals became the nation's monopolist employer rather than trainer of nurses (Kurian 55–57).

In the early 1970s, nurses integrated words such as *diagnosis* and *treatment* into a new nursing lexicon. In 1973, nursing diagnoses were elaborated (NANDA International), with nursing practice redefined as "diagnosing and treating human responses to actual or potential physical and emotional health problems" ("Nurse"). Colleges began to graduate nurse practitioners with independent practice. From the late nineteenth century to the present, language has become the major tool wielding power for nursing.

The Role of Genre in Nursing

In our research, genre plays a central role. Faculty members require written assignments to achieve course objectives. When assignments link to nursing-specific writing genres, they may be evaluated as evidence of competence in the scope of practice. This shift to written assignments categorized according to NSWGs reifies students' appreciation of their evolving competence in the discipline. We note that this sense of genre is especially important to those colleagues in this volume who must prepare their students for careers in which licensure is integral to professional practice. In their contribution in this volume, Jeffrey Hogrefe and Vladimir Briller describe architecture writing genres as practice in the discipline. This orientation that architecture writing genres demonstrate writing as architecture practice empowers architecture faculty members to assume responsibility for writing in their discipline, instead of displacing responsibility to the English department. Julia M. Williams writes in this volume that STEM faculty members "model the forms of discourse appropriate to their professions," creating writing experiences that shape thought in the disciplines themselves instead of simply employing writing as a vehicle for thought. For nursing, architecture, and engineering, writing in these disciplines has evolved as practice in the disciplines.

Initially, faculty members involved in our study explored the word *genre* in its contemporary form: as a vehicle for professional practice and thus disciplinary and career success. As we learned, genre mediates intention, exigency, and context, thus providing a way to understand professional behavior and organizational structure (Coe et al. 6–7). As Clay Spinuzzi observes, "genres are not discrete artifacts, but traditions of producing, using, and interpreting artifacts" (41). A constrained view of writing without reference to nursing genres may therefore limit students' opportunities to use rhetorical moves required to communicate effectively using evidence. Thus, students may not be exposed to genres central to their professional lives, and fairness would be denied. As is the case for nursing students—indeed for all careers involving licensure—there must be explicit curricular connection between classroom work and professional practice. As Patricia Benner, Christine Tanner, and Catherine Chesla observe in their study of expertise, nursing requires both techne and phronesis, as described by Aristotle in *Nicomachean Ethics*. They write:

> Techne can be captured by procedural and scientific knowledge, knowledge that can be made formal, explicit, and certain except for the necessary timing and adjustments made for particular patients. Phronesis, in contrast to techne, is the kind of practical reasoning engaged in by an excellent practitioner lodged in a community of practitioners who through experiential learning and for the sake of good practice continually lives out and improves practice.   (xiii)

In the classroom, knowledge can be made explicit but remains limited unless enacted in a community of practice. Connections are required if students are to be engaged, experiential learners. Vital to connecting classroom and professional practice is genre. As we came to understand, genre provides referential frameworks to understand practice. Genre is granular. Attention to genre reveals professional functions. Genre is also expansive. From written to computer notes, genre expands as nursing expands. Also, genre is assessable and thus can be evaluated, with scores used to offer learning opportunities for students (Moss et al.).

Christine L. Latham and Nancy Ahern write that techniques to teach and evaluate writing in nursing are not well reported in nursing literature (615). A systemic review of literature on writing instruction by baccalaureate nursing faculty illustrates a striking paucity of research (Troxler et al. 280–81); nevertheless, NSWGs are visible in nursing education and clinical practice literature but simply not named as such (Long and Beck 14–19). A disjuncture between curricular approach and profession practice is apparent.

Program of Research: A Generative Case Study

The setting for our research was the Bachelor of Science in Nursing program in a public, research-oriented university in the midwestern United States, with selective admission and a graduation rate at seventy-eight percent on average. The study was approved by the university's Institutional Review Board in spring 2016.

We aimed to identify, implement, and assess NSWGs integral to the practice of nursing. Evidence-based practice provides the foundation of quality, cost-effective health care delivery in the United States (Melynk and Fineout-Overholt

3–9). As practice, writing must also be evaluated as evidence-based. We therefore articulated five questions for our research: Can NSWGs be identified so that instruction and assessment may complement each other? Can grading rubrics with delineated traits for essential criteria be developed so that the rubrics are meaningful for faculty members? Can NSWG assignments be independently scored and yield acceptable levels of interreader agreement? What standpoints do students hold toward these NSWGs and rubrics? Can recommendations be offered for subsequent study?

In our study, we believe that rubrics tailored to task are essential to genre exposure. We thus view traits as dimensions of the assignment itself, rhetorical moves by students to demonstrate proficiency. We report on three assignments selected for study: Patient Health History writing assignment (sophomore level); Clinical Skills writing assignment (junior level); and Nursing Diagnosis and Plan of Care writing assignment (senior level).

In fall 2016, thirty-three sophomores, thirty-six juniors, and fifty-two seniors consented. Due to time limitations of scoring, twelve sophomore, fourteen junior, and eighteen senior assignments were randomly selected. Following collection of other information, these samples were further reduced to six sophomore, ten junior, and five senior assignments. These small samples allowed for the descriptive information that follows.

The sampling plan for the pre- and post-surveys was larger since consent was not required, with a range of pre-survey sample sizes from forty sophomores to eighty-two juniors. Our exploratory, descriptive design enabled us to identify phenomena of interest regarding NSWGs (Loeb et al. 1–17; Sutherland 39). Surveys queried students regarding NSWGs and grading rubrics. Consistent with contemporary empirical research, the study was designed to yield evidence of fairness (*Standards* 63–72), validity (23–31), and reliability (42–47).

Phase 1 involved the identification of nursing-specific writing genres. Phase 2 involved design of grading rubrics for fall 2016. Rubrics designed by faculty consensus included criteria evaluated on a rating scale with operationally defined attributes. Rubrics resulted in trait and holistic scores. Detailed trait scores were developed, with fourteen traits for the Patient Health History writing assignment, thirty-four for the Clinical Skills writing assignment, and fifteen for the Nursing Diagnosis and Plan of Care writing assignment. Table 1 shows the first trait used for these three assignments. Phase 3 involved scoring NSWG assignments for three courses using revised rubrics. Two nursing faculty members independently scored de-identified student papers for interreader agreement on trait and holistic scores for each assignment (Stemler 6–7). Third readers rated for adjudication purposes on holistic scores, as needed.

Table 1. Selections from Rubrics for Patient Health History, Clinical Skills, and Nursing Diagnosis and Plan of Care Writing Assignments

Trait	4	3	2	1
	Meets Standards	Nearly Meets Standards	Does Not Meet Standards	No Evidence
Patient Health History Writing Assignment, Sophomore-Level Course (Fall 2016)				
Demographic data, occupational history, and financial status	• Clear, concise description of pertinent data	• Descriptions adequate but some pertinent data missing (1% to 25%) OR • Data unclear or illogical	• Descriptions adequate (missing 26% to 50%) but poorly differentiates pertinent and nonpertinent data OR • Information lacks clarity or logic	• Descriptions inadequate (missing > 50%); limited inclusion of pertinent data OR • Information lacks clarity or logic
Clinical Skills Writing Assignment, Junior-Level Course (Fall 2016)				
Chief complaint on arrival	• Chief complaint clear • Patient demographics • Through Emergency Department, Operating Room, or direct admit • Via ambulance, family vehicle, etc. • Symptom analysis of chief complaint (eight characteristics) • Pertinent other history identified • Pertinent previous admissions	• No more than two items from four-point column missing or inaccurate OR • Information is all present but presented unclearly or illogically	• Partially or completely missing three to four items from four-point column AND • Information lacks clarity or logic	• Partially or completely missing more than four items from the four-point column. AND • Presentation lacks clarity or logic
Nursing Diagnosis and Plan of Care Writing Assignment, Senior-Level Course (Fall 2017)				
Nursing Diagnoses: Correct selection	• Lists four highest priority diagnoses • Must be true nursing diagnoses for this patient • Uses Carpenito or Ackley et al. to select diagnoses supported by defining characteristic	• Includes one family diagnosis that is not in top three, but still pertains to patient and is an actual nursing diagnosis.	• Missing one top priority diagnosis • Inaccurate diagnosis included • May not pertain to patient or may not be actual nursing diagnosis	• Missing two or more top priority diagnoses • Inaccurate diagnosis included • May not pertain to patient or may not be actual nursing diagnosis

Case Study Results: Inferences from Descriptive Information

Faculty members identified specific assignments as NSWGs. Colleagues revised grading rubrics to develop evaluation tools correlated with course outcomes, ensuring justice through fair evaluation. The methodology enabled standardization of grading rubrics with interreader agreement exercises for reliability. Although the final data sets obtained had small sample sizes insufficient for inferential statistics and probability testing, there was adequate data to postulate themes or trends. The data from pre- and post-surveys were rich in findings.

If the samples were larger, inferential statistics would be used to determine interreader reliability, and probabilistic methods could be used to establish relations among measures and subgroup differences. Nevertheless, descriptive inferences can be made. In reviewing table 2, we see scorer consistency of the holistic scores awarded by readers 1 and 2 of the six papers reviewed. Only one set of trait scores was discrepant (defined in this study as scores that are not adjacent). No adjudication by a third reader was required for any holistic score. Interreader agreement was good. Patterns between trait and holistic scores are also apparent, with readers often awarding higher scores for the first trait. Although distinct from scores, the range of faculty grades on these assignments was seventy-nine to ninety-six—a moderate to high level of academic performance. These students were young, non-Hispanic females with high GPAs who, in general, performed well across the three assignments.

Student responses on the pre- and post-surveys were revealing. Response choices were on a semantic differential scale from 1 (i.e., the statement does not describe my opinion at all) to 7 (i.e., the statement describes my opinion perfectly). Response choices 1, 2, and 3 were combined, as were choices 5, 6, and 7. Six items assumed prominence relative to implications at a local level on the scale of 5 + 6 + 7 for all pre- and post-surveys—the end of the scale slanted toward "this statement describes my opinion perfectly." Table 3 provides survey responses for these courses.

Items 1, 4, and 6 in table 3 are broadly written, whereas items 7, 11, and 13 reflect local characteristics. On post-surveys the majority believe that writing is an essential skill in nursing practice and that grading rubrics for writing assignments in nursing promote fairness in evaluation. The majority of students in Clinical Skills and Nursing Diagnosis, however, characterized writing assignments as less important than other nursing skills. In contrast, responses to items 7, 11, and 13 reflect opinions of students at a local level. For example, for item 7, the data for Patient Health and Clinical Skills indicated that students' opinions regarding fair application of grading rubrics across all course sections and different faculty members decreased. On this same item for those in Nursing

Table 2. Student Performance on Patient Health History, Clinical Skills, and Nursing Diagnosis and Plan of Care Writing Assignments (Note: H = Hispanic; L = Latinx)

Student	Reader 1 Trait 1 Score	Reader 2 Trait 1 Score	Reader 1 Holistic Score	Reader 2 Holistic Score	Adj. Holistic	Final Holistic Score	Assignment Grade	Course Grade	Fall GPA	Age	Gender	Race	Ethnicity
Patient Health History Writing Assignment (Fall 2016)													
1	4	4	2	3	NA	5	89	86	3.50	21	F	white	not H or L
2	3	4	3	4	NA	7	88	91	3.63	21	F	no resp.	not H or L
3	2	4	2	3	NA	5	96	93	3.65	20	F	white	not H or L
4	4	4	4	3	NA	7	79	81	3.47	21	M	white	no resp.
5	1	1	2	1	NA	3	79	90	3.71	20	F	white	not H or L
6	4	4	4	4	NA	8	91	90	3.74	22	F	white	not H or L
NURS 301: Clinical Skills Writing Assignment (Fall 2016)													
1	4	3	2	3	NA	5	97	91	3.50	21	F	white	not H or L
2	4	4	3	2	NA	5	86	86	3.60	22	F	Asian	not H or L
3	3	3	2	3	NA	5	92	89	3.70	21	F	white	not H or L

4	4	4	4	4	NA	8	92	93	3.88	20	F	white	not H or L
5	4	4	4	3	NA	7	98	92	3.66	20	F	white	not H or L
6	4	3	4	4	NA	7	95	91	3.60	22	F	white	not H or L
7	4	4	4	4	NA	8	100	96	3.90	20	F	white	not H or L
8	4	4	3	3	NA	7	98	91	3.60	20	F	black	not H or L
9	3	4	4	3	NA	7	95	88	3.79	22	F	white	not H or L
10	3	2	2	2	NA	4	97	95	3.83	20	F	white	not H or L
NURS 401: Nursing Diagnosis and Plan of Care Writing Assignment (Fall 2017)													
1	4	4	3	3	NA	7	83	85	3.17	21	F	white	not H or L
2	4	4	4	4	NA	8	100	95	3.80	21	F	white	not H or L
3	2	3	4	4	NA	8	100	97	3.83	21	F	white	not H or L
4	2	2	3	3	NA	6	100	94	3.87	21	F	white	no resp.
5	3	3	3	2	NA	5	100	94	3.60	22	F	white	not H or L

Table 3. Surveys about Patient Health History, Clinical Skills, and Nursing Diagnosis and Plan of Care Writing Assignments

SURVEY QUESTIONS	Patient Health History (Fall 2016)						Clinical Skills (Fall 2016)						Nursing Diagnosis and Plan of Care (Fall 2017)					
	Pre-Survey (N = 43)			Post-Survey (N = 40)			Pre-Survey (N = 82)			Post-Survey (N = 72)			Pre-Survey (N = 52)			Post-Survey (N = 66)		
Scores	1+2+3	4	5+6+7	1+2+3	4	5+6+7	1+2+3	4	5+6+7	1+2+3	4	5+6+7	1+2+3	4	5+6+7	1+2+3	4	5+6+7
1. Writing is an essential skill in nursing practice.	6; 14%	12; 28%	25; 58%	5; 13%	9; 23%	25; 63%	10; 12%	20; 24%	52; 64%	9; 13%	18; 25%	45; 62%	11; 21%	11; 21%	30; 58%	12; 18%	13; 20%	41; 62%
2. Skills for nursing-specific writing assignments can be learned.	0	13; 30%	29; 67%	2; 5%	6; 15%	32; 80%	5; 6%	9; 11%	68; 83%	1; 1%	11; 16%	59; 82%	6; 12%	9; 17%	37; 71%	6; 10%	11; 17%	49; 73%
3. Writing is best taught by English faculty rather than by nursing faculty.	15; 35.0%	15; 35%	13; 30%	22; 55%	8; 20%	10; 25%	38; 46%	17; 21%	27; 33%	39; 54%	13; 18%	20; 28%	27; 52%	10; 19%	14; 27%	32; 49%	19; 30%	14; 21%
4. Writing assignments in nursing are less important than other nursing skills.	13; 30%	6; 14%	24; 56%	11; 28%	13; 33%	15; 38%	14; 17%	14; 17%	54; 66%	14; 19%	15; 21%	43; 60%	5; 10%	8; 15%	39; 75%	16; 24%	12; 18%	38; 58%
5. I am confident in my ability to successfully complete writing assignments in nursing courses.	5; 12%	8; 19%	30; 70%	2; 5%	7; 17%	31; 78%	5; 1%	9; 11%	68; 83%	11; 15%	9; 13%	52; 72%	5; 10%	7; 13%	40; 77%	4; 6%	9; 14%	52; 79%
6. Grading rubrics for writing assignments in nursing promote fairness in evaluation.	1; 2%	11; 26%	31; 72%	4; 10%	5; 12%	31; 78%	3; 4%	5; 6%	74; 90%	13; 18%	15; 21%	44; 61%	15; 29%	12; 23%	25; 48%	12; 18%	13; 20%	41; 62%

Statement																		
7. For courses with multiple groups and different faculty members, grading rubrics for written assignments are applied fairly across all groups.	3; 7%	12; 28%	26; 60%	15; 38%	5; 12%	19; 48%	17; 21%	19; 23%	46; 56%	42; 58%	11; 15%	19; 27%	29; 56%	15; 29%	8; 15%	23; 35%	17; 26%	26; 39%
8. Nursing faculty members have the skills to evaluate my nursing-specific written assignments.	1; 2%	7; 16%	34; 79%	3; 8%	4; 10%	33; 82%	1; 1%	7; 9%	74; 90%	6; 8%	15; 21%	51; 71%	6; 12%	9; 17%	37; 71%	4; 6%	16; 24%	45; 68%
9. Scholarly writing assignments in nursing make me apprehensive.	9; 21%	8; 19%	25; 58%	9; 22%	11; 28%	20; 50%	11; 13%	12; 15%	59; 72%	9; 12%	22; 31%	41; 57%	8; 15%	11; 21%	33; 64%	10; 15%	20; 30%	36; 55%
10. Effective writing in nursing-specific assignments is necessary for professional success.	4; 9%	7; 16%	32; 74%	3; 8%	10; 25%	27; 67%	9; 11%	11; 13%	62; 76%	9; 12%	17; 24%	46; 64%	9; 17%	14; 27%	29; 56%	4; 6%	16; 24%	45; 68%
11. Grades on written assignments do not adequately reflect my knowledge of nursing.	13; 30%	13; 30%	17; 40%	7; 17%	15; 38%	18; 45%	26; 32%	20; 24%	36; 44%	14; 19%	10; 14%	48; 67%	6; 12%	7; 13%	39; 75%	13; 20%	13; 20%	39; 59%
12. Requiring use of a specific citation style (e.g., APA format) for written assignments is restrictive in evaluation.	12; 28%	13; 30%	18; 42%	16; 40%	12; 30%	12; 30%	31; 38%	23; 28%	28; 34%	25; 35%	22; 30%	25; 35%	18; 35%	14; 27%	19; 37%	29; 44%	19; 30%	18; 27%
13. The number of nursing-specific written assignments is aligned to course objectives.	6; 14%	19; 44%	18; 42%	5; 13%	15; 38%	20; 50%	5; 6%	27; 33%	49; 60%	13; 18%	21; 29%	38; 53%	15; 29%	23; 44%	14; 27%	8; 12%	30; 46%	28; 42%

Diagnosis, student opinions did not decrease, but the majority described their opinions somewhere between response choices 1 and 4.

Survey themes addressed local concerns regarding consistent use of grading rubrics across clinical sections and excessive emphasis on writing assignments. As these themes demonstrate, issues of fairness, validity, and reliability across the courses are paramount. These issues center on the need for multiple sections of clinical courses, due to enrollment limits set by state nursing boards. Administrators must recruit credentialed clinical adjunct faculty members to supervise student education in clinical settings. Clinical faculty members generally have full-time positions and assume adjunct posts on a semester basis. Although adjuncts receive course syllabi and evaluation tools, it is possible that clinical NSWG assignments may not be reviewed in detail. For administrators, identifying adjunct clinical faculty members is a challenge, given that programs can run only with full clinical teams. The themes identified in the survey returns provide actionable information regarding the curriculum and the divergent groups teaching it—that is, full-time and adjunct faculty members. To students, fairness, validity, and reliability are inextricably linked. Interestingly, in their essay in this volume, Hogrefe and Briller offered similar conclusions from their student survey—that is, that curricular change is necessary in order for students to view writing as practice and for faculty members to ensure fairness by providing comparable instruction across sections.

Our results are best summarized relative to our questions, as follows: Can NSWGs be identified so that instruction and assessment may complement each other? We now understand the difficulties that occur when these genres become central to the curriculum by being defined, developed through traits on rubrics, and assessed collectively by faculty members. Implementation of NSWGs is complex, requiring faculty development. Can grading rubrics with delineated traits for essential criteria be developed so the rubrics are meaningful for faculty members? Meaningful rubrics must be collaboratively developed and defined by faculty members. Such rubrics provide detailed specificity that can be used to drive nursing instruction through assessment. Can NSWG assignments be independently scored and yield acceptable levels of interreader agreement? Although our sample is small, we are encouraged by the interreader agreement. With larger samples and further faculty development, we are confident that our nursing colleagues can obtain acceptable levels. What standpoints do students hold toward these NSWGs and rubrics? Although students embrace the combined NSWG and rubric approach, they remain skeptical of the reliability of rubric use across faculty members. This failure is related to issues of fairness and validity. Can recommendations be offered for subsequent study in this area? We end our essay by answering this question.

Recommendations: Still on Duty

The goal of obtaining normative data in 2016–17 was to provide baseline information on this first sample employed in the design and implementation of NSWG assignments and grading rubrics. If findings suggested that assignments and rubrics adequately represented NSWG, then they would be employed subsequently, pending annual review, in association with a writing-in-nursing curriculum. Limitations of the genres themselves, as well as assignments and rubrics, will be evaluated regularly as part of curricular review. Particularly important will be the evaluation of the genres, assignments, and rubrics as appropriate to both the mission and outcomes of the Bachelor of Science in Nursing program and the structure of opportunity to learn for students (Moss et al.). It is especially important that assessment designers align genres, assignments, and rubrics. Such alignment can best be understood in terms of the rubrics themselves. When rubrics fail to capture the NSWG task at hand, they fail to adequately depict performance expectations (Shipman et al. 246–47). In terms of measurement, use of a poorly designed rubric can result in construct underrepresentation and introduce construct irrelevant variance into the assessment—a fundamental violation of fairness (*Standards* 63–72). Conversely, a well-designed rubric aligned to genre and assignment results in an effective evaluation tool that minimizes construct-irrelevant variance and sets clear expectations for nursing students— the fundamental elements of fair assessment. It is this sense of unified purpose and commitment to fairness that informs our recommendations.

The research team recommends the following: inclusion in professional conferences of the topics writing as practice in nursing and identification and ownership of NSWGs; annual review and revision of grading rubrics for NSWG assignments; research exploring the construct writing as practice, with larger sampling plans and subgroup analyses; criteria for annual merit, promotion, and award of tenure to include consistent use of grading criteria; continuing education on writing as practice, with training in rubric development and evaluation for fairness, validity, and reliability; and dissemination of information on NSWGs.

Although nursing's history reveals traditions that do not resonate with the view that writing is practice, nurses now embrace evidence-based nursing practice. Writing as practice requires that nurses engage intentionally in writing as essential to professional life. Writing is an opportunity to define the work of nursing; thus, writing illuminates the relation between nurse and society. Nurse as author of the profession shifts the narrative, positioning nurses as the authentic voice of the profession.

If what we describe is taken as too difficult, we should remember that there are those who will sit behind desks as we stand, ready to limit our writing to checks on a sheet of observed symptoms. If we fail in our obedience, they will raise an eyebrow, investigate our status as single women or widowers, and ask in passing if we have any uterine complaints. Perpetually, there are those ready to take away our authority to write sentences that go all the way to the end of the page.

Assessment beyond Accreditation: Improving the Communication Skills of Engineering and Computer Science Students

Julia M. Williams

Perspective

This essay reflects on the issues of fairness, assessment, and professionalism as they are enacted in science, technology, engineering, and mathematics (STEM) educational contexts. Many STEM programs must meet accreditation requirements regarding achievement of student learning outcomes, driven in large part by professional societies. The drive for meeting accreditation requirements has, however, provided a lever by which revisions to curricula and teaching methods can be achieved. I offer the case of one STEM educational context to illustrate how assessment of students' communication competencies has produced corollary benefits to students, faculty members, administrators, and academic staff members: greater transparency regarding faculty pedagogies, increased attention to issues of fairness to students, and deeper learning with regard to professionalism.

Introduction

Published in 2004, the National Academies of Engineering's *The Engineer of 2020: Visions of Engineering in the New Century* looks forward, painting a picture of engineers and their work that differs starkly from traditional notions of the field. As the authors state:

> The engineers of 2020 will be actively involved in political and community arenas. They will understand workforce constraints, and they will recognize the education and training requirements necessary for dealing with customers and the broader public. Engineering will need to expand its reach and thought patterns and political influence if it is to fulfill its potential to create a better world for our children and grandchildren. (44)

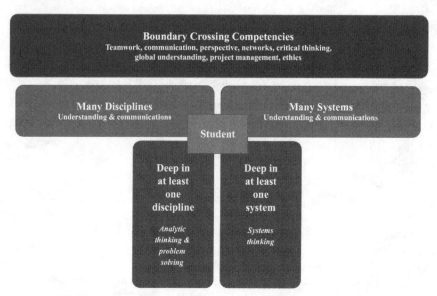

Figure 1. T-Shaped Student Engineer (© 2019 Michigan State University).

The publication of *The Engineer of 2020* in 2004 was followed by numerous other calls for change in STEM education, calls that have been uniform in their emphasis on professional skills, sometimes referred to as *soft skills*, as the basis for students' success in the technical workplace and their contributions to beneficial technologies in all regions of the world. For example, the T-Summit conference has promoted the development of T-shaped STEM graduates shown in figure 1. Derived from the concept of "T-shaped managers" who can operate successfully in both the technical and professional realms (Hansen and Von Oetinger 106), a T-shaped STEM professional possesses both deep disciplinary expertise and "boundary crossing competencies," including teamwork, global understanding, and communication (Rogers and Freuler 2).

The use of the T-shape metaphor informing figure 1 and the associated calls for changing STEM curricula both reflect growing interest in deepening students' learning and professionalism. As James W. Pellegrino and Margaret L. Hilton argue, these skills as not new, but they reflect the need for competencies and associated comprehension that were not required for success previously (National Research Council 9). The current calls for changing engineering education are also explicit in their demands for communication and professional competencies (Harris et al. 74; Williams et al. 3). Embedded in the explicit demands are implicit assumptions about how changing engineering education will produce a different kind of engineering student: a socially aware, technically skilled graduate who possesses not only superior communication skills but also a developed sense of ethics and fairness. To achieve this set of educational goals—which represent the highest ideals that industry and educators have expressed for those who enter the engineering profession—those of us who work in STEM education see writing as vital. Unlike college-level writing in some non-STEM-focused institutions, however, writing in STEM environments requires integration across multiple disciplines and engagement with faculty and professional staff members in a variety of departments and offices. Students must learn to write not only from writing instructors but also from engineering faculty members, who model the forms of discourse appropriate to their professions. This deep learning means that writing in STEM environments serves as more than mere professional training to meet career goals (see Rhonda Maneval and Frances Ward's essay in this volume for insights on how writing figures in the professional preparation of nursing students).

Many of us in STEM higher education are endeavoring to ensure that students graduate from our institutions well prepared to take on both the technical and nontechnical demands of their jobs, specifically the ability to communicate effectively in both written and oral forms with keen insight into the contexts that give their communication meaning and significance. These forms range widely, from communication between team members, as they design, prototype, test, and deliver a product to customer specifications, to communication across disciplinary boundaries, as engineers and computer scientists work together with nonengineers in communities, in government, and across the globe to address important social challenges. The task, therefore, is not merely to produce effective technical writers. For instance, Juan Lucena, Jen Schneider, and Jon Leydens have emphasized the importance of incorporating the tenets of social justice and sustainability in engineering design curricula (17). Similarly, Donna Riley has highlighted the importance of gender equity and liberative pedagogies in core technical courses, such as the study of thermodynamics (24). Justin L. Hess and Grant Fore have likewise foregrounded the incorporation of engineering ethics in the curricula (555). These examples place into stark relief the goals of STEM educators. We want to ensure that STEM students are cognizant of the ethical issues that pertain when they write and speak in professional contexts, particularly since our students graduate with technical skills that can be used for good or for ill. We want our students to understand the need for diversity and inclusion in STEM professions that have too long been exclusive and unwelcoming to women and members of underrepresented groups. In addition to industry demands, engineering program accreditation through ABET ("Criteria") has helped us focus on the assessment of students' professional skills in order to meet program accreditation standards. Since the shift of focus to learning outcomes assessment in 2000, engineering and computer science educators have sought effective, efficient methods by which students can develop their communication abilities, inspiring collaboration in academic settings between faculties in engineering and computer science and composition and communication (Darling and Dannels 2). The result has been a variety of assessment tools and resources. Thus, we see writing in STEM contexts as not merely a vehicle for thought, but a way to shape thought in STEM disciplines (Spinuzzi 28).

This essay addresses the development of communication pedagogies and assessments for STEM contexts by analyzing the ways engineering and communication faculties have responded to demands from various stakeholders— industry, society, and students themselves, to name a few. In order to understand the interactions of STEM and written and oral communication, the essay presents one institutional context and our efforts as composition and communication faculty members to collaborate with engineering and computer science faculty members in order to develop assessment tools that both challenge students and reflect our culture as an undergraduate-focused institution. Rose-Hulman Institute of Technology, Terre Haute, Indiana (Carnegie classification: special-focus four-year engineering schools; see *Carnegie*) is a small residential college (2,245 students) that grants bachelor of science degrees in engineering, science, and math only ("Rose-Hulman"). All students are required to take nine courses in the humanities and social sciences, two of which are writing courses, and the humanities and social sciences faculty is the largest of any department on campus.

In 1998, teams of faculty members representing a wide variety of disciplines embarked on a comprehensive project to define criteria for evaluating students' technical and professional skills and to develop online tools for collecting and evaluating evidence of those skills. Twenty years later, we are still assessing students' learning outcomes using an online tool, the *RosEvaluation* process, developed on our campus. The assessment process begins with faculty members in all disciplines identifying student artifacts as evidence of their achievement in ten defined student learning outcomes (Williams, "Evaluating" 8). Artifacts are collected through the *RosEvaluation* tool, integrated into the campus learning management system, *Moodle*. At the end of each academic year, a team of faculty members drawn from departments across our campus spend two days evaluating these student artifacts using a set of established evaluation rubrics. The assessment results are compiled and sent back to each department for use in both program and institutional continuous improvement efforts.

ABET, Outcomes, and Assessment

Reflecting on the reports demanding change in how engineers are educated, perhaps no single development has had a greater impact on engineering and computer science curricula than the adoption of the ABET Engineering Criteria 2000. Like most professional degrees, engineering and computer science degrees must be conferred by accredited programs. These programs earn their accreditation status through a voluntary peer-review process conducted by ABET. Until the advent of the Engineering Criteria 2000, engineering programs were accredited on the basis of requirement validations that mandated that the program offer a specific number and type of courses (e.g., a defined number of credit hours in basic mathematics, basic sciences, general education, and so on) and provide evidence that students graduating from the program had taken those courses. Student transcripts provided the primary source of data, and evidence regarding faculty member qualifications, suitable facilities, and institutional support was collected into a program self-study report.

Dissatisfaction with the performance of program graduates while on the job, as well as changing demands from industry that hired these graduates, led to the major change in program accreditation (beginning in 2001), from an input focus to an outcome focus. No longer was it sufficient for students merely to take the program's required courses. Instead, programs needed to provide evidence of students' performance in each of the defined outcomes. ABET adopted eleven student learning outcomes and required that each program under review provide proof that evidence of student performance was collected, assessed, and then used to make improvements in that program. The move to outcomes assessment was initiated in the mid-1990s, with the first reviews under the new criteria beginning in 2000. To support these objectives, the ABET Engineering Criteria 2000 required that programs provide evidence of their graduates' performance on eleven student learning outcomes, one of which is "an ability to communicate effectively" ("Criteria").

The move to outcomes assessment necessitated several important changes to the practice of engineering education (and, later, computer science education, when similar outcomes were adopted for computer science program accreditation), not least of which was the development of valid assessment tools and regular collection of evidence of performance. Foremost among these changes was the effort to align course content to outcomes, with the addition of appropriate methods to collect and analyze evidence of student learning. Needless to say, the move to outcomes assessment provoked questions and some expressions of fear, since engineering faculty members are trained as disciplinary experts, not as education assessment specialists. Beginning in the late 1990s, there was a sharp rise in the number of conference presentations, educational workshops, and journal articles that provided faculty members with assessment resources and methods (see Eichhorn et al., Ollis et al., Scales et al., Shuman et al., and Spurlin et al.). By aligning course objectives to the ABET Engineering Criteria, then collecting data on student performance, engineering and computer science programs seeking accreditation could demonstrate how they used data to improve courses and curricula (Felder and Brent 10).

The impact of the Engineering Criteria (the "2000" designation was dropped soon after the new criteria were adopted) was profound across the spectrum of undergraduate engineering programs in the United States and on the campus of Rose-Hulman Institute of Technology, particularly with regard to communication skills. Until 1995, all students were required to take the freshman writing course, but only one department—civil engineering—required that students also take the junior-level technical communication course. Recognizing that communication faculty members were the best prepared to develop and deploy effective communication pedagogies, more departments added the course to their list of requirements. By the time of this essay, the course is required of all students in all majors except chemistry (which offers its own "communication in the profession" seminar). Coincident with the increasing number of students taking the course, however, was a rising interest among engineering and computer science faculty members to incorporate communication work in their technical courses. As a result, we collaborated with faculty members in a variety of departments to help them develop appropriate writing and oral communication assignments, along with effective, efficient assessment methods, so they could build students' knowledge, skills, and abilities in a technical context (Hanson and Williams). We look on the work by technical faculty members to include communication in their technical courses as a crucial partnership on our campus. Granted, Rose-Hulman is small and its focus is narrowly on technical education. Even so, engineering and computer science faculty members (many of whom have experience working in industry) acknowledge that effective communication skills are the foundation of a successful technical career. Moreover, the partnership between the communication faculty and the STEM faculty has produced two significant outcomes. First, our efforts in assessment signify our commitment as educators to improve faculty teaching and student learning through a rigorous process of assessment. The data we collect has immediate and important impacts on our classrooms, reflected in improved curricula. Second, we ensure that our efforts in the classroom are transparent, fair, and aligned with best educational practices as they are reflected in STEM education research.

Communication Outcome Definitions and Assessment Process

Assessment of communication learning objectives poses two distinct challenges. First, the communication objective must be defined. This specificity is particularly important since the ABET communication criterion was unmeasurable (i.e., "an ability to communicate effectively"). Work among communication faculty members began when we decided to focus solely on written communication, although oral communication is still taught and assessed in the curriculum in communication courses as well as in engineering and computer science courses. We also restricted the number of performance criteria (what a student can demonstrate and can be measured with an appropriate assessment method), using both industry practice and academic models as a guide for selection, in a manner similar to the choice of criteria found in the Society for Technical Communication Body of Knowledge, whose effort was produced in the late 2000s (Coppola 11). For instance, we defined the communication objective using five performance criteria; one criterion related to audience analysis, a foundational communication concept: "Adapt technical information for a non-specialized audience" (Williams, "Evaluating" 5). This performance criterion reflected an important construct in our technical communication course that matched demands from industry; many engineers have difficulty adapting highly technical information for other users, such as engineers in other fields, government representatives, customers, or community members. In order to support students in their understanding of audience, we provided them opportunities to develop their skills in audience analysis and content adaptation through assignments such as a detailed audience analysis that initiated work on a technical report. We also designed revisions into both the audience analysis document and the technical report, since writing and rewriting are important skills in both communication and engineering (no product design or work proposal is sent out to clients or sponsors without numerous drafts, rounds of review, and revision). The emphasis on audience provides an important avenue for expanding students' empathy and awareness of audiences made up of real users of technology. Our use of audience constructs, furthermore, shares much with the realm of software engineering, where audience constructs, referred to as "use cases," provide software designers with clearer, more concrete understanding of the needs of product users (Adolph et al. 10). Of course, we must struggle against students' perceptions that the audience construct does not represent a "real" audience (Ong 10). Engineering and computer science faculty members collaborate with us in this regard; they employ the same rhetorical terminology and concepts when they engage students in the follow-on courses, and they emphasize to their students the importance of eliciting user needs as a part of the design process. As a result, we have aligned the content of the communication course with both our objectives as teachers of written communication and the pedagogical goals of our STEM faculty colleagues.

A few caveats are necessary here. Communication faculty members in other program contexts could adopt a different stance on the communication outcome and make different choices, such as targeting oral rather than written communication. In addition, there is an important distinction between communication assessment for the purpose of accreditation and communication assessment for the purpose of assigning a grade in the technical communication course. Engineering and computer science program accreditation represents a minimum standard that all students must meet. In our context, the intent is not to track an individual student's development from the first year to the final year and show growth in communication skills. The emphasis for accreditation is to assess cohorts of students (e.g., all students majoring in electrical engineering or computer science). We were able to align the assignments assessed for the purpose of program accreditation to course objectives assessed for a grade, but the assessment for accreditation is performed separately through a different process by a team of assessment evaluators who did not teach the course (Williams, "Evaluating" 7). In addition, the assessment process ensures all students have the opportunity to learn and develop through pedagogies that reflect best practices in STEM education; thus, assessment is the vehicle by which we can ensure equity for all students in their learning and all faculty members in their teaching (Moss et al. 127).

The assessment for the accreditation process is conducted on our campus through the *RosEvaluation* system. In this process, each engineering and computer science program creates a Curriculum Map; the map identifies where students are given the opportunity to develop their knowledge, skills, and abilities, what assignment will be assessed to measure student performance, and how the assessment results will be collected. For program-specific objectives, such as developing a skill like using visualization software or defining the scope of a client-based project, the program collects, assesses, and analyzes student assignments within the department. The results are then used by the department to make improvements in the course and the curriculum, if needed. For outcomes that cross many programs, such as communication, a required ABET outcome for all programs, the process is conducted through the *RosEvaluation* system.

A detailed explanation of the system is provided elsewhere (Williams, "Evaluating"), but two important observations are useful here. First, the move from input to outcomes assessment had a profound impact on the way we talk about communication on our campus. In order to develop specific performance criteria for the communication objective, we conducted numerous discussions with engineering and computer science faculty members to clarify what each disciplinary group understood "effective communication" to mean. These conversations revealed both the stark differences and close parallels between disciplines. For example, faculty members stressed the differences between chemical engineering design projects (initiated primarily within a company for its own benefit, like improving an insulin production process) and civil engineering design projects (initiated through a request for proposals from a community or government entity for the benefit of the public, like a bridge or stormwater management system). As disciplinary experts in communication, we were able to analyze the differences in final product while identifying the similarities in communication genre (a technical proposal that describes work to be done). From that point, we could develop the technical proposal assignment for the technical communication course with the confidence that all students would need to learn about the genre and have practice in writing proposals. By partnering with all engineering and computer science departments on our campus, we also succeeded in distinguishing the technical communication course and its focus on teaching rhetoric from the disciplinary courses that incorporated communication strategies specific to their disciplines and professions. As technical communication faculty members, we could not pretend to know engineering communication practices expected of our students when they enter a technical workplace (Winsor 25). Engineering and computer science faculty members are, however, the experts in this dimension of workplace communication, and they take up this aspect of communication instruction when students move from our technical communication course into other courses within engineering and computer science programs. As we developed and deployed our assessment process, our understanding of the construct representation evolved. We were able to see that the robustness of the communication construct enabled fairness as students learned and then produced writing in genres appropriate to their professions, thereby ensuring their success as both STEM professionals and as citizens.

The second notable achievement was the dissemination of communication pedagogy among technical faculty members to inform the way they use the language of rhetoric in their technical courses. Through the communication objective discussions, technical faculty members expressed willingness to reinforce and extend students' communication development in their classes. Through workshops and one-to-one work, engineering and computer science faculty members have partnered with us by adopting communication pedagogy in their courses. Peer review is an expected step in the writing process of students who are preparing documents in the computer science specifications course, the biomedical mechanics course, and the technical communication course. Engineering faculty members refer to the "rhetorical triangle" and "the rhetorical appeals" as they help students understand how persuasion figures into genres as diverse as a failure report, a design change memo, and an e-mail to a supervisor. The collaboration has even produced an engineering communication textbook, authored by two technical communication faculty members together with two mechanical engineering faculty members (House et al., *Engineering*). Although this was not an explicit objective in our original project, the evolution of our assessment project has made our work more transparent to students, thus creating important opportunities for our entire academic community—students, faculty members, administrators, and staff members—to learn.

It is tempting to see the positive, productive collaboration between faculty members as a unique occurrence, the result of the focused mission of our institution, the small size of the faculty (192, at last count, with women representing twenty-five percent), and accreditation demands. In order to assess the interest of engineering faculty members in communication and related pedagogy, we were funded in 2008 to gather information on faculty member engagement with communication as part of their technical courses (see Williams, "Transformations"). The Mapping the Future of Engineering Communication Project, funded by a grant from the Engineering Information Foundation, measured the impact of ABET and Engineering Accreditation Council accreditation criteria on the pedagogy of faculty members in engineering departments. We surveyed engineering faculty members to determine to what degree accreditation demands influenced their incorporation of communication into their technical classes. The project included the development of an electronic survey instrument that collected 110 responses from engineering faculty members at programs and departments in the United States. In addition to survey results, we conducted focus groups with faculty members, both at our home institution and at the 2008 Frontiers in Education Conference. The results from this project point to higher levels of interest in incorporating communication into technical courses than one might assume. For many engineering faculty members, incorporating communication stemmed from their experience in industry, where effective communication was a key component of their technical work. In preparing engineering students for their professions, engineering faculty members saw communication as an integral component of this preparation. We also determined a high level of interest in creating partnerships with technical communication faculty members, and many of the engineering faculty members commented on successful partnerships between faculty members across the disciplines. The primary obstacles to incorporating communication and creating partnerships were the lack of recognition for these efforts (e.g., not acknowledged by tenure committees as valid professional development, research, or service), the already crowded content of engineering courses, and an inability to locate interested partners in the composition, rhetoric, or English departments (House et al., "Elements"). We plan to revisit these data with a new round of surveys and interviews to determine how the landscape of engineering and computer science communication has changed over the past ten years.

Conclusion

Whereas our assessment effort (through the *RosEvaluation* process) has remained the same since its inception in 1998, the communication outcomes we assess have been reviewed and revised to reflect the needs of our students as they enter the practice of engineering, mathematics, and science. For instance, we have adopted the Written Communication outcomes developed in the VALUE Rubrics initiative led by the American Association of Colleges and Universities (see McConnel and Rhodes). These outcomes and rubrics have allowed us to raise the expectations we have for student performance while still providing important accreditation data for the technical programs on our campus. Revisions to the communication outcome and our pedagogy have also helped us to emphasize the importance of context, fairness, and social responsibility to our students as part of their development as professionals. This emphasis is reinforced by input from industry and graduate schools, which have collaborated with us on changes to our curricula and pedagogy. As Patricia Wojahn and colleagues have noted, the STEM classroom is often disconnected from the technical workplace where students will eventually apply their communication skills (130). Consequently, we believe that STEM programs best serve their students when they adopt professional workplace standards, tenets of fairness, and pedagogies of social justice in their communication classrooms. For instance, workplace genres, such as team meeting minutes, have been part of academic communication curricula (Wolfe 5), while the importance of collaborative writing has been identified as a component of communication pedagogy. These developments suggest that teaching written and oral communication in STEM contexts is linked both to applied, workplace practice and to understanding the impacts of technological developments on individuals and communities, both in the United States and around the world. We understand the level of effort required to ensure that our teaching is fair, ethical, and socially responsible, but if we are to reach the lofty goal set by the National Academies of Engineering to fulfill the potential of STEM to "create a better world for our children and grandchildren" (44), nothing less would suffice.

Part Four

Location

Teaching Composition in the Two-Year College: Approaches for Transfer Students and Career and Technical Education Students

Angela B. Rasmussen and Andrea Reid

Perspective

This essay discusses an expanded pedagogical approach in first-year composition for both transfer and career and technical education (CTE) students, and it explains methods for facilitating conversations with colleagues about expanding curricular approaches to serve the needs of both student groups. We link genre exposure to fairness and approach fairness in terms of curricular design. This connection requires teaching broader forms of writing instead of privileging one type of writing over another. For a classroom to be fair, all students must have an equal opportunity to succeed, which cannot be attained if genres associated with workplace success are denied them.

Introduction

As instructors at Spokane Community College (SCC), a comprehensive, though predominantly professional and technical, institution, we are aware of the constant negotiation between meeting the needs of both transfer and CTE students. In our first-year English composition courses, we often learn about our students' diverse academic and career plans but, unfortunately, do not always address that diversity in our course curriculum and assessments. In the most general terms, academic students plan to transfer to earn four-year degrees, whereas CTE students plan to take courses, earn credentials, or complete a two-year degree that emphasizes direct workforce applications. No matter the type of student enrolled in the course, the academic essay is still a standard writing form for many first-year composition classes, both at SCC and elsewhere. Relying solely on that thesis-support structure, however, can work against institutional goals of engaging and preparing students for a breadth of discipline-specific transfer courses and workplace communication skills, especially when many students are unlikely to use that genre beyond first-year composition. First-year composition may be a student's only writing class at SCC, and that alone challenges us to design a course curriculum that serves all students, regardless of their academic or career goals.

In this essay, we first outline an approach that encourages creating composition curricula relevant for both transfer and CTE students—classrooms that include transparent, real world, and reflective curricula. This approach can bridge the gap between skills traditionally defined for transfer students and those for CTE students. Second, we include a discussion protocol designed to guide the departmental conversations necessary for systemic buy-in and implementation of this approach. This how-to protocol is meant to generate conversations around instructors' own experiences teaching composition; around ways instructors can create a fair and inclusive curriculum that is transparent, real-world, and reflective; and around identifying the resources necessary to support this work.

Fundamental to our approach is the concept of fairness within the discipline of composition. We borrow heavily from Norbert Elliot's discussion of fairness in writing assessment, one that allows "all student groups . . . to display their knowledge of the specified construct in writing performance" ("Theory"). In a similar way, we approach fairness in writing curricula as one that builds writing across many disciplines instead of privileging one type of writing over another. Despite recent innovations in the field of composition, the most common curricular approach in first-year composition courses continues to emphasize topics and genres useful for transfer students and relies heavily on literary analysis, academic research, argumentative essays, and similar forms and topics (for a good historical overview of how writing has been taught, see Yancey, *Writing*). This approach might work when every student needs those skills for future academic courses, but that is not the case with many community college students. Fairness in first-year composition classes means adopting a curricular approach that serves both groups equally well.

Our professional work in the classroom, in the college, and in the state of Washington grounds our perspectives in this essay. As longtime English faculty members, we have both perpetuated and been troubled by privileging the academic essay over real-world composing. Within leadership roles in the department, we have led curricular reform and innovation that address some, but not enough, of the varying needs of our student population. Throughout our careers, we have participated in K–16 curricular alignment and partnerships in our state, and we are working to create more opportunities for cross-sector collaboration. Now, through college-wide assessment and faculty professional development positions, we recognize and appreciate that systemic change takes time, energy, and resources. At the intersection of this work is where we hope to include our contribution to this collection—curricular reform in the two-year college composition classroom.

Institutional Context

For those unfamiliar with community college missions, an overview of our college demographics may prove useful. Like many comprehensive community colleges, student success at SCC can have radically different definitions. The college served almost 18,000 students during the 2017–18 academic year, with fifty-two percent declaring an intention to complete a certificate or professional degree program ("Annual Overview"). The college's top enrolled courses of study include Nursing, Welding and Fabrication, Medical Assisting, Dental Assisting, and Baking. During fall 2017, more than seventy-eight percent worked or were looking for work, and the average age was thirty-seven years old. Of all students, more than twenty percent were first-generation college students, and for award-seeking students, forty-nine percent were low income ("CCS Fast Facts").

Both the CTE and transfer populations that comprise SCC's student body enroll in first-year composition. During the academic year 2016–17, the percentage of students enrolled in first-year composition who intended to transfer ranged between about sixty-one and seventy-seven percent. The numbers for 2015–16 were similar: between about forty-nine and sixty-nine percent. The average enrollment percentage for the last three academic years is approximately sixty-five percent transfer and thirty-three percent CTE students. Consequently, we can expect anywhere from a quarter to almost half the students in any SCC first-year composition class to be CTE-focused ("Annual Overview").

For the thirty percent of our students who will transfer, completing first-year composition is a requirement for the Associate of Arts and Associate of Applied Science degrees. For the remaining seventy percent of students, first-year composition is not a consistent requirement. Career and technical education programs that require students to take transfer-level first-year composition courses include Nursing, Allied Health, Cosmetology, Criminal Justice, and others. Those CTE programs (including Culinary, Heavy Diesel, Automotive, Carpentry, and others) that do not require transfer-level first-year composition do require a technical writing course through SCC's Applied Education department. Although there is a portion of the CTE population that does not take first-year composition, enough do to warrant a curriculum that serves both groups. Ultimately, all students—transfer as well as CTE—will enter the workforce at some point, bringing with them composition content and abilities we hope they have gained in part from our classes. As composition instructors committed to student success, we can and should equip every student with essential critical reading, thinking, and writing skills for the twenty-first century. Certainly, the Common Core State Standards Initiative in K–12 has pushed higher education to consider new ways to build on the career and college readiness skills students need. Additionally, the P21 Partnership for 21st Century Learning Initiative provides a framework for student outcomes around the knowledge, skills, and expertise students need to master to succeed beyond college—in work and life.

Creating a Fair and Inclusive Composition Curriculum for Transfer Students and Career and Technical Education Students

Important conversations are happening across academic institutions about fairness and inclusivity, including how composition placement, language usage, text selection, pedagogy, and assessment impact student success. Fairness in writing assessment, for example, is most often concerned with creating opportunity and success for those "least advantaged" (Elliot, "Theory"). And, whereas most discussions of fairness rightfully focus on systemically underrepresented groups (writers who may be low-income, historically underserved, linguistically diverse, or first-generation), in this discussion we focus on a different divide: that between transfer and CTE students in the same composition classroom. For a more thorough examination of fairness and inclusivity in composition, see the 2016 special issue on writing assessment as social justice in *College English* (Poe and Inoue, *Toward*) and the 2016 special issue on a theory of ethics for writing assessment in the *Journal of Writing Assessment* (Kelly-Riley and Whithaus, *Theory*). And because fairness and inclusivity reach beyond composition, see Beckie Supiano's "Traditional Teaching May Deepen Inequality. Can a Different Approach Fix It?" for another viewpoint.

Our approach to creating a more fair composition curriculum—though by no means a comprehensive one—highlights three key concepts to help instructors and departments. We believe a curriculum that is transparent, real world, and reflective can better bridge the gap between the respective skills and abilities needed by CTE and transfer students. To create these fair and inclusive classrooms, we will need to consider, as Kathleen Blake Yancey says in *Writing in the Twenty-first Century*, how to develop and teach new models of composing that "operat[e] simultaneously, each informed by new publication practices, new materials, and new vocabulary" (7). The three concepts we discuss are an attempt to begin conversations that do just that.

For a classroom to be fair, all students must have an equal opportunity to succeed. For many community college students, previous classrooms have not prepared them well for academic writing. Whether they have been out of the classroom for an extended period of time or taken a high school pathway that did not emphasize college preparatory skills, many SCC students arrive without the same vocabulary and shared understanding of academic writing as traditional students.

One of the most potentially transformative practices for moving toward fairness comes from the Transparency in Learning and Teaching (TILT) in higher education framework for assignment design. From Mary-Ann Winkelmes and colleagues' "A Teaching Intervention that Increases Underserved College Students' Success," the TILT framework offers strategies for creating assignments that are clear and transparent for students. Led by Winkelmes at the University of Nevada, Las Vegas, a 2015 study examined the effects of this teaching intervention at seven minority-serving institutions. Students whose assignments were more transparent and problem-centered made "gains in three areas that are important predictors of students' success: academic confidence, sense of belonging, and mastery of the skills that employers value most when hiring" (Winkelmes et al.). Best of all, whereas all students benefited from the increased transparency, at-risk students (low income, first-generation, underrepresented) saw greater benefits, making significant gains in closing the achievement gap. Students who are most likely to struggle perform best when faculty members break down the hidden agendas of assignments and avoid assuming that all students are familiar with academic expectations.

Making assignments more transparent includes three major components: purpose, or explaining the skills and knowledge that students will gain or practice through completing the assignment; task, or the steps or specific processes that students should do or perform for the assignment; and criteria for success, or the characteristics of a successful finished product, including a rubric, sample, or checklist (Winkelmes et al.). These seemingly simple changes clarify the unwritten rules of instructor expectations and articulate assignment components in a way that invites all students to excel.

Transfer and CTE students alike can benefit from the transparency framework, as many students struggle to understand academic expectations but are afraid to ask questions that suggest confusion or unpreparedness. This framework is especially important for nontraditional students who often arrive at community college with little experience of academic writing forms. Even more important, the exercise of articulating purpose can help writing instructors examine how their assignments and activities support both transfer and CTE students. When faculty members articulate the transferability of knowledge and skills directly in their course assignments, students' metacognitive awareness and engagement increase. For all these reasons, using a proven equity strategy like the TILT framework can be one of the most effective ways to create a more fair and equitable curriculum.

The fact that many CTE students are heading into the workforce after a short course of study makes our time with them more significant. Often, only one composition course is required for program or degree completion, and that means that composition faculty members must be intentional with the limited amount of time we have with those students. Whereas transfer students may have their writing instruction spread out over four years in college, CTE students require the essential skills to be covered in their very first (and possibly only) course. A common complaint among composition instructors is that we are being asked to be "all things to all people." Simply meeting the course's multiple formal and informal course outcomes (reading, writing, critical thinking, information literacy, and college success) can pose challenges for instructors. We suggest that, instead of trying to do it all, instructors refocus the content onto real-world assignments and topics that position composition as a lifelong, relevant skill.

Students need to become rhetorically agile as twenty-first-century communicators, adept in analyzing and producing texts for diverse audiences, purposes, contexts, and mediums. In our composition courses, we can help them gain these skills by including opportunities for rhetorical analysis that better connects them to their diverse academic or CTE fields. In their essay "Informing Automated Writing Evaluation Using the Lens of Genre: Two Studies," Jill Burstein and colleagues suggest this shift toward multigenre composing as part of their examination of the disconnected types of writing emphasized in K–12, higher education, and workplaces. The authors suggest that "the predominant requirement of the genre of the essay remains a problematic barrier to students becoming effective writers across many genres" and, that although assessing students' ability to write essays remains the norm in many composition classrooms, "[s]uch a restricted vision of genre and audience may limit students' ability to understand the professional discourse communities and rhetorical situations that will govern their professional lives" (134). Composition programs looking to include more CTE students in their curriculum should consider the variety of genres called for in the workplace and to integrate more real-world audiences and assignments.

As writing instructors, our responsibility should be to provide not only the *how-to* of structures called for in different genres (essay, blog post, memo, report, etc.) but also the *why* and *for whom*. We must encourage students to be conscious creators of writing and language within varied situations. Real-world and discipline-specific professional writing can grow students' skills as communicators in ways that benefit both CTE and transfer students. By using real-world assignments in first-year composition courses, teachers communicate that professional writing is as important as academic writing.

Reflection at its best encourages students to become agents of their own learning and theorize about their own writing. Current research suggests that metacognition plays a significant role in students' abilities to transfer and apply skills into different writing situations. Raffaella Negretti's 2012 study of metacognition's connection to academic writing concludes that "[m]etacognitive awareness . . . helps students know how to adapt their strategic choices to the specific requirements of the task and why" (170). Students who become aware of the "communicative practices of academic written communication and develop rhetorical consciousness" make better writing choices and are more skilled at self-evaluation (142).

Over and above the internal work that happens through reflection, reflection also has a practical external application in the composition classroom. As students understand their own learning, they are able apply that learning to their writing through transferability. When faculty members emphasize transferring writing skills from one situation to another—building explicit bridges between composition classroom tasks, other college writing, and real-world situations—they further students' metacognitive awareness. Building on Kathleen Blake Yancey, Liane Robertson and Kara Taczak's 2014 work in *Writing across Contexts*, Howard Tinberg discusses his application of the teaching for transfer concept. This model challenges students to "develop a portable theory of writing applicable across broad and varied contexts, including the workplace" directly, instead of hoping students make the cognitive leaps between the classroom and beyond. By employing a variety of assignments (readings, writing assignments, blog posts), he provides students opportunities to "articulate and apply concepts critical to becoming successful writers," a habit of mind that serves, as Tinberg says, as a "passport" for students as they move into new writing contexts. He asks students to develop personal theories of writing in tandem with reflection on their writing choices of audience, purpose, and genre necessary for different assignments.

Similar to the transparency framework, the teaching for transfer approach invites students to see the purpose and application of classroom skills in their future studies and careers. In their contribution to this volume, Brooke A. Carlson and Cari Ryan support the notion that metacognitive practices allow students the opportunity "to integrate, adapt, and wield prior knowledge in new ways." Additionally, in their essay in this collection, Karen Singer-Freeman and Linda Bastone posit that reflective writing can be useful in acquiring and assessing multiple general education learning outcomes. Reflection is vital to both transfer and CTE students. Using reflective writing in a composition classroom is one of the best ways to encourage students to internalize their own growth and development as writers and to externalize what they have learned by transferring skills and abilities to new situations.

Facilitating Conversations

Our faculty and administrative roles at the college inform our approach to curriculum change. Without department support and targeted professional development, we know that changes will always remain small in scale. To have an impact on more than a handful of students, meaningful conversations with colleagues about making first-year composition classrooms more inclusive for both transfer and CTE students must take place. These conversations can be difficult for faculty members. Not only can they challenge the status quo and require significant curricular revision but they can also appear to question the value of the liberal arts education that many faculty members received and believe in. Curricular revision can reach into the territory of academic freedom, making it important to ground conversations within the shared priority of student success. To bring about significant change, the slow, deliberate process of consensus-building must happen.

Our discussion protocol shown below is designed to engage individuals, groups, and departments in the difficult work of composition curriculum reform.

Beyond the Academic Essay:
Creating Fair Composition Curriculum in Comprehensive Two-Year Colleges

This discussion protocol is designed for longer department meetings or retreats that encourage individual reflection and significant group conversations about how to effectively meet the needs of both career and technical education and transfer students in first-year composition tasks and assessments.

The protocol can be beneficial for faculty members to read several texts ahead of time as shared points of comparison for these conversations. Three key texts referred to in the protocol are Tinberg's "Teaching for Transfer: A Passport for Writing in New Contexts," Yancey's *Writing in the Twenty-First Century: A Report from the National Council of Teachers of English*, and the *Framework for Success in Postsecondary Writing* by the Council of Writing Program Administrators, National Council of Teachers of English, and National Writing Project.

The facilitator should keep the group focused and synthesize perspectives. For each protocol question set, facilitators should engage everyone in the conversation by using a mix of reflective or timed writing, partner discussions, small- or large-group share out, poster papers, and so on.

Note: Having an outside facilitator can be useful for dealing with faculty resistance, providing expertise or experience with teaching for transfer concepts, or offering a fresh perspective.

1. Getting Started: Positioning Ourselves in the Conversation
   - Reflect on ways graduate experience and training influences how we teach composition.
   - What composition content, skills, and abilities do we hope (expect, assume) students bring into first-year composition courses?
   - Where do we see students struggle most in composition courses? Where do they struggle most in courses that require writing in other disciplines?
   - What key characteristics of teaching for transfer and twenty-first-century writing could benefit both transfer and CTE students at our institution?
   - Which areas—transparent, real world, or reflective—do we already include in our department's composition curriculum and assessments? Which do we not include? Why?

2. Creating a Transparent Composition Curriculum
   - Where do students often struggle with assignments? What directions would be helpful when they start their work? What additional resources do they need to perform well?
   - Thinking about a specific first-year composition assignment, how do we articulate underlying assumptions and expectations about concepts and terminology embedded in the assignment (e.g., standard edited English, knowledge of thesis statements, understanding what makes a good paragraph)?
   - What composition content, skills, and abilities do we hope (expect, assume) students learn and transfer from first-year composition into their next courses? into discipline-specific writing? into workplace writing?
   - What key characteristics of TILT could benefit both transfer and CTE students at our institution?

3. Creating a Real-World Composition Curriculum
   - What activities and class discussions can further an understanding of audience? How can existing assignments be revised to allow for multiple revisions for multiple audiences?
   - What kinds of genres and structures might students need to be familiar with for future classes or workplace writing situations? (Use examples from *Framework for Success*.)
   - What's a specific writing opportunity that could help students develop transferable rhetorical knowledge? Considering a set of first-year composition summative assignments, how might we revise course assessments to encourage a mix of increasingly rigorous skills and abilities that also include authentic audiences and genres?

- What resources are available on campus or locally to bring in professional writers or employers to share their perspectives?

4. Creating a Reflective Composition Curriculum

- Which habits of mind do we emphasize in teaching and hope (expect, assume) students learn and transfer from first-year composition courses? into discipline-specific writing? into workplace writing?
- Which habits of mind do we hope (expect, assume) students bring to first-year composition courses (e.g., metacognition, flexibility, responsibility, persistence, creativity)?
- According to Tinberg, students should develop their own theories of writing. Why is having a theory of writing important, given that a majority of students aren't English majors and may never take another writing course?
- How might reflective writing assignments be included in both formative and summative student assessment?
- How might writing reflection and literacy narratives help students develop rhetorical agility?

5. Resources to Support This Work

- Who are our strategic partners and key stakeholders in discussing writing across the college (e.g., K–12 partners, faculty members in other transfer disciplines or professional technical programs, employers, four-year institutions)? How can we learn more about their expectations for student writing?
- What professional development is needed to continue this effort?
    ◊ What training would be useful (e.g., using multimodal or visual formatting assignment design and assessment, embedding metacognition into assignments, teaching writing in the twenty-first century)?
    ◊ What structures can provide opportunities for faculty members to reflect on and share what they learn (e.g., reading and discussion group, TILT revised assignment sharing)?
    ◊ What readings and resources do faculty members need access to (e.g., collection of current articles and books)?

Because real change requires time and sustained energy, leaving each discussion with a plan for what comes next can be an encouraging and practical way to wrap up. The facilitator might lead a wrap-up identifying major themes or ideas that emerged from discussion of the question sets. It is also recommended that participants decide on two or three things that are the most important next steps to further explore or address.

This protocol may be used in longer meetings or retreats that allow for significant reflection and conversation. The question sets also can be broken up if the only practical approach to meeting is in short time periods; for some institutions, subdividing question sets can allow for an ongoing and potentially more productive discussion.

To create the best conditions possible for conversation, skillful facilitation of the protocol is vital. Most likely, the person(s) bringing the protocol to the department will be convinced of the value of change; not all faculty members will share that same conviction. Including an outside facilitator in this process can be an effective way to guide conversations. Additionally, considering some prediscussion approaches can aid the facilitator in contextualizing the discussion and anticipating potential arguments. Depending on the department, the following approaches may be useful, though they may require adaptation.

Numbers Approach. Providing a program-level view of enrollment can be a good place to start. Individual faculty members find it easy to use anecdotal experience and paint a picture of enrollment patterns that may or may not be true. Without the data to describe actual patterns, some faculty members may be in denial about who is actually taking their classes.

Strengths-Based Approach. Approaching curriculum changes as additions to the beneficial assignments faculty members already use is more effective than starting with a deficit model—what we are supposedly failing to teach. For faculty members reluctant to make changes, whether from a practical stance ("I always do it this way, and my students are fine") or a philosophical view ("I firmly believe that students need the academic essay"), building on existing classrooms strengths invites buy-in.

Pilot or Small-Group Approach. Few people can argue with conducting a short-term, small-scale experiment to improve student learning, especially one with as much composition research and evidence behind it. If the department outright resists or is slow to adapt to changes, name the project a pilot study. Working with a college's institutional researchers to identity retention rates before and after the changes may lead to better conversations about student success.

Guided Pathways Approach. Many community colleges in the United States are engaged in conversations around supporting student success through metamajors or interest areas at the start of students' educational careers. Accordingly, providing a contextualized first-year composition course for groups of students interested in discipline-specific and career pathways writing (e.g., health care, STEM, humanities, etc.) is likely in all our futures. It is vital that composition faculty members lead the design of new pathway composition curricula to ensure that essential composition theory connects with disciplinary and workplace applications. This approach assumes that faculty members would prefer to be on the giving rather than receiving end of curriculum reform. (For more information on Guided Pathways, see Thomas R. Bailey, Shanna Smith Jaggars, and Davis Jenkins's *Redesigning America's Community Colleges: A Clearer Path to Student Success* and Bailey's "Guided Pathways at Community Colleges: From Theory to Practice.")

Conclusion

Creating inclusive curricula is one approach to fair opportunity structures and, more important, it is in the control of individual composition faculty members. When writing tasks privilege transfer-related knowledge and skills, inequities are created that disadvantage CTE students. To avoid these inequities, faculty members must create writing tasks that "allow all student groups . . . to display their knowledge of the specified construct in writing performance" ("Theory"). Elliot continues, "[F]or those students whose scores reveal that they are at a disadvantage because of the task design, opportunity structures are to be created that include a range of support, from resources allocated for individual tutoring to curricular support for teams of instructors." Expanding curriculum and assessments to those with a "rich view of writing" rather than a narrow one ensures that students with the fewest advantages "will not be further victimized by constrained pedagogical practices" ("Theory").

For curriculum revision to have the greatest impact on students, a system-level approach is necessary; it is not enough to have a few faculty members adopt fair practices. We expect most readers will be aware of current composition theory and may even be convinced of the need for real-world first-year composition curricula, but it is not always easy to individually lead the charge for change. To create real change for our students, we need to bring departments, disciplines, and even institutions to the table to have candid conversations with our colleagues about how and why first-year composition must benefit both transfer and CTE students.

Distributed Learning: Fairness, Outcomes, and Evidence-Based Assessment in Online, Hybrid, and Face-to-Face Writing Courses

Carl Whithaus

Perspective

This essay examines how a programmatic assessment based on student learning outcomes in a first-year writing program can develop nuanced recommendations for programmatic decisions. In this study, I describe ways a localized assessment built on techniques of descriptive analysis was attentive to issues of construct validity, reliability, and fairness. The assessment process determined that differences in student experience and success were not tied to the different versions of distributed learning—online, hybrid, or face-to-face—but rather were related to administrative, cross-campus enrollment issues. The descriptive analysis approach used in this case study demonstrates that localized assessments can attend to fairness, as well as validity and reliability. Effective use of technologies connecting writers to each other and to their readers is central to professional discourse and holds a great deal of possibility for reconceptualizing educational practice.

Introduction

Mapping connections between situated, localized writing assessments and large-scale assessments of student learning is a complex task. This essay works at one of the seams where these inquiries meet: distributed learning technologies and the development of students' writing abilities and rhetorical knowledge. Considering fairness and construct validity in distributed learning environments becomes even more pressing when we consider the pragmatics of writing program administration. Evidence-based decision-making on institutional levels—as well as for and by individual students—requires us to understand validity, reliability, and fairness as more than the result of one simple claim or judgment. Rather, we need to see validity, reliability, and fairness as overlapping and acknowledge the ways they create complex ecologies that should take into account local variables and conditions.

Distributed Learning in Writing Instruction

Using distributed learning for writing instruction fosters forms of interaction and collaboration that parallel processes and interpersonal domains that students are likely to use in their academic and professional careers beyond first-year composition. As a general term, *distributed learning* has been used to describe instructional delivery methods ranging from fully online instruction through hybrid or blended learning—where some classroom time is replaced by online activities—to face-to-face instruction that is supplemented with online modules. Distributed learning in first-year composition can include, but almost always reaches beyond, an instructor's use of a campus-wide learning management systems (LMS) such as *Canvas*, *Moodle*, *Sakai*, or *Blackboard*. Distributed learning approaches to writing instruction embrace models that emphasize writing and learning processes occurring across delivery platforms.

Distributed learning acknowledges that student writers can now—and will in their futures—work on writing projects around conference tables in groups; turn in assignments through their campus's LMS for instructor and peer feedback; present themselves as professionals in networking sites such as *LinkedIn*; participate as both producers and consumers of texts in social media spaces; and engage in rich, detailed, and varied correspondences through e-mail and shared online documents (e.g., *Google Docs*). All these composing activities and environments offer affordances for learning as well as for writing, and a distributed learning approach to first-year composition attempts to incorporate and build on these affordances.

This sort of approach acknowledges that as much learning about writing happens when students are physically at a distance from one another and from the instructor as when they are in a classroom together. Distributed learning includes the deliberate shaping of learner-to-learner activities as well as instructor-to-learner interactions. Increasingly, businesses as well as colleges and universities are using distributed learning for staff development and technical training. First-year college writing programs that embrace and develop distributed learning appear posed not only to provide students meaningful writing instruction but also to expose them to writing processes they are likely to encounter in future educational and professional environments.

To date, however, research on distributed learning, particularly in composition studies and writing across the curriculum work, has focused mostly on online writing instruction (e.g., Hewett and DePew's *Foundational Practices of Online Writing Instruction* and Warnock's *Teaching Writing Online*). There is a growing body of research on how writing programs are using combinations of face-to-face and online activities to deliver writing instruction through hybrid forms of distributed learning. Jason Allen Snart's *Hybrid Learning* as well as Joyce Magnotto Neff and Carl Whithaus's *Writing across Distances and Disciplines* sketch some of the dynamics around these emerging, alternative delivery methods. Understanding these changes to delivery methods not only relates to student learning outcomes but also suggests changes to the construct of writing as it is used in today's academic and professional settings.

Learning Outcomes and Writing as a Psychological Construct

Assessing student learning and the effectiveness of writing instruction in distributed learning can be complicated. It is even more so when we wrestle with questions of fairness as well as validity and reliability. Recent tensions within both psychometrics and writing assessment around questions of validity, reliability, and fairness of medium- to large-scale writing assessment systems help shed light on the process of defining particular constructs we want to measure when we assess student learning and reveal the overall effectiveness of a writing program's curriculum and instruction. In this volume, Mya Poe traces how these developments in writing assessment theory and research in the last twenty years have begun to address issues of fairness when considering access, cultural responsiveness, and social justice. Her essay extends the work done in Bob Broad's *What We Really Value* and his coauthored *Organic Writing Assessment*, articulate visions of localized forms of writing assessment that can accommodate the richly digital, often multimodal compositions found in many distributed learning environments. On a national level, documents such as the "WPA Outcomes Statement" and the *Framework for Success in Postsecondary Writing* sketch the contours of a broad, yet widely shared, consensus-based construct or definition of what writing is valued in postsecondary institutions. At the same time, the *Standards for Educational and Psychological Testing* provides techniques for evidence-based forms of assessment. Susanna Loeb and colleagues' "Descriptive Analysis in Education" and Grover J. Whitehurst's *Identifying and Implementing Educational Practices Supported by Rigorous Evidence* complement the concepts within *Standards* by outlining techniques for empirical data collection and analyses. For college writing assessments, the key is the seam between those two broader conceptual categories. We need to examine the space where contemporary definitions of the construct of writing meet evidence-based, psychological measurement

techniques. Creating localized assessments that use valid, reliable, and fair practices to account for the distributed forms of writing students will produce at
college and in their lives is not abstract work; rather, it ties into day-to-day curricular, instructional, and administrative issues.

Distributed Learning in First-Year Composition

This essay describes how an assessment of student learning outcomes in first-
year composition (FYC) courses in general, and those delivered in hybrid and
online formats in particular, engage issues beyond the genre-based writing activities and enhance students' learning about digital and multimodal literacies.
At the University of California, Davis, the first-year composition program had
used a genre-based, writing-about-writing approach as the standardized base
syllabus for first-year composition starting in 2008–09. The writing-about-
writing approach had been heavily influenced by Elizabeth Wardle's critiques
of "mutt genres" (774) as well as Doug Downs and Elizabeth Wardle's work to
develop more meaningful composition curricula. When graduate students and
faculty members in the program reconceptualized the curriculum for both hybrid and online learning environments in 2011–12, we expanded the writing-
about-writing focus into one that included more explicit work on building and
developing multimodal, digital literacies.

Later the assessment of a stratified sample of student portfolios as part of
the University of California Office of the President (UCOP) Innovative Learning
Technology Initiative (ILTI) grant helped us to continue to revise the curriculum
not only for the hybrid and online sections but also for the entire first-year composition program. The assessment project helped faculty members and graduate
students gain a greater awareness of the ways composition should not be separated from the digital tools used to facilitate learning. The development and assessment associated with the ILTI project highlighted how distributed learning
environments reshape the way the construct of writing itself is shifting.

This essay draws on five years of data from the development of these hybrid
and fully online versions of first-year composition at the University of California, Davis. Classified as a comprehensive doctoral research university, UC Davis
is a residential campus. In fall 2016, 36,441 students were enrolled. Of those
students, 29,546 were undergraduates. The vast majority of both undergraduate and graduate students (35,845) were full-time. As a land grant, public institution, the university draws on the diverse population of California as well
as a significant number of students from around the United States, and indeed,
from around the world. Among undergraduates, fifty-nine percent are women. A
little over one-third identify themselves as Asian or Pacific Islander, while one-

quarter identify as white; about twelve percent are international students, and six percent of undergraduates are age twenty-five and older ("UC Davis").

The initial development of the online version of the course was funded by the ILTI grant as part of developing UC online course options. The project involved contributions from faculty members and graduate students at UC Davis, UC Irvine, and UC Santa Barbara. University of California, Davis focused on developing the first-year composition course; UC Irvine developed the online Entry Level Writing (basic writing) course; and UC Santa Barbara worked on modules to supplement writing in the disciplines and professions courses. Figure 1 provides an overview of how hybrid and online versions of first-year composition were developed at UC Davis. This process began in academic year (AY) 2011–12; by 2014–15 the initial development stages were complete. The program continued to adjust based on assessments and decisions made by the faculty and administration.

During summer of 2012, faculty members and graduate students at UC Davis worked on developing short, technologically mediated modules (i.e., activities) within our *Sakai* learning management system. The ultimate goal was for these modules to be used in hybrid and fully online courses. We beta tested and refined the activities in 2012–13. This year involved intense research into best practices for online writing instruction as well as development work. In summer 2013, we created the hybrid and online course shells within *Sakai*. During 2013–14, we offered the first sections of hybrid and online first-year composition. By 2014–15 we had stable, regular course offerings of both hybrid and fully online

AY 2011–12	Identify core learning outcomes for hybrid and online FYC.
Summer 2012	Develop short technologically mediated modules (i.e., activities) within the UC Davis LMS to incorporate into face-to-face classes.
AY 2012–13	Beta test and refine modules.
	Review literature on online writing instruction.
	Plan full hybrid and online course development.
Summer 2013	Create online course shells for hybrid and online FYC.
AY 2013–14	Offer hybrid and online FYC courses.
Summer 2014	Offer summer sessions versions of hybrid and online FYC courses.
AY 2014–15	Increase number of offerings of hybrid and online FYC courses.

Figure 1. Development Time Line for Hybrid and Online Versions of First-Year Composition.

sections. Different course designations were developed for face-to-face, hybrid, and online first-year composition courses. The thirty-two sections of the online and hybrid courses were just over twenty percent of the total number of sections of first-year composition offered by UC Davis in 2013–14 and 2014–15; this total includes summer 2014 and summer 2015 sessions.

Our empirically based, locally developed assessment effort traced the project's efforts to offer first-year composition courses in multiple, distributed learning environments. We reported on both the successes and failures involved with fostering digital literacies practices in fully online, hybrid, and face-to-face courses to UCOP. The assessment projects described in this essay are based on reports on only the first-year composition courses offered by UC Davis; the assessment was designed as a program assessment to compare learning outcomes across delivery media, consider student success and future developments of the curriculum, and report back to UCOP. This discussion includes insights gained from program and learning outcomes assessment projects that examined program data, including work from fifty sections that enrolled 1,159 students and were taught by twenty different instructors. In addition, the assessment and research work included analyzing the collaborative teaching journals that were an important part of the development process for instructors as well as for the course materials (see Stewart et al.).

Program Assessment Design

A stratified random sample of thirty-six portfolios were selected for analysis. These represented work at the A-, B-, C-, and DFW-levels across each type of course: fully online, hybrid, and face-to-face. The stratification process, followed by a random selection of sample portfolios from within each of the twelve groups allowed the faculty members conducting the assessment to divide the student work into homogeneous subgroups before randomly selecting the samples. The strata were mutually exclusive (i.e., each student portfolio was assigned to a unique group); all possible levels of performance and course types were included. Following this process of stratified random sampling, eight raters examined the thirty-six sample portfolios for achievement in relationship to four stated learning outcomes: audience and purpose, organization and coherence, support, and style and mechanics.

The ILTI assessment of student learning outcomes and discussions among writing program administrators about cross-campus enrollment issues led to our decision to continue offering the hybrid version but to suspend offerings of the fully online version. In fact, not only did the program continue to offer the hybrid version, but the curriculum from the hybrid and online versions of the course that emphasized multimodal composition informed the revision of the face-to-face curriculum.

This decision was based in part on the programmatic assessment of student learning outcomes across the three different delivery formats. Based on the primary-trait analysis of the concurrent evidence found in the stratified random sample portfolios, we determined that the hybrid courses were as successful as traditional, face-to-face courses at developing our stated student learning outcomes. The analysis of the portfolios from the online sections also indicated that students who completed the quarter were able to achieve similar learning outcomes to those in face-to-face or hybrid sections; our analysis of institutional data, however, showed that students withdrew or did not complete the fully online versions of the course at higher rates than students enrolled in the hybrid and face-to-face sections. Closer examination of these data indicated that students from other UC campuses who were taking advantage of cross-campus enrollment options were less likely to complete the course than UC Davis students taking the online, hybrid, and face-to-face version of the course.

This programmatic decision was based on discussions that considered institutional data as well as the detailed work from the learning outcomes assessment project. Contextual, institutional information about students withdrawing or earning Ds or Fs because they did not complete an online section enabled us to better understand data from the learning outcomes assessment that had focused on the stratified random sample of thirty-six portfolios. That is, our first-year composition courses were designed to prepare students for their later writing-in-the-disciplines coursework. If students from other UC campuses were not completing the online versions of UC Davis's first-year composition course, the failure was tied to the delivery format for this subpopulation rather than to the curriculum or instructional materials. In short, the learning outcomes assessment indicated there was concurrent validity across delivery formats and portfolio grade strata; successful completion of the course (and hence achievement of learning outcomes), however, was limited for cross-campus students enrolled in the fully online sections. Curriculum and instruction were working effectively across all three delivery formats, but outside factors were impacting cross-campus students in the online sections to such a degree that we decided to discontinue offering these sections until we better understood those factors.

Using Descriptive Analysis for Localized Program Assessment

The UC Davis case study was informed by work in descriptive analysis. The student portfolios were scored according to a trait-based rubric as part of the program assessment. These scores were compared with course grades, but the assessment was designed to see how well stated learning outcomes were achieved across A, B, and C, and DWF portfolios. This methodology resonates with Susanna Loeb and colleagues' study for the Institute of Education Sciences, "Descriptive Analysis in Education." The Institute of Education Sciences is the evaluation arm of the United States' Department of Education; its mission is to provide scientific evidence on which to ground education practice and policy. Loeb and colleagues' work on descriptive analysis in the social sciences, particularly in education, demonstrates how descriptive analyses are as foundational to empirical research as causal analyses (39). Employing descriptive analysis techniques provides nuanced ways of understanding empirical, evidence-based research; it encourages connections with localized assessment practices. Our mixed-methods approach allowed the program to consider insights about digital literacies and distributed learning environments from the teachers' collaborative journals as well as insights gained from the learning-outcomes-based assessment of student portfolios.

This case shows that a detailed, evidence-based assessment can allow a nuanced programmatic assessment to develop. A programmatic assessment of distributed learning in writing courses may conclude that aspects of the courses are successful (i.e., the validated, established learning outcomes were achieved across delivery formats) and other aspects (i.e., the ability of students from other UC campuses to enroll in and complete the online courses) are not successful. In this case, the empirically based assessment of learning outcomes included samples of student writing and was part of an iterative assessment process that influenced future course offerings.

Construct Validity for Multimodal, Digital Forms of Writing

While the development and assessment work was occurring on the hybrid and fully online first-year composition courses at UC Davis, a national conversation was developing among the Council of Writing Program Administrators (CWPA), National Council of Teachers of English (NCTE), and National Writing Project (NWP). This conversation resulted in the production of the *Framework for Success in Postsecondary Writing*. Defining the construct of writing in ways that value a rhetorical approach is a key part of *Framework for Success in Postsecondary Writing*. At UC Davis, we recognized this as an important move if student and program learning outcomes were going to align with the writing tasks students are likely to encounter in their futures. The "habits of mind" approach embodied in the *Framework for Success in Postsecondary Writing* complemented our work on distributed learning and on writing as a multimodal construct. By developing the habits of mind identified in the *Framework*, the CWPA-NCTE-NWP authors believe that writing teachers will help students develop their rhetorical knowledge, critical thinking, writing processes, knowledge of conventions, and abilities to compose in multiple environments.

Measuring how students are increasing their rhetorical knowledge, critical thinking, writing processes, and knowledge of conventions in a way that is fair across contexts is a challenge. It is even more complicated when we also consider—as we did for this project—how students' abilities to compose in multiple environments has an impact on what we consider the construct of writing. The categories of reliability and validity frequently referred to in writing assessment alone are not enough to provide a conceptual framework for this sort of assessment work. Fairness provides a further vehicle to mitigate the tensions between proponents of localized writing assessment and those who seek to work from larger, national consensus statements. In "An Integrated Design and Appraisal Framework for Ethical Writing Assessment," David Slomp establishes the importance of focusing "on fairness from the outset of the design work." His process for developing an integrated design and appraisal framework "begins by identifying stakeholders who will most be affected by the design and implementation of the assessment system." This emphasis on assessment design tied to the most-affected stakeholders squares assessment practice with fairness instead of beginning with the categories of validity and reliability.

Slomp's project fits with evidence-based approaches to writing assessment. In many ways, his work parallels the evidence-centered design practices described by Robert J. Mislevy and Norbert Elliot ("Ethics") and by Mislevy and colleagues ("'Conditional' Sense"). As a criterion-based model, their evidence-centered design promotes the use of complex tasks for more accurate assessments of performances where simpler, standardized assessments fail to represent adequately the complexity of the tasks. Evidence-based approaches like those of Slomp, Mislevy and Elliot, and Mislevy and colleagues represent an evolving multimodal construct of writing that includes room for a variety of types of peer and audience interactions. This sort of evidence-based work can be powerfully situated within Michael Kane's work on ethics, scoring, generalization, extrapolation, and implication in relationship to validity ("Validating" and "Validation").

Fairness in Writing Assessments

Whereas the technical aspects of different forms of reliability and validity have long occupied a central position in writing assessment research, an increasing amount of attention has been paid to fairness in recent years. This concern with uses of tests and test scores can been seen in projects such as the 2014 edition of the *Standards for Educational and Psychological Testing*, which discusses fairness as "a fundamental issue in protecting test takers and test users" (49). As both psychometricians and writing researchers have articulated the importance of fairness along with validity and reliability in the development of assessments, the need to operationalize a mechanism for evaluating the consequences of test and score use has become more apparent. This need is particularly pressing when we consider writing assessments that address newer forms of writing emerging in distributed work and learning environments.

Within writing studies, the amount of literature on transfer has surged in the last eight years (e.g., Robertson et al.; Adler-Kassner et al.; "Elon Statement"; National Research Council). A full review of that literature is beyond the scope of this essay, but the importance of construct validity, as we look to facilitate connections between classroom contexts and distributed contexts, cannot be underestimated.

Fairness and the Local

In interesting ways, distributive learning returns us to questions about fairness and localized writing assessments. The move to situate writing as a construct defined in terms of the local has been developed in Diane Kelly-Riley and Norbert Elliot's "The 'WPA Outcomes Statement,' Validation, and the Pursuit of Localism" as well as in Slomp's "An Integrated Design and Appraisal Framework for Ethical Writing Assessment." Kelly-Riley and Elliot's and Slomp's work approaches validity, reliability, and fairness from the local or microlevel; in *On Solid Ground*, the VALUE rubric development project of the Association of American Colleges and Universities (AAC&U), approaches validity, reliability, and fairness from the macrolevel of multi-institutional collaboration and accreditation (McConnell and Rhodes). Further, the most recent version of the *Standards for Educational and Psychological Testing* provides an opening into these debates around validity and writing constructs. In this volume, Terrel L. Rhodes describes the dynamics around macrolevel work on validity, reliability, and fairness. He examines how encouraging institutions to articulate localized student-learning outcomes for writing relate to accreditation and AAC&U's Multi-State Collaborative to Advance Quality Student Learning. The dynamics between macrolevel issues for accreditation agencies and microlevel campus issues that he explores has parallels with the issues among the University of California system and individual UC campuses when the development of online basic and first-year writing courses occurred. The work on the UC Davis writing program, its connections with the writing programs at UC Irvine and UC Santa Barbara, and its place with UC Online embodied exactly these negotiations between macro- or system-level concerns and micro-level or local concerns from faculty members at UC Davis.

These questions about valuing fairness and the local are particularly fraught for writing courses when the mode of delivery includes distributed learning formats. Distributed learning can be seen as a threat to traditional instruction and even to the potential for students to learn effectively. In *Changing Course*, their survey-based work for the Sloan Foundation, I. Elaine Allen and Jeff Seaman describe how traditional, Web-facilitated, blended or hybrid, and online courses are influencing instruction at American colleges and universities. One of their most interesting findings is that a significant amount of work on hybrid and online course development is occurring at traditional, residential colleges, not at for-profit, online universities. Their findings indicate that distributed learning is supplementing, not replacing, classroom instruction. For writing courses, it is helping instruction more closely resemble the writing environments students will encounter later in their educational and workplace experiences.

Consequences and Connections: Implications for Assessing Distributed Learning

Both educational measurement and writing assessment research have focused on fairness in relation to the social consequences of assessment. The development of validity theory in particular has been a rich area for these projects. Samuel J. Messick's work from the 1980s connected construct validity and social consequences ("Test"). He helped us understand that negative social consequences arising from the use of an assessment can undermine the validity of that assessment. In addition, Kane's work ("Validating" and "Validation") on interpretation-use argument encourages test developers and educational administrators to consider how an exam's use is connected to a student's score on the exam. That is, Kane wants developers and administrators to integrate and understand the chain inferences that move from scoring, generalization, and extrapolation to a decision based on the score. The significance of Messick's ("Validity") and Kane's ("Validation") work—and the extensions into writing assessment research—is that assessments should have construct validity (i.e., they need to measure what they were designed to measure) and be fair (i.e., the consequences that result from their use should consider societal values and evidential reasoning and chain of inferences). The programmatic assessment of the hybrid and online courses at UC Davis aimed to put into practice these principles.

Research into writing assessment practices that enhance construct validity and fairness is as important as work on reliability. Peggy O'Neill has argued that writing assessment work needs to move away from research and practices focused primarily on interrater reliability. In "Reframing Reliability," she calls for an approach that does not "side step" reliability, but rather values performance-based assessments and the development of scoring systems that consider concepts of reliability more in sync with the work of Jay Parkes. This sort of work on more expansive concepts of reliability can be seen in the research publications of writers such as Jesse R. Sparks and colleagues. It is leading us toward the development of operational mechanisms that would value construct validity, fairness, and reliability in ways that reflect the complex, distributed forms of writing found in postsecondary and professional contexts today.

The program assessment of hybrid and online first-year composition courses at UC Davis has implications for other colleges and universities working on delivering writing instruction through distributed learning environments. First-year composition should not be about isolated writers completing a requirement; rather, it should be about how students are emerging as writers within their majors and within their fields. In his contribution to this volume, Mislevy suggests the consequences of writing assessments should be seen from a situated perspective on written communication. His argument in favor of viewing assessment as evidentiary argument extends the ecology of assessment beyond the categories of validity and reliability to include fairness. This stance promotes opportunities to learn and can provide faculty members and instructional designers information vital to program improvement. The effective use of technologies that connect writers to each other and to their readers is now a central writing skill and a central part of professional discourse. The key issues we found at UC Davis were developing valid and fair local program assessment connected with student learning outcomes. Descriptive analyses of student work and instructors' journals were used to shape, in an iterative fashion, curriculum and instruction. Programmatic assessments of student learning outcomes based on descriptive analysis protocols can lead to subtle and accurate localized accounts of how distributed learning techniques are—or are not—helping faculty members and students accomplish their goals.

Note

I am indebted to Jenae Cohn, Mary Stewart, Beth Pearsall, and Dan Comins, who contributed to the development and assessment of UC Davis's hybrid and fully online first-year composition courses. I am also thankful for the leadership that Dana Ferris, Aliki Dragona, Heather Milton, Dan Melzer, and Sarah Faye provided for the writing program.

Accreditation for Learning: The Multi-State Collaborative to Advance Opportunities for Quality Learning for All Students

Terrel L. Rhodes

Perspective

This essay examines the continuing emphasis among regional and specialized accreditation bodies for evidence of the types of learning expected from college graduates. To frame the discussion, I emphasize the long history of using rubrics to assess student writing as a fundamental learning outcome that underlies virtually all areas of study. To lend focus to the discussion, I present information on the origin of the VALUE collaborative, information from the assessment results, and directions for future research. I envision a future where the point of accreditation is to be able to affirm institutional commitment to fairness for students' access to, and achievement of, quality learning.

Accreditation

Too often accreditation is viewed by individuals in higher education as an onerous duty that periodically must be endured, both to receive a stamp of approval for prospective students and as a requirement for receipt of federal (and sometimes state) financial aid resources for enrollees. Having been a faculty member and administrator in three different accreditation regions and an institutional liaison for accreditation, I can say with certainty that compliance with standards was a paramount preoccupation that typically translated into a desire to receive multiple commendations for the institution while minimizing any recommendations describing needed improvements. Since higher education institutions regularly receive reaffirmation of their accredited status, I was always struck by two central purposes of accreditation that should have connected the work of the campus to the meaning of the self-study (and the accreditation review and report) but often seemed to recede during the review process and visit. Specifically, the point of accreditation is to be able to affirm institutional documentation of fairness for students' access to and achievement of quality learning. And, second, the reason to focus on the institution as a whole is the shared nature of the day-to-day work necessary to accomplish the goal of quality for all students; namely, higher education institutions and programs are expected to provide quality learning for all students supported by and through enacting the criteria contained in accreditation standards. This essay focuses on what can occur when fairness and opportunity to learn are goals of assessment.

Accreditation encompasses all aspects of program activities, not just learning. Here, we attend to learning as a process that occurs over time both inside and outside the formal classroom and curriculum, positing that as a fundamental learning outcome written communication competence needs to be demonstrable in every major or program of study at any level of higher education. As such, every faculty member should be able to assign student work that requires appropriate written communication and, even though they are not experts in rhetoric and composition, make basic judgments about the quality of the communication students provide in response to an assignment they have been given. Specifically, attention now focuses on demonstrated competence in writing for all students regardless of their area of study.

Not just in the United States but also internationally the ability to evaluate writing across disciplines requires articulated, shared statements of core criteria that characterize effective writing generally, as well as criteria that underlie the articulation of specifics associated with a disciplinary domain—an example of the shared nature of developing learners' fundamental competence as effective communicators through writing in multiple contexts (Klenowski and Wyatt-Smith; Martin and Mahat).

Assessment for Learning and Writing

The broad theme of this essay, illustrated through written communication, is that it is possible and desirable to assess student learning in a way that faculty members and other educators can generate actionable information that can be utilized by individual, program, departmental, and institutional actors to enhance effectiveness and effect learning improvement. The actual work educators are already doing in the classroom can and needs to be the best evidence of student learning; the professional judgments of faculty members and other educators can and need to be validated as worthy of trust both for self-understanding and for those who doubt the worth of higher education and its integrity; and evidence from assessments can be disaggregated and interrogated to identify patterns of systematic success and the need for improvement in addressing issues of equity and fairness in access to quality educational practices.

Work prompted by assignments represents one of the best and ubiquitous opportunities to capture demonstrations of student accomplishment. This focus on broad construct representation in student work

- bases measurement on work that reflects the level of student motivated learning (direct assessment);
- allows assessments to examine what students can do across a set of key dimensions of a learning outcome (validity);
- places faculty members' and other educators' shared expert judgment at the critical center of quality (reliability); and
- produces assessment results that, unlike many current institutional assessment metrics, are useful and actionable feedback for learning improvement (fairness, validation, and accountability simultaneously).

In short, this approach to quality education and quality learning mirrors the 2014 *Standards for Educational and Psychological Testing.* The *Standards* were built on a hundred years of focused attention on the validity of outcomes measures, joined along the way by attention to reliability of the measures. The 2014 addition of fairness as equally important for measurement recognized the changing nature of measures and measurement since 1906 and the critical need to attend to the differential effects of language, background, and circumstances of learners to attain desired outcomes.

Can This Work?

Since writing competence is ubiquitous across the curriculum and cocurriculum and valued for student success in life beyond the academy, it is important that all faculty members and students have access to a shared, valid guide for judging the general quality of student writing across an institution. Rubrics can provide this shared guidance for faculty experts and novices, as well as for students. Even nonexpert faculty members can recognize basic writing quality through calibration training on the use of common rubrics. The ability to engage faculty members across disciplines has the potential to enhance student learning beyond specified writing-designated courses that can at times leave students with the perception of writing as something siloed or relegated to specific academic locations rather than as a critical capability for communicating in all facets of their lives. The preceding essays in this volume have presented a multitude of ways writing in disciplinary contexts is being measured, integrated, and molded to reflect effective communication in chosen areas of study, amply demonstrating the necessity and nuance of quality communication as students develop expertise in deep exploration of focused studies. The challenge remains from an institutional accreditation standpoint, how do we know what learning looks like across the institution?

The VALUE Rubrics

Rubrics have been a long-standing resource and tool in education for helping faculty members judge the quality of student work. Writing programs have led the development of rubrics to articulate expected performance in writing, as well as the necessity for writing to occur across all disciplinary contexts if students are to develop effective writing abilities for expressing meaning to others both within and outside more-focused areas of study. For some this balance between the fundamentals of writing and specific concentrations of knowledge has surfaced as an argument that the only legitimate judgment of writing quality is manifested between a student and an educator in a specific writing context. Although this may be the ultimate and the best demonstration of writing that brings all facets of writing together for a specific student, it in no way obviates the worth and importance of making a case that all programs and institutions can and are providing high-quality learning in written communication for all students regardless of the specific course, educator, or area of study a learner chooses.

A *Test of Leadership*, a much-heralded 2006 report for the Department of Education on the future of higher education in the United States, championed the need for a set of standardized tests to judge the performance of all higher education institutions and students. In response, a broad set of objections was raised to the report, not least of which was the lack of recognition of the role of faculty members in its vision for improving the quality of higher education. The Association of American Colleges and Universities (AAC&U) responded immediately to an ensuing call in 2007 from the Department of Education to develop an alternative. The resulting approach was entitled the Valid Assessment of Learning in Undergraduate Education (VALUE). The starting point of VALUE was a set of learning outcomes synthesized from a decade of surveys and focus groups with faculty members, other educators, employer feedback, and research on the essential learning outcomes all groups cited as critical for postsecondary learners to be successful in life, work, and society. Three key principles guided the VALUE approach to assessing learning: develop shared understanding of essential learning outcomes; improve direct assessment of student learning (in text and other modalities); and encourage transparency and student self-evaluation of learning.

In 2007, the AAC&U sent calls for higher education professionals to help develop a set of corresponding rubrics for each of the essential learning outcomes. Each rubric team consisted of individuals from a cross-section of campus types, disciplinary specializations, formal positions in the academy, and familiarity with utilization of rubrics. Every team was asked to follow a set of guidelines in accomplishing their work:

Provide the basic perspective the rubric developers took in addressing the specific rubric, some background information, the definition for the outcome, and definitions of key terms.

Develop a rubric that expressed expectations for learning as a learner moved from minimal understanding of the dimensions of the specific learning outcome to descriptions of what sophisticated, complex learning would look like (i.e., reflect learning growth through a portfolio of student work across the arc of learning).

Keep the use of expert jargon to a minimum so nonexperts could use the rubric to inform judgments about the level of learning demonstrated (i.e., consider these metarubrics, not disciplinary-specific ones).

Keep the language for the descriptors of the key dimensions and levels of learning focused on what the reviewer was seeing rather than on what was missing from the student work under review.

As draft rubrics were developed, over one hundred individuals on campuses across the country tested the rubrics in their own classes with work produced by their students. Feedback was provided to the development teams and revisions made to improve understanding and effectiveness of the rubrics.

Since the VALUE rubrics were released in fall 2009, over seven thousand unique organizations have accessed and downloaded the sixteen rubrics, including all types and sizes of institutions (domestic and international), professional associations, and consortia of campuses and states.

The VALUE/MSC and the VALUE Institute

To test the VALUE arguments, the Multi-State Collaborative (MSC) to Advance Quality Student Learning initiative used the AAC&U's VALUE rubrics as the shared articulation of core dimensions of writing and levels of demonstrated achievement. From 2013 to 2017, the MSC was a partnership between the Association of American Colleges and Universities and the State Higher Education Executive Officers Association, the professional organization of state higher education governing and coordinating boards found in most states. The VALUE/ MSC effort was designed to address a glaring shortcoming that historically emerged in accreditation reports: the lack of verification of systematic collection of evidence that demonstrated student higher-order abilities.

The VALUE/MSC—a collaboration of thirteen states and ninety-two two- and four-year institutions—is the only nationwide effort to systematically address the challenge of demonstrating through direct evidence the progressive levels of student learning across essential learning outcomes. Participating states and institutions collected samples of student work to assess written communication. All student work was de-identified to protect student, department, program, institution, and state identities. All student work was evaluated by faculty members and other educators from the participating institutions who underwent calibration sessions on the VALUE rubrics. In 2014, two other consortia joined the effort, bringing four-year private liberal arts colleges into the VALUE/MSC work.

By the third year of collecting and scoring work (2017), the initiative amassed assessment evidence that began to reveal the landscape of learning across selected learning outcomes—written communication, critical thinking, and quantitative literacy—as well as evidence on the fairness, validity, and reliability of the results. Initiative-level results are being used by individual and program faculty members and institutions to improve pedagogy and assignment design in ways that support and strengthen student learning achievement within and beyond individual classes and programs and to demonstrate evidence of learning for accreditation. In 2017, building on the VALUE/MSC collaboration, the AAC&U established the VALUE Institute to invite any state, higher education institution, or program seeking external validation of student learning to collect samples of student work artifacts to be scored by faculty members trained to use the VALUE rubrics.

VALUE Data from Scoring

The data discussed below are from the three nationwide VALUE initiatives. Comparison of key demographic information about the students closely approximated the demographic profiles of graduating students at the respective participating institutions. Over 29,000 pieces of student work were collected. Although not representative of all states and students in higher education, participating states stretch from Maine to Hawai'i and Minnesota to Texas, representing rural and urban, large and small, research university and community college, and minority-serving institutions. Randomized samples of student work were collected for scoring. All student work was subject to respective Institutional Review Board guidelines. The VALUE/MSC participants followed shared sampling parameters for size and variables to allow institutional level results within methodologically acceptable ranges to permit generalizability about quality in the aggregate, not about individual students (Maxwell).

What follows are examples of data displays showing the distribution of scores from certified scorers across student work submitted from all institutions. The results are presented as illustrative, not as standards or goals that institutions should strive to achieve. The initial results reveal variations in levels of achievement found in student work designed in this case for written communication. Figure 1 summarizes scoring results for written communication from students who had completed at least seventy-five percent of the requirement for the degree being sought. The capstone score reflects expected levels for students approaching attainment of a baccalaureate degree; milestones are progressive markers of expertise; benchmark reflects performance for beginning learners at collegiate institutions. As hoped, students nearing completion of a baccalaureate degree show higher levels of achievement than students nearing completion of an associate degree. It is also clear that, regardless of degree level being sought, there are students who demonstrate learning at all levels of the rubric (McConnell and Rhodes 39).

Numerous questions ensue as faculty members and other educators explore the implications of the results. Are the levels of achievement surprising? Is the distribution within and across the dimensions of the learning outcome expected? Is there a specific dimension where percentages are higher or lower than desired? Are there implications from a comparison of the two-year and four-year results that prompt efforts by faculty members to better align expectations that might enhance student transfer success?

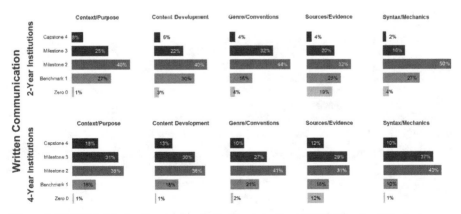

Figure 1. VALUE Initiative Results for the Refinement Year (2017) Sample of Students Completing At Least Seventy-Five Percent of Degree Requirements (*N* = 2,855).

The results create a space for discussing student learning across multiple dimensions of a learning outcome as well as across institutions with the focus on student learning evidence rather than on course titles and credits, individual faculty members, or even programs. These summary results can be examined in relation to other variables collected along with the student work samples to provide other possible factors that might shed light on how faculty members could concentrate attention to influence student learning. For example, student socioeconomic status and race are often identified as important influences on student academic success (Sullivan and McConnell 22).

Figure 2 presents results for student responses disaggregated on the basis of race (see figure 2 note). A quick look for initial impressions might focus on the low percentage of students scoring at the capstone level desired for graduating students with a baccalaureate.

What might explain this? Do the stronger skills in syntax and mechanics of writing evidence that writing programs and repeated opportunities built into and across the curriculum do indeed improve student achievement? Are patterns of student performance similar to patterns for other outcomes? What is the relation between assignments and outcomes? Did assignments not ask students to include evidence in their work? Are the capstone expectations too aspirational? How do these findings align with our expectations for underrepresented populations?

This provocation of inquiry is exactly what was hoped would result from the VALUE approach—multiple questions related to patterns of learning among and across student populations on key dimensions or characteristics. There

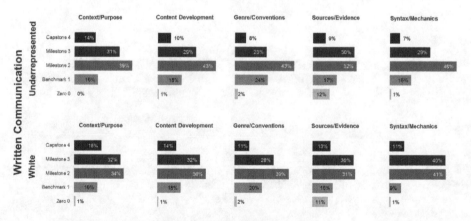

Figure 2. Underrepresented Groups* at Four-Year Institutions.

* Underrepresented includes American Indian or Alaska Native, Pacific Islander, Hispanic, Black, nonresident alien, and two or more races; white n = 2245; underrepresented n = 804.

were variations in statistically significant relations. Disaggregating the results suggests that underrepresented groups perform similarly to other populations across dimensions but that there are variables that significantly affect performance for all groups of students. Initial findings suggest that what educators do is equally or more influential in student performance over time than student factors often assumed to be determinative for learning.

These are the same types of conversations and explorations that accreditors expect at institutions through their insistence on "closing the loop" on assessment for learning (Banta and Blaich). The general scoring results for an institution create a starting point to engage colleagues from across the institution in discussing student learning and to join in making meaning and sense out of the results by asking the questions that can be more fully answered only by bringing in the locally generated assessment data.

In addition to the face validity and content validity of the rubrics derived from the rubric development process (McConnell and Rhodes 29), figure 3 summarizes responses from faculty members and other educators who have used the VALUE rubrics during the last three years. The scorers represent multiple disciplines and positions across the range of campuses that have participated. The scorers report high levels of usefulness and applicability in utilizing the rubrics to score student work gathered from the variety of assignments and courses. Indeed, in the context of accreditation, the VALUE process lifts up the institution's shared, institutional commitment to gathering evidence and utilizing it to enhance the quality of student learning (Cumming and Maxwell 10).

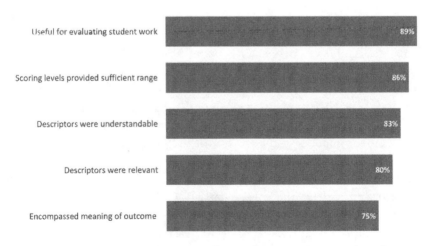

Figure 3. Percentage of Scorers Who Reported Strongly Agree or Agree with Each Aspect of Rubric Use (*n* = 400).

In practice, we are learning from participating institutions that the VALUE findings allow institutions to connect institutional-level data to program- and course-level data in order to chart pedagogical changes that improve student learning. This connection allows institutions to bridge a gap in the current accreditation process by providing educators and students with information that is useful in their day-to-day lives. Also, the VALUE-generated institutional evidence can support the identification and growth of higher-order essential learning across learning outcomes necessary for graduation and success. Through VALUE, institutions report they are effectively using the VALUE results as documentation to move their institutions closer to solid evidence in support of their primary mission of quality student learning as discussed by Rhonda Maneval and Frances Ward in this volume. Already, accreditation visiting teams are commenting positively on institutional use of the VALUE-initiative-based assessment results—the provision of evidence on the general, broad outlines of learning from a sample of students across an entire institution. This framing allows the more localized assessments that have emerged in specific programs and departments that are better able to capture greater specificity about where, how, and why student learning can be enhanced to achieve higher-order learning, to be viewed as evidence-informed actions educators closest to the teaching and learning interaction on the ground can implement to effectuate improvements. The VALUE approach brings many programmatic pieces into a picture of the whole, which is the primary focus of institutional accreditation reviews.

Writing, Fairness, and Evidence-Based Assessment

The centrality of writing—to communicate competence or mastery of content, to share learning with others, and to apply learning to solve problems—requires higher education providers to ensure that all students pursuing postsecondary education attain skills and practice to improve writing by providing evidence of learners' written abilities. In earlier essays in this volume, Ruth Benander and Brenda Refaei (in their work at Blue Ash College) and Erick Montenegro (in his work at the National Institute for Learning Outcomes Assessment), respectively, demonstrate the importance for equity in assessment to encompass and encourage diverse ways for students to demonstrate their learning connected to identity and culture. Accreditation, especially regional accreditation, has increased its insistence on evidence that all graduates have obtained a level of competence but without specifying how to gather the evidence or defining the level of quality expected (Ambrose et al. 121–52; Bali et al.; Gaston 111–38).

Reliability in Using VALUE Rubrics

Many sources of research on sampling, interrater reliability, validity, fairness, generalizability, and rubric development were examined as part of the VALUE initiative (Broad et al. 144–50; White, *Very*). Basic learning theory and cognitive development and resultant challenges were also incorporated into the development of the VALUE approach.

Early in the VALUE initiative, AAC&U began investigating the reliability of the VALUE assessment process with several small-scale studies between 2008 and 2010. There were no statistically significant differences across the scorer groups, demonstrating that faculty members from a range of disciplines could indeed score student work from within or beyond their own disciplines and reach relatively high levels of agreement on the general quality of the work. Interrater reliability continues to be an important methodological concern of the newly established VALUE Institute. Although there are a range of statistical tests available to ascertain interrater reliability, preliminary examinations included weighted percent agreement between raters, weighted Cohen's Kappa (which, for a design like the VALUE approach to assessing student learning, is limited in a number of ways), and Gwet's AC (which adjusts for chance by considering how difficult or easy it is to rate a subject). Using Gwet's AC, the range of agreement across the dimensions for critical thinking, written communication, and quantitative literacy shows that agreement can be described as moderate to strong (.56 to .85) (McConnell and Rhodes 30).

Fairness, Validity, and Reliability Needed for Learning Assessment and Accreditation

Although comparing the fairness, validity, and reliability of the VALUE process to standardized tests will always be an "apples to oranges" proposition, establishing the methodological soundness of VALUE was and remains a key priority. This work, however, must take into consideration the inherent complexity— methodological, philosophical, and pedagogical—that VALUE entails. It is critical to acknowledge there is no other existing available model for this important work (McConnell and Rhodes 30).

The VALUE/MSC initiatives collected and scored work for students early in their academic pursuits and those nearing completion of their academic studies. By collecting demographic information for every student whose work is collected for scoring, the initiatives can explore multiple dimensions of fairness by disaggregating scoring results on the quality of students' written communication (and other outcomes) to reveal patterns of scores and the relation to demographic variables, such as race, gender, first-generation status, or year in school (Finley and McNair 5–20).

With the ongoing emphasis on access and completion of postsecondary education for life success, higher education institutions must in fairness have evidence to indicate the learning quality for all students at our institutions if we are to have confidence that graduates are accessing quality learning in practice. Gone are the days when high-impact, highly effective practices associated with strengthening quality education can be reserved for the most talented students attending higher education (Gordon 14–15). Many of the preceding essays in this collection focus on high-impact, highly effective practices in their respective disciplines that exemplify learning engagement that builds higher-order skills and abilities.

Preliminary analysis of the VALUE initiative data supports the important influence of effective assignments, examining the relations among level of course from which the student work was collected, the student's year in school, faculty member's indication of difficulty of the assignment in terms of demonstrating higher-order skills and abilities, and VALUE scores received on student work. The scoring patterns indicate clearly that "regardless of class year[,] students completing assignments that are more demanding achieve higher scores on the . . . Written Communication Rubrics. The . . . mean Written Communication score when the assignment was at the Mastery level was .91 higher than when the assignment was at the introductory level. When asked to do more, students did more" (Sullivan and McConnell 8).

In short, the VALUE approach embraces the messiness of teaching and learning. It embraces the imperfections in any approach to assessment *for* learning (focused on learning improvement as demonstrated through student-generated work), as distinguished from assessment *of* learning (single tests of learning often divorced from the curriculum and student experience).

Several principles are emerging from the initial VALUE efforts:

Demonstrated learning is the key to student success, and assessment of student learning should be based on actual student work across a broad array of essential learning outcomes.

Student work should be subjected to expert judgment through reliable and valid methods and processes that represent clearly articulated and transparent findings across broadly shared standards for proficiency.

Learning is a complex process that is about meaning and sense making that cannot be reduced to single numbers or sound bites.

Administrators, faculty members, and other educators themselves must act to reconstruct a culture of learning based on evidence of fairness, shared expectations, and standards for liberal learning, proficiency, and student agency.

Consequences

A challenge of assessment for learning at programmatic and institutional levels—the focus of accreditation—is that reporting aggregate results tends to mask the variations that exist within the collectivity (Cumming and Miller 164; Hubley and Zumbo 219). Through collecting information on student performance across multiple learning outcomes using rubrics, it is possible to deconstruct learning into critical dimensions while also focusing on pedagogy and practice to improve attainment. By utilizing demographic information about students and disaggregation of results, patterns of inequitable performance associated with groups of students can be examined and revealed. The use of VALUE provides two critical components expected by accreditors: direct assessment of learning quality linked to the curriculum at an institution (unlike results from most standardized tests) and external validation of local efforts to measure and report on quality student learning that to date has relied on individual programmatic or departmental efforts.

Looking Forward

Accreditation is moving slowly but surely in the direction of demanding evidence that measurements of student learning and student learning improvement are being used by faculty members and other educators in their work with students, and that student learning has improved as a result of assessment efforts, an improvement that is also recognized by qualified experts outside the local context. Demand for assessment evidence that captures fairness for student learning, validity in measurement of important components of learning standards, and reliability in judgments of quality are mandatory, not just at a program or course level, but also across the curriculum and cocurriculum. Writing across disciplines is a rich focus for learning assessment, and VALUE takes fairness seriously in its evidence gathering and transparency. Accreditors are accrediting a collective, not the individual pieces or students. Accreditors are increasingly demanding direct assessment evidence that students are exhibiting desired levels of learning and not just isolated pockets of evidence drawn from a single program that has specialized assessment criteria or robust engagement of faculty members in student learning improvement. There is no value dualism of local versus generic assessment—good occurs when one is seen in terms of the other.

Afterword

Diane Kelly-Riley and Norbert Elliot

Now is a moment of possibility. To improve educational outcomes related to writing, our contributors have examined values, knowledge foundations, the role of disciplinarity, and the complexity of distribution. This collection illustrates new possibilities in the evolutions of scholarship and practices of teaching and assessing writing in the disciplines that have flourished since the publications of the first two books in MLA's Research and Scholarship in Composition series thirty years ago. Documenting the diverse ways that students learn about and demonstrate knowledge of their disciplines in postsecondary settings, our contributors illustrate the wide reach of learning that has become standard postsecondary practice. Collectively, our contributors establish two visions: that disciplinary identity is enacted through written communication, and that, if this vision of language-informed identity is to be realized, then traditional views of instruction and assessment must continue to evolve. Tradition will not suffice if we are to structure success for the diverse students who will enter our classrooms, laboratories, and studios over the next forty years.

As editors, we believe that this is a significant moment, one that requires us to consider carefully ways to enact change. The authors and editors of this volume believe that the lens of fairness is the primary means through which educational outcomes associated with written communication may substantially evolve postsecondary education—and by extension our broader society—through attention to our practices of disciplinary writing and local assessment. Consider first the aim of fairness, variously defined but unified under principles of equity and opportunity to learn. That aim can be contextualized within a specific institutional site, where attention is paid to the ability of admitted students to access the knowledge, skills, and attitudes of fields of study within the major of their choice—and with special attention paid to the affordances and barriers that accompany intersectionality (of socioeconomic status, ability, gender, race, and other individual differences) in the United States. Contextualism further occurs as faculty members in each campus major define disciplinarity as they have experienced it. In making tacit understanding explicit, those practitioners create a community for students in which professionalization occurs. As students experience writing for different aims and audiences in different genres, their cognitive and affective powers increase. To ensure that educational silos are not the sole basis of knowledge, collaborative efforts across the curriculum may be undertaken that result in group assessments advancing distinct institutional mission, articulated professional goals, and unique student desires.

This collection is the first to weave together fairness with evolving scholarship in writing in the disciplines and writing assessment. We hope that it leads to a long line of promising next-generation work. We look forward to future explorations that consider how theory building and street-level knowledge produce new perspectives to this line of inquiry. In light of the diverse future that benefits us all, we no longer have to believe that some things will never change.

New to this context are collaborative possibilities with faculty members across the disciplines—those whose primary expertise falls outside of the study of language, but nevertheless are devoted to its power to create meaning. These faculty members operate both as producers and shapers of knowledge within their specific disciplinary contexts and develop communicative practices within their fields. As teachers, they instruct legions of undergraduates and graduate students about dynamic expectations of communication in their areas of study. Here, faculty scholars of field-appropriate rhetoric derive, theorize, and apply language reflecting emerging knowledge, and their communicative practice is reinforced through instruction imparted to students in the ways in which they learn and communicate about these new concepts. Writing assessment—reconceptualized to emphasize its formative role in local settings—is one strategy that codifies these dynamic systems of knowledge. Thus, our contributors do more than reinforce a narrow and reductive focus on writing as correctness. They actively shape and are shaped by language use embodied in diverse forms of writing instruction and formative assessment.

Although enlightened pedagogical and assessment approaches have evolved within our scholarship, the reality is that reductive, high-stakes assessments remain the predominant topic in our institutional conversations. The obstacles to this kind of attitude toward teaching and assessing writing are breathtaking, with critical voices rising from the very disciplines who will lose turf and those who will gain responsibility. For many of us, our lived experience includes high-stakes discussions about assessment and accountability—tied to institutional performance and resources. These conversations result in an ever-increasing educational environment of utilitarian values that disenfranchise students and continue the long history of inequity and exclusion embedded within our language and social structures. There is a long road ahead to the work of justice and fairness. Publications in the field of writing studies have started to move toward more gender parity, but we have much to do in terms of the inclusion of other importance voices representing the many characteristics that make us what we are. Something has been started here in this collection, and yet much remains.

As editors and authors in this collection, we optimistically believe that change can be made, and that where it can happen is at the intersection of disciplinary conversations reinforced through assessments. There is something remarkably appealing and enduring about the varied approaches to change documented in this volume: the reliance on theory-building, the countering impact of a rubber-meets-road orientation, the willingness to embrace students as they are, the many ways we can see them if we are willing to look in nontraditional ways, the thrill of proposals that get just ahead of what is known, the chance that something different might work to the benefit of all. Again, we reiterate: now is a moment of possibility for humanities and language scholars to actively participate in critical conversations with colleagues across disciplinary settings that will determine our collective future.

Notes on Contributors

Linda Bastone is chair of the School of Natural and Social Sciences and associate professor of psychology at Purchase College, State University of New York. Bastone received the SUNY Chancellor's Award for Excellence in Teaching and for Excellence in Faculty Service. She is codirector of the Purchase College MARC U-STAR honors program, funded by the National Institutes of Health and the National Institute of General Medical Sciences.

Ruth Benander is professor in the Department of English and Communication at the University of Cincinnati, Blue Ash College. She teaches basic writing, first-year composition, and intermediate composition. Her teaching is informed by her research in e-portfolio pedagogy, experiential learning, and transfer of learning. Her research can be found in the *International Journal for the Scholarship of Teaching and Learning*, the *International Journal of E-Portfolio*, and the *Journal of General Education*. She is the general editor of the *Journal for Research and Practice in College Teaching*.

Vladimir Briller is retired from Pratt Institute in New York. He is currently a visiting professor at the Institute of Education of Higher School of Economics in Moscow. He is involved in educational research and consulting with the World Bank, UNICEF, and UNESCO. His work includes analysis of the PISA (Programme for International Student Assessment) test for the CIS countries, a Tajikistan country study, research on Islam and education in Central Asia for the United States' Department of State, and a number of articles on portfolio assessment.

Beth Buyserie is director of composition and assistant professor of English at Utah State University. She has previously served as both the assistant and interim director of composition and clinical assistant professor at Washington State University. She teaches graduate and undergraduate courses in composition, rhetoric, pedagogy, and English education. Her research interests include language and power, critical pedagogies, queer rhetorics, teacher preparation, and professional development.

Brooke A. Carlson is assistant professor of English at Chaminade University. He teaches writing, literature surveys, and Shakespeare, both online and in brick-and-mortar classrooms. His research interests include composition and rhetoric, early modern drama, Korean Shakespeare, assessment, and sustainable pedagogy. Central to his work is the notion of being human, the articulation of that being, and what being human with others means.

Norbert Elliot is professor emeritus at New Jersey Institute of Technology and currently serves as research professor at the University of South Florida. With Alice Horning, he is coeditor, most recently, of *Talking Back: Senior Scholars and Their Colleagues Deliberate the Past, Present, and Future of Writing Studies*. With Richard Haswell, he is coauthor, most recently, of *Early Holistic Scoring of Writing: A Theory, A History, A Reflection*.

Patricia Freitag Ericsson is an emeritus faculty member at Washington State University. While at WSU, she was director of the composition program (2010–17) and director of the Digital Technology and Culture program (2003–2010). She has taught a variety of undergraduate composition classes, digital writing classes, and graduate courses in pedagogy and critical technology studies. Her research interests include technologically influenced composing practices, bureaucracy and education, and composition pedagogy.

Christine Farris is professor emeritus of English at Indiana University. Her publications include *Subject to Change: New Composition Instructors' Theory and Practice* and several coedited collections: *Under Construction: Working at the Intersection of Composition Theory, Research, and Practice*; *Integrating Literature and Writing Instruction*; and *College Credit for Writing in High School: The "Taking Care of" Business*, which won the Council of Writing Program Administrators 2012 Best Book Award.

Matt Frye is assistant professor of communication at Oregon Institute of Technology and formerly a graduate teaching assistant at Washington State University. While at WSU, he coauthored several institutional reports on the university's writing program and the services it offers. He currently teaches primarily technical writing and professional writing courses. His research interests center on the intellectual and epistemological development of college students, particularly as expressed in their writing.

Anne Ruggles Gere is Arthur F. Thurnau Professor of English and Gertrude Buck Professor of Education at the University of Michigan, where she chairs the Joint PhD in English and Education. A former chair of CCC and a former president of NCTE, she was the 2018 president of MLA. Her most recent work is *Developing Writers in Higher Education: A Longitudinal Study*, and she is currently studying the integration of writing-to-learn pedagogies into STEM courses.

William Hart-Davidson is professor of writing and rhetoric and associate dean for Research and Graduate Education in the College of Arts and Letters at Michigan State University. His research focuses on writing analytics and feedback and the digital systems that facilitate them, both in teaching and learning and other areas, such as information warfare and the treatment of chronic illness.

Valerie M. Hennings is an associate professor of political science at Morningside College, where she teaches courses on the government of the United States, state and local politics, political behavior, and gender and politics. She is the director of the Col. Bud Day Center for Civic Engagement and the director of the Gender Studies Program. She has published several essays relating to gender, media, and politics. Her current research centers on issues of civic engagement and cocurricular assessment.

Jeffrey Hogrefe is associate professor of humanities and media studies and founder of the Architecture Writing Program, a transdisciplinary initiative of the School of Liberal Arts and Sciences and School of Architecture at Pratt Institute. He is the coeditor with Scott Ruff of *In Search of African American Space*, an anthology of essays, and is at work on *The Abolitionist Landscape Project for Utopian Futures*, an archive of critical practices that propose a remapping of the Potomac River Valley to reveal African and Indigenous knowledge.

Diane Kelly-Riley is associate professor of English and associate dean for research and faculty affairs at the University of Idaho. She studies writing assessment theory and practice, validity theory, race and writing assessment, public humanities, and multimodal composition. She is coeditor of the *Journal of Writing Assessment*.

Tialitha Macklin is lecturer at Boise State University, where she teaches courses in composition and rhetoric. Her research interests center on writing assessment, with a particular focus on assessment at the individual, classroom, and programmatic levels. She is also associate editor of the *Journal of Writing Assessment* and editor of the *JWA* Reading List.

Rhonda Maneval is professor of nursing and senior associate dean for the College of Health Professions and the Lienhard School of Nursing at Pace University. She has held academic appointments and administrative roles at Michigan State University and Temple University. She has received funding from several sources to explore clinical research questions and has published widely in scholarly nursing journals. Throughout her career, she has undertaken major curriculum reform and expansion of nursing's scope of practice.

Melissa Graham Meeks is director of professional development for *Eli Review*, a peer learning app for feedback and revision. She partners with instructors and administrators to design revision routines and build helpful feedback cultures. Her research focuses on writing analytics for classes and programs.

Robert J. Mislevy is the Frederic M. Lord Chair in Measurement and Statistics at Educational Testing Service and professor emeritus at the University of Maryland. His research applies developments in statistics, technology, and cognitive science to practical problems in educational assessment. He is the author of *Sociocognitive Foundations of Educational Measurement* and, with Roy Levy, *Bayesian Psychometric Modeling*.

Erick Montenegro is a doctoral candidate in the Education Policy, Organization and Leadership program at the University of Illinois at Urbana-Champaign. He is the communications coordinator and research analyst for the National Institute for

Learning Outcomes Assessment, colocated at the University of Illinois and Indiana University. His research focuses on issues of equity in assessment and culturally responsive assessment practices at Hispanic-serving institutions.

Ruth Osorio is assistant professor of English and women's studies at Old Dominion University. She has published articles in *Peitho* and *Rhetoric Review*. Her research focuses on disability studies, activist rhetoric, and feminist methodologies.

Mya Poe is associate professor of English and director of the writing program at Northeastern University. Her books include *Learning to Communicate in Science and Engineering* (CCCC Advancement of Knowledge Award, 2012), *Race and Writing Assessment* (CCCC Outstanding Book of the Year, 2014), and *Writing, Assessment, Social Justice, and Opportunity to Learn*. She is series coeditor of the *Oxford Brief Guides to Writing in the Disciplines*.

Angela B. Rasmussen serves on the English faculty at Spokane Community College, where she also serves as coordinator for the Teaching and Learning Center. Her professional development work focuses on equitable teaching strategies, transparent assignment design, and integrative learning.

Brenda Refaei is associate professor in the Department of English and Communication at the University of Cincinnati, Blue Ash College. She teaches basic writing, first-year composition, and intermediate composition. Her work has appeared in *Teaching English in the Two-Year Colleges*, *International Journal of E-Portfolio*, and *College Teaching*. She is an Engaging Excellence in Equity Fellow, sponsored by the Bill and Melinda Gates Foundation

Andrea Reid is an English instructor at Spokane Community College and director of composition for the English department. Additionally, she serves as the college's faculty assessment coordinator for transfer programs. She is involved in several K–16 collaborations, such as the Washington State Board for Community and Technical College's twelfth-grade English transition course, Bridge to College English, and the College Spark Washington/CCS grant, Collaboration for Rural Students College and Career Readiness.

Terrel L. Rhodes is vice president for Quality, Curriculum, and Assessment and executive director of VALUE at the Association of American Colleges and Universities. He was a faculty member for twenty-five years before joining national higher education efforts to focus issues of equity and quality in student learning through assessment of student work, e-portfolios, and assignments.

Cari Ryan was formerly an assessment specialist at Chaminade University's Teaching and Learning Center and is now an educational specialist at the University of Hawai'i, Manoa.

Jeremy Schnieder is director of the Center for Teaching and Learning at the University of La Verne. Previously, he served as associate professor of writing and rhetoric and faculty coordinator of assessment at Morningside College.

Karen Singer-Freeman is director of Academic Planning and Assessment at The University of North Carolina, Charlotte. She was previously an associate professor of psychology at Purchase College, State University of New York. Singer-Freeman received the SUNY Chancellor's Award for Excellence in Teaching and served as an Association of American Colleges and Universities Scientific Thinking and Integrative Reasoning Scholar. She was codirector of the Purchase College MARC U-STAR honors program and the Bridges to the Baccalaureate program, both funded by the National Institutes of Health and the National Institute of General Medical Sciences.

Frances Ward is professor emerita of nursing at Temple University and currently teaches graduate research methods and biostatistics at Drexel University. The founding dean of the School of Nursing, University of Medicine and Dentistry of New Jersey (Legacy), she is the author of *The Door of Last Resort: Memoirs of a Nurse Practitioner* (2013) and *On Duty: Power, Politics, and the History of Nursing in New Jersey* (2009).

Carl Whithaus is professor of writing and rhetoric at the University of California, Davis. He studies digital culture and rhetoric, writing in the sciences and engineering, and writing assessment. His books include *Multimodal Literacies and Emerging Genres* (2013), *Writing across Distances and Disciplines* (2008), and *Teaching and Evaluating Writing in the Age of Computers and High-Stakes Testing* (2005). He is coeditor of the *Journal of Writing Assessment*.

Julia M. Williams is professor of English at Rose-Hulman Institute of Technology. Williams's publications on assessment, engineering and professional communication, and tablet PCs have appeared in the *Journal of Engineering Education*, *IEEE Transactions on Professional Communication*, *Technical Communication Quarterly*, and *The Impact of Tablet PCs and Pen-based Technologies in the Classroom*, among others. She has been awarded grants from Microsoft, HP, the Engineering Communication Foundation, and the National Science Foundation.

Works Cited

"About Us." *National Institute for Learning Outcomes Assessment* (NILOA), www
.learningoutcomesassessment.org/about/niloa-mission/. Accessed 4 Dec. 2019.

Ackley, Betty, et al. *Nursing Diagnosis Handbook: An Evidence-Based Guide to Planning
Care.* 11th ed., Elsevier, 2017.

Addison, Joanne. "Shifting the Locus of Control: Why the Common Core State
Standards and Emerging Standardized Tests May Reshape College Writing
Classrooms." *Journal of Writing Assessment*, vol. 8, no. 1, 2015,
journalofwritingassessment.org/article.php?article=82. Accessed 4 Dec. 2019.

Adelman, Clifford. "To Imagine a Verb: The Language and Syntax of Learning
Outcomes Statements." National Institute for Learning Outcomes Assessment
(NILOA), 2015. Occasional Paper 24.

Adler-Kassner, Linda. *The Activist WPA: Changing Stories about Writing and Writers.*
Utah State UP, 2008.

———. "Because Writing Is Never Just Writing." *College Composition and
Communication*, vol. 69, no. 2, 2017, pp. 317–40.

Adler-Kassner, Linda, and Susanmarie Harrington. *Basic Writing as a Political Act:
Public Conversations about Writing and Literacies.* Hampton Press, 2002.

Adler-Kassner, Linda, and Elizabeth Wardle. *Naming What We Know: Threshold
Concepts of Writing Studies.* Utah State UP, 2015.

Adler-Kassner, Linda, et al. "The Value of Troublesome Knowledge: Transfer and
Threshold Concepts in Writing and History." *Composition Forum*, vol. 26, Fall
2012, compositionforum.com/issue/26/troublesome-knowledge-threshold.php.
Accessed 4 Dec. 2019.

Adolph, Steve, et al. *Patterns for Effective Use Cases.* Addison-Wesley Longman
Publishing, 2002.

Alexander, Jonathan. "Queered Writing Assessment." *College English*, vol. 79, no. 2,
2016, pp. 202–05.

Allen, I. Elaine, and Jeff Seaman. *Changing Course: Ten Years of Tracking Online
Education in the United States.* Sloan Consortium, 2013.

Allen, Stanley. "The Future That Is Now." *Architecture School: Three Centuries of
Educating Architects in the United States*, edited by Joan Ockman, MIT P, 2015,
pp. 204–29.

Ambrose, Susan A., et al. *How Learning Works: Seven Research-Based Principles for Smart
Teaching.* John Wiley and Sons, 2008.

Anderson, Judith H., and Christine R. Farris, editors. *Integrating Literature and Writing Instruction: First-Year English, Humanities Core Courses, Seminars*. Modern Language Association of America, 2007.

"Annual Overview, 2017–2018." *Community Colleges of Spokane*, scc.spokane.edu/About -Us/Quick-Facts. Accessed 4 Dec. 2019.

Anson, Chris, and Deanna Dannels. "Profiling Programs: Formative Uses of Departmental Consultations in the Assessment of Communication across the Curriculum." *Across the Disciplines*, vol. 6, 2009, wac.colostate.edu/atd/ assessment/anson_dannels.cfm. Accessed 4 Dec. 2019.

Applebee, Arthur N. "Common Core State Standards: The Promise and the Peril in a National Palimpsest." *English Journal*, vol. 103, no. 1, 2013, pp. 25–33.

Aristotle. *Nicomachean Ethics*. Translated by Terence Irwin, Hackett Publishing, 1999.

Arola, Kristin L., et al. *Writer/Designer: A Guide to Making Multimodal Projects*. Macmillan Higher Education, 2014.

Artemeva, Natasha, and Janna Fox. "Awareness versus Production: Probing Students' Antecedent Genre Knowledge." *Journal of Business and Technical Communication*, vol. 24, no. 4, 2010, pp. 476–515.

"The Assignment Charrette Toolkit." *National Institute for Learning Outcomes Assessment* (NILOA), 2019, www.learningoutcomesassessment.org/ourwork/ assignment-charrette/#1549481918909-4e924c6d-3b02201920192019201. Accessed 4 Dec. 2019.

Aull, Laura. *How Students Write: A Linguistic Analysis*. Modern Language Association of America, 2020.

Bailey, Thomas R. "Guided Pathways at Community Colleges: From Theory to Practice." *Diversity and Democracy*, vol. 20, no. 4, Fall 2017.

Bailey, Thomas R., et al. *Redesigning America's Community Colleges: A Clearer Path to Student Success*. Harvard UP, 2015.

Baker, Gianina R. "North Carolina A&T State University: A Culture of Inquiry." *National Institute for Learning Outcomes Assessment* (NILOA), 2012, www .learningoutcomesassessment.org/documents/CaseStudyNCAT.pdf. Accessed 4 Dec. 2019.

Baldwin, Doug. "Fundamental Challenges in Developing and Scoring Construed-Response Assessments." *Writing Assessment in the Twenty-First Century: Essays in Honor of Edward M. White*, edited by Norbert Elliot and Les Perelman. Hampton, 2012, pp. 327–41.

Bali, Maha, et al. "Pedagogy of Imperfection." *ProfHacker, The Chronicle of Higher Education*, 13 Jan. 2017.

Banks, Adam. *Digital Griots: African American Rhetoric in a Multimedia Age*. Southern Illinois UP, 2011.

Banta, Trudy W., and Charles Blaich. "Closing the Assessment Loop." *Change: The Magazine of Higher Learning*, vol. 43, no. 1, 2010, pp. 22–27.

Bartholomae, David, and Anthony Petrosky. *Ways of Reading: An Anthology for Writers.* 8th ed., Bedford / St. Martin's, 2008.

Bass, Randy. "Social Pedagogies in E-Portfolio Practices." *High-Impact E-Portfolio Practice: A Catalyst for Student, Faculty, and Institutional Learning*, edited by Bret Eynon and Laura M. Gambino, Stylus Publishing, 2017, pp. 65–73.

Bateson, Gregory. *Steps to an Ecology of Mind: Collected Essays in Anthropology, Psychiatry, Evolution, and Epistemology.* U of Chicago P, 2000.

Bawarshi, Anis S., and Mary Jo Reiff. *Genre: An Introduction to History, Theory, Research, and Pedagogy.* Parlor Press / WAC Clearinghouse, 2010.

Bazerman, Charles. "From Cultural Criticism to Disciplinary Participation: Living with Powerful Words." Herrington and Moran, *Writing*, pp. 61–68.

Bazerman, Charles, et al. *Reference Guide to Writing across the Curriculum.* Parlor Press / WAC Clearinghouse, 2005.

Bazerman, Charles, et al. "Taking the Long View on Writing Development." *Research in the Teaching of English*, vol. 51, no. 3, 2017, pp. 351–60.

Bean, John C. *Engaging Ideas: The Professor's Guide to Integrating Writing, Critical Thinking, and Active Learning in the Classroom.* Jossey Bass, 1996.

Beaufort, Anne. *College Writing and Beyond: A New Framework for University Writing Instruction.* Utah State UP, 2007.

———. "Developmental Gains of a History Major: A Case for Theory Building." *Research in the Teaching of English*, vol. 39, no. 2, 2004, pp. 1136–85.

Benander, Ruth, and Brenda Refaei. "Helping Faculty in Two-Year Colleges Use E-Portfolios for Promoting Student Writing." *Teaching English in the Two-Year College*, vol. 45, no. 1, 2017, pp. 89–106.

Benkler, Yochai, and Helen Nissenbaum. "Commons-Based Peer Production and Virtue." *Journal of Political Philosophy*, vol. 14, no. 4, 2006, pp. 394–419.

Benner, Patricia, et al. *Expertise in Nursing Practice: Caring, Clinical Judgment, and Ethics.* 2nd ed., Springer, 2009.

Bennett, Randy Elliot. "On the Meanings of Constructed Response." *Construction versus Choice in Cognitive Measurement: Issues in Constructed Response, Performance Testing, and Portfolio Assessment*, edited by Bennett and William C. Ward, Erlbaum, 1993, pp. 1–27.

Bereiter, Carl, and Marlene Scardamalia. *The Psychology of Written Composition.* Erlbaum, 1987.

Berkenkotter, Carol, and Thomas N. Huckin. "Rethinking Genre from a Sociocognitive Perspective." *Written Communication*, vol. 10, no. 4, 1993, pp. 475–509.

Bitzer, Lloyd F. "The Rhetorical Situation." *Philosophy and Rhetoric*, vol. 25, pp. 1–14.

Blake, Michelle F., et al. "Self-Regulated Strategy Instruction in Developmental Writing Courses: How to Help Basic Writers Become Independent Writers." *Teaching English in the Two-Year College*, vol. 44, no. 2, 2016, pp. 158–75.

Blakeslee, Ann. *Interacting with Audiences: Social Influences on the Production of Scientific Writing.* Erlbaum, 2000.

Borrego, Maura, et al. "Systematic Literature Reviews in Engineering Education and Other Developing Interdisciplinary Fields." *Journal of Engineering Education*, vol. 103, no. 1, 2014, pp. 45–76.

Borton, Sonya C., and Brian Huot. "Responding and Assessing." *Multimodal Composition: Resources for Teachers*, edited by Cynthia L. Selfe, Hampton Press, 2007, pp. 99–111.

Boyer, Ernest. *Scholarship Reconsidered: Priorities of the Professoriate*. Princeton UP, 1990.

Brandt, Deborah. *Literacy in American Lives*. Cambridge UP, 2001.

Brandt, Mark J., et al. "The Replication Recipe: What Makes for a Convincing Replication?" *Journal of Experimental Social Psychology*, vol. 50, 2014, pp. 217–24.

Brewer, Elizabeth, et al. "Creating a Culture of Access in Composition Studies." *Composition Studies*, vol. 42, no. 2, 2014, pp. 151–54.

Broad, Bob. *What We Really Value: Beyond Rubrics in Teaching and Assessing Writing*. UP of Colorado, 2003.

Broad, Bob, et al. *Organic Writing Assessment: Dynamic Criteria Mapping in Action*. UP of Colorado, 2009.

Brown, Ester Lucille. *Nursing for the Future: A Report Prepared for the National Nursing Council*. Russell Sage Foundation, 1948.

Brueggemann, Brenda Jo. "An Enabling Pedagogy: Meditations on Writing and Disability." *JAC*, vol. 21, no. 4, 2001, pp. 791–820.

Brueggemann, Brenda Jo, et al. "Becoming Visible: Lessons on Disability." *College Composition and Communication*, vol. 52, no. 3, 2001, pp. 368–98.

Burstein, Jill, et al. "Informing Automated Writing Evaluation Using the Lens of Genre: Two Studies." *Calico Journal*, vol. 33, no. 1, 2016, pp. 117–41.

Butler, Janine. "Embodied Captions in Multimodal Pedagogies." *Composition Forum*, vol. 39, Summer 2018, compositionforum.com/issue/39/captions.php. Accessed 4 Dec. 2019.

———. "Where Access Meets Multimodality: The Case of ASL Videos." *Kairos*, vol. 21, no. 1, 2016, kairos.technorhetoric.net/21.1/topoi/butler/index.html.

Butler, Judith. *Bodies That Matter*. Routledge, 1993.

Buyserie, Beth, et al. "Retention, Critical Pedagogy, and Students as Agents: Eschewing the Deficit Model." *Retention, Persistence, and Writing Programs*, edited by Todd Ruecker et al., Utah State UP, 2017.

Cambridge, Barbara. Introduction. *Electronic Portfolios 2.0: Emergent Research on Implementation and Impact*, edited by Darren Cambridge et al., Stylus Publishing, 2009, pp. xi–xvi.

Carillo, Ellen C. *Securing a Place for Reading in Composition: The Importance of Teaching for Transfer*. Utah State UP, 2015.

The Carnegie Classification of Institutions of Higher Education. Trustees of Indiana University, Indiana University Center for Postsecondary Research, 2018, carnegieclassifications.iu.edu/.

Carpenito, Lynda. *Handbook of Nursing Diagnosis*. 15th ed., Lippincott, Williams, and Wilkins, 2016.

Carroll, Lee Ann. *Rehearsing New Roles: How College Students Develop as Writers*. Southern Illinois UP, 2002.

Carter, Michael, et al. "Writing to Learn by Learning to Write in the Disciplines." *Journal of Business and Technical Communication*, vol. 21, no. 3, 2007, pp. 278–302.

"CCS Fast Facts." *Community Colleges of Spokane*, 2019, ccs.spokane.edu/About-Us/About-CCS/Quick-Facts. Accessed 4 Dec. 2019.

Cedillo, Christina V. "What Does It Mean to Move? Race, Disability, and Critical Embodiment Pedagogy." *Composition Forum*, vol. 39, Summer 2018, compositionforum.com/issue/39/to-move.php. Accessed 4 Dec. 2019.

Ceraso, Steph. *Sounding Composition: Multimodal Pedagogies for Embodied Listening*. U of Pittsburgh P, 2018.

Chen, Xianglei, and Sean Simone. *Remedial Coursetaking at U.S. Public Two- and Four-Year Institutions: Scope, Experiences, and Outcomes*. United States, Department of Education, National Center for Educational Statistics, Institute of Education Sciences, 2016.

Cho, Kwangsu, and Charles MacArthur. "Learning by Reviewing." *Journal of Educational Psychology*, vol. 103, no. 1, 2011, pp. 73–84.

Cho, Kwangsu, and Christian D. Schunn. "Scaffolded Writing and Rewriting in the Discipline: A Web-Based Reciprocal Peer Review System." *Computers and Education*, vol. 48, no. 3, 2007, pp. 409–26.

Civil Rights Act of 1964. United States Code, Title 42, section 2000e. *U.S. Equal Opportunity Employment Commission*, www.eeoc.gov/laws/statutes/titlevii.cfm. Accessed 4 Dec. 2019.

Clifford, James, and George Marcus. *Writing Culture: The Poetics and Politics of Ethnography*. Berkeley, U of California P, 2010.

Coe, Richard M., et al., editors. *The Rhetoric and Ideology of Genre: Strategies for Stability and Change*. Hampton Press, 2001.

Cohen, Nicole, et al. "Becoming Strategic Readers: Three Cases Using Formative Assessment, UDL, and Technology to Support Struggling Middle School Readers." *New Frontiers in Formative Assessment*, edited by Pendred E. Noyce and Daniel T. Hickey, Harvard Education Press, 2011, pp. 129–40.

Collins, Harry, and Robert Evans. *Rethinking Expertise*. U of Chicago P, 2007.

Common Core State Standards for English Language Arts and Literacy in History / Social Studies, Science, and Technical Subjects. Common Core State Standards Initiative (CCSSI), www.corestandards.org/wp-content/uploads/ELA_Standards1.pdf. Accessed 4 Dec. 2019.

Conant, James B. *The Child, the Parent, and the State*. Harvard UP, 1960.

Coppola, Nancy W. "The Technical Communication Body of Knowledge Initiative: An Academic-Practitioner Partnership." *Technical Communication*, vol. 57, no. 1, 2010, pp. 11–25.

"Criteria for Accrediting Engineering Programs, 2017–2018." *ABET*, www.abet.org/accreditation/accreditation-criteria/criteria-for-accrediting-engineering-programs-2017-2018/. Accessed 4 Dec. 2019.

Cronbach, Lee J. "Five Perspectives on the Validity Argument." *Test Validity*, edited by Howard Wainer and Henry I. Braun, Erlbaum, 1988, pp. 3–17.

Cumming, J. Joy., and Graham S. Maxwell. "Contextualising Authentic Assessment." *Assessment in Education: Principles, Policies, and Practices*, vol. 6, no. 2 (1999), pp. 177–94.

Cumming, Tammie, and M. David Miller. *Enhancing Assessment in Higher Education: Putting Psychometrics to Work*. Stylus Publishing, 2017.

Cushman, Ellen. "Forum: Issues and Reflections on Ethics and Writing Assessment." *Journal of Writing Assessment*, vol. 9, no. 1, 2016, journalofwritingassessment.org/article.php?article=95. Accessed 4 Dec. 2019.

Darling, Ann L., and Deanna P. Dannels. "Practicing Engineers Talk about the Importance of Talk: A Report on the Role of Oral Communication in the Workplace." *Communication Education*, vol. 52, no. 1, 2003, pp. 1–16.

Davidson, Cathy N. *The New Education: How to Revolutionize the University to Prepare Students for a World in Flux*. Basic Books, 2017.

"Define First Generation Students." *First Generation Programs, Washington State University*, firstscholars.wsu.edu/define-first-gen/. Accessed 4 Dec. 2019.

Deleuze, Gilles, and Felix Guattari. *A Thousand Plateaus: Capitalism and Schizophrenia*. Translated by Brian Massumi. U of Minnesota P, 1987.

Derrida, Jacques. *Of Grammatology*. Translated by Gayatri Chakravorty Spivak, Johns Hopkins UP, 2016.

Diefes-Dux, Heidi A., et al. "A Framework for Analyzing Feedback in a Formative Assessment System for Mathematical Modeling Problems." *Journal of Engineering Education*, vol. 101, no. 2, 2012, pp. 375–406.

Dijk, Teun. A. van. "Critical Discourse Studies: A Sociocognitive Approach." *Methods for Critical Discourse Analysis*, edited by Ruth Wodak and Michael Meyer, Sage, 2009, pp. 62–85.

Dolmage, Jay. *Academic Ableism*. U of Michigan P, 2017.

———. *Disability Rhetoric*. Syracuse UP, 2014.

Double Operative: Language/Making. Pratt Institute School of Architecture and School of Liberal Arts and Sciences, doubleoperative.com/. Accessed 4 Dec. 2019.

Dowd, Alicia C. "Community Colleges as Gateways and Gatekeepers: Moving Beyond the Access 'Saga' toward Outcome Equity." *Harvard Educational Review*, vol. 77, no. 4, 2007, pp. 407–19.

Downs, Doug, and Elizabeth Wardle. "Teaching about Writing, Righting Misconceptions: (Re)Envisioning First Year Composition as 'Introduction to Writing Studies.'" *College Composition and Communication*, vol. 58, no. 4, 2007, pp. 552–84.

Dressel, Paul L., editor. *Evaluation in Higher Education*. Houghton Mifflin, 1961.

Dryer, Dylan B., et al. "Revising FYC Outcomes for a Multimodal, Digitally Composed World: The 'WPA Outcomes Statement for First-Year Composition (Version 3.0).'" *WPA: Writing Program Administration*, vol. 38, no. 1, 2014, pp. 129–43.

Dunn, Patricia A., and Kathleen Dunn De Mers. "Reversing Notions of Disability and Accommodation: Embracing Universal Design in Writing Pedagogy and Web Space." *Kairos*, vol. 7, no. 1, 2002, kairos.technorhetoric.net/7.1/coverweb/dunn _demers/. Accessed 4 Dec. 2019.

During, Simon. "The Postcolonial Aesthetic." *PMLA*, vol. 129, no. 3, 2014, pp. 498–503.

Dweck, Carol S. *Mindset: The New Psychology of Success*. Ballantine Books, 2006.

———. *Self-Theories: Their Role in Motivation, Personality, and Development*. Psychology Press, 1999.

Eccles, Jacquelynne S., et al. "Expectancies, Values, and Academic Behaviors." *Achievement and Achievement Motives: Psychological and Sociological Approaches*, edited by Janet T. Spence, W. H. Freeman, 1983, pp. 75–138.

Eichhorn, Kristen, et al. "Infusing Communication Skills in an Engineering Curriculum." *Proceedings for American Society for Engineering Education Conference*, 2010, peer.asee.org/15778. Accessed 4 Dec. 2019.

Elliot, Norbert. "A Theory of Ethics for Writing Assessment." *Journal of Writing Assessment*, vol. 9, no. 1, 2016, journalofwritingassessment.org/article.php?article =98. Accessed 4 Dec. 2019.

Ellis, Katie, and Mike Kent. *Disability and New Media*. Routledge, 2011.

"Elon Statement on Writing Transfer." *Elon University*, 2013, www.elon.edu/e-web/ academics/teaching/ers/writing_transfer/statement.xhtml. Accessed 4 Dec. 2019.

Englander, Karen. *Writing and Publishing Science Research Papers in English: A Global Perspective*. Springer Dordrecht Heidelberg, 2014.

Englander, Karen, et al. "Doing Science within a Culture of Machismo and Marianismo." *Journal of International Women's Studies*, vol. 13 no. 3, 2012, pp. 65–85.

"Ensuring Every Student Succeeds." *Partnership for Assessment of Readiness for College and Careers*, parcc-assessment.org.

"E-Portfolios." *Association of American Colleges and Universities* (AAC&U), 2017, www .aacu.org/eportfolios. Accessed 4 Dec. 2019.

Ericsson, K. Anders, et al. *The Cambridge Handbook of Expertise and Expert Performance*. Cambridge UP, 2006.

Fanon, Frantz. *Black Skin, White Masks*. Translated by Richard Philcox, Grove Press, 2008.

Farris, Christine. "Literature and Composition Pedagogy." *A Guide to Composition Pedagogies*, edited by Gary Tate et al., Oxford UP, 2014, pp. 163–76.

Farris, Christine, and Raymond Smith. *Writing and Reading Alignment Project (WRAP): Final Report*. Improving Teacher Quality Partners Program, Indiana University Center for P–16 Research and Collaboration, Indiana Commission for Higher Education, Sept. 2015.

"Fast Facts: Students with Disabilities." United States, Department of Education, National Center for Education Statistics, nces.ed.gov/fastfacts/display.asp?id=60. Accessed 4 Dec. 2019.

Felder, Richard M., and Rebecca Brent. "Designing and Teaching Courses to Satisfy the ABET Engineering Criteria." *Journal of Engineering Education*, vol. 10, no. 1, 2003, pp. 7–25.

Felski, Rita. *Uses of Literature*. Wiley-Blackwell, 2008.

Finkenstaedt-Quinn, S. A., et al. "Characterizing Peer Review Comments and Revision from a Writing-to-Learn Assignment Focused on Lewis Structures." *Journal of Chemical Education*, vol. 96, 2019, pp. 227–37.

Finley, Ashley, and Tia McNair. *Assessing Underserved Students' Engagement in High-Impact Practices*. Association of American Colleges and Universities, 2013.

Flower, Linda. *The Construction of Negotiated Meaning: A Social Cognitive Theory of Writing*. Southern Illinois UP, 1994.

Flower, Linda, and John R. Hayes. "A Cognitive Process Theory of Writing." *College Composition and Communication*, vol. 32, no. 1, 1981, pp. 365–87.

Fordham, Traci, and Hillory Oakes. "Rhetoric across Modes, Rhetoric across Campus: Faculty and Students Building a Multimodal Curriculum." *Multimodal Literacies and Emerging Genres*, edited by Fordham and Carl Whithaus, U of Pittsburgh P, 2012, pp. 313–35.

Foucault, Michel. *The Order of Things: An Archaeology of the Human Sciences*. Vantage, 1970.

Fox, Charles. "A Liberal Education for the Twenty-First Century: Some Reflections on General Education." *Currents in Teaching and Learning*, Sept. 2016, pp. 5–17.

Framework for Success in Postsecondary Writing. Council of Writing Program Administrators (CWPA), National Council of Teachers of English (NCTE), and National Writing Project (NWP), 2011.

"Framework for Twenty-First Century Learning." P21 Partnership for 21st Century Learning, 2019, static.battelleforkids.org/documents/p21/P21_Framework_Brief .pdf. Accessed 4 Dec. 2019.

Fundamental Principles of Disability, Union of the Physically Impaired Against Segregation / The Disability Alliance, 1976.

Gallagher, Chris W. "Being There: (Re)Making the Assessment Scene." *College Composition and Communication*, vol. 62, no. 3, Feb. 2011, pp. 450–76.

———. *Reclaiming Assessment: A Better Alternative to the Accountability Agenda*. Heinemann, 2007.

———. "Symposium: Standardization, Democratization, and Writing Programs." *College Composition and Communication*, vol. 70, no. 3, 2019, pp. 476–507.

Garland-Thomson, Rosemarie. "The Case for Preserving Disability." *Journal of Bioethical Inquiry*, vol. 9, no. 3, 2012, pp. 339–55.

Gaston, Paul L., III. *Higher Education Accreditation: How It's Changing, Why It Must*. Stylus Publishing, 2013.

Gee, James Paul. "Reflections on Understanding, Alignment, the Social Mind, and Language in Interaction." *Language and Dialog*, vol. 5, no. 2, 2015, pp. 300–11.

———. *The Social Mind: Language, Ideology, and Social Practice*. Bergin and Garvey, 1992.

———. "A Sociocultural Perspective on Opportunity to Learn." Moss et al., pp. 76–108.

Gere, Anne Ruggles. "The Way Our Students Write Now." *PMLA*, vol. 133, no. 1, 2018, pp. 139–45.

Gere, Anne Ruggles, et al. "Interrogating Disciplines/Disciplinarity in WAC/WID: An Institutional Study." *College Composition and Communication*, vol. 67, no. 2, Dec. 2015, pp. 243–66.

Gielen, Mario, and Bram DeWever. "Scripting the Role of Assessor and Assessee in Peer Assessment in a Wiki Environment: Impact on Peer Feedback Quality and Product Improvement." *Computers and Education*, vol. 88, 2015, pp. 370–86.

Gilbuena, Debra, et al. "Feedback on Professional Skills as Enculturation into Communities of Practice." *Journal of Engineering Education*, vol. 104, no. 1, 2015, pp. 7–34.

Gladwell, Malcolm. "The Courthouse Ring." *The New Yorker*, 3 Aug. 2009, www.newyorker.com/magazine/2009/08/10/the-courthouse-ring.

Good, Victor Carter. *Dictionary of Education*. McGraw-Hill, 1945.

Gordon, Edmund W. *To Assess, To Teach, To Learn: A Vision for the Future of Assessment*. The Gordon Commission on the Future of Assessment in Education, 2013.

Graham, Steve, et al. "Writing: Importance, Development, and Instruction." *Reading and Writing*, vol. 26, no. 1, 2013, pp. 1–15.

Greeno, James G., and Melissa S. Gresalfi. "Opportunities to Learn in Practice and Identity." Moss et al., pp. 170–99.

Hamp-Lyons, Liz. "Farewell to Holistic Scoring: Part Two: Why Build a House with Only One Brick?" *Assessing Writing*, vol. 29, July 2016, pp. A1–A5.

Hansen, Kristine, and Christine Farris. *College Credit for Writing in High School: The "Taking Care of" Business*. National Council of Teachers of English (NCTE), 2010.

Hansen, Morten T., and Bolko Von Oetinger. "Introducing T-Shaped Managers." *Harvard Business Review*, vol. 79, no. 3, 2001, pp. 106–16.

Hanson, James, and Julia M. Williams. "Using Writing Assignments to Improve Self-Assessment and Communication Skills in an Engineering Statics Course." *Journal of Engineering Education*, vol. 97, no. 4, 2008, pp. 515–29.

Harackiewicz, Judith M., et al. "Closing Achievement Gaps with a Utility-Value Intervention: Disentangling Race and Social Class." *Journal of Personality and Social Psychology*, vol. 111, no. 5, 2016, pp. 745–65.

Harbour, Wendy, and Daniel Greenberg. *Campus Climate and Students with Disabilities*. NCCSD Research Brief, vol. 1, no. 2, 2017, National Center for College Students with Disabilities, www.nccsdonline.org/uploads/7/6/7/7/7677280/nccsd_campus_climate_brief_final_pdf_with_tags2.pdf. Accessed 4 Dec. 2019.

Harris, James G., et al. "Journal of Engineering Education Round Table: Reflections on the Grinder Report." *Journal of Engineering Education*, vol. 83, no. 1, 1994, pp. 69–94.

Harris, Joseph. *Rewriting: How to Do Things with Texts*. Utah State UP, 2006.

Hart Research Associates. *Falling Short? College Learning and Career Success. Association of American Colleges and Universities* (AAC&U), 2015, www.aacu.org/sites/default/files/files/LEAP/2015employerstudentsurvey.pdf. Accessed 4 Dec. 2019.

Haswell, Richard H. *Beyond Outcomes: Assessment and Instruction within a University Writing Program*. Ablex Publishing, 2001.

———. *Gaining Ground in College Writing: Tales of Development and Interpretation*. Southern Methodist UP, 1991.

Hayes, John R. "Modeling and Remodeling Writing." *Written Communication*, vol. 29, no. 3, 2012, pp. 369–88.

Herrington, Anne, and Charles Moran, editors. *Genre across the Curriculum*. Utah State UP, 2005.

———. *Writing, Teaching, and Learning in the Disciplines*. Modern Language Association of America, 1992.

Hess, Justin L., and Grant Fore. "A Systematic Literature Review of US Engineering Ethics Interventions." *Science and Engineering Ethics*, vol. 24, no. 2, 2018, pp. 551–83.

Hewett, Beth L., and Kevin Eric DePew. *Foundational Practices of Online Writing Instruction*. WAC Clearinghouse / Parlor Press, 2015, wac.colostate.edu/books/owi/. Accessed 4 Dec. 2019.

Higher Education Act of 1965. Public Law 89-329, www.gpo.gov/fdsys/pkg/STATUTE-79/pdf/STATUTE-79-Pg1219.pdf. Accessed 4 Dec. 2019.

Holiday, Judy. "Competing Discourses within the 'WPA Outcomes Statement.'" *The "WPA Outcomes Statement"—A Decade Later*, edited by Nicholas N. Behm et al., Parlor Press, 2013, pp. 242–56.

hooks, bell. *Teaching to Transgress: Education as the Practice of Freedom*. Routledge, 1994.

House, Richard, et al. "Elements of Effective Communication: Results from a Research Study of Engineering Faculty." IEEE International Professional Communication Conference, 20 July 2009, Hilton Hawaiian Village Hotel, Honolulu, Hawai'i.

House, Richard, et al. *The Engineering Communication Manual*. Oxford UP, 2016.

Howard, Rebecca Moore. "A Plagiarism Pentimento." *Journal of Teaching Writing*, vol. 11, no.3, 1993, pp. 233–46.

Hubley, Anita. M., and Bruno. D. Zumbo. "Validity and the Consequences of Test Interpretation and Use." *Social Indicators Research*, vol. 103, no. 2, 2011, 219–30.

Huddart, David. *Involuntary Associations: Postcolonial Studies and World Englishes*. Liverpool UP, 2014.

Huot, Brian. *(Re)Articulating Writing Assessment for Teaching and Learning*. Utah State UP, 2002.

Huot, Brian, et al. "A Usable Past for Writing Assessment." *College English*, vol. 72, no. 5, 2010, pp. 495–517.

Hussar, William J., and Tabitha M. Bailey. *Projections of Education Statistics to 2028.* United States, Department of Education, National Center for Education Statistics (NCES), 2020-024, nces.ed.gov/pubs2020/2020024.pdf. Accessed 4 July 2020.

Hyland, Ken. *Disciplinary Discourses: Social Interactions in Academic Writing.* U of Michigan P, 2004.

Inoue, Asao B. "Community-Based Assessment Pedagogy." *Assessing Writing*, vol. 9, no. 3, 2004, pp. 208–38.

———. *Labor-Based Grading Contracts: Building Equity and Inclusion in the Compassionate Writing Classroom.* WAC Clearinghouse / UP of Colorado, 2019.

———. "Self-Assessment as Programmatic Center: The First Year Writing Program and Its Assessment at California State University, Fresno." *Composition Forum*, vol. 20, Summer 2009, compositionforum.com/issue/20/calstate-fresno.php. Accessed 4 Dec. 2019

———. "Theorizing Failure in US Writing Assessments." *Research in the Teaching of English*, vol. 48, no. 3, 2014, pp. 330–52.

Inoue, Asao B., and Mya Poe, editors. *Race and Writing Assessment.* Peter Lang, 2012.

Jakobson, Roman. *Selected Writings: Vol. I. Phonological Studies.* 2nd ed., Mouton, 1971.

Jameson, Frederick. "Future City." *New Left Review*, vol. 21, 2003, newleftreview.org/II/21/fredric-jameson-future-city. Accessed 4 Dec. 2019.

Kafer, Alison. *Feminist, Queer, Crip.* Indiana UP, 2013.

Kane, Michael. "Validating the Interpretations and Uses of Test Scores." *Journal of Educational Measurement*, vol. 50, 2013, pp. 1–73.

———. "Validation." *Educational Measurement*, edited by R. L. Brennan, 4th ed., American Council on Higher Education / Praeger, 2006, pp. 17–64.

Kant, Immanuel. *Critique of Pure Reason.* Translated and edited by Paul Guyer and Allen W. Wood, Cambridge UP, 1998.

Kellogg, Ronald T., and Allison. P. Whiteford. "Training Advanced Writing Skill: The Case for Deliberate Practice." *Educational Psychologist*, vol. 4, no. 4, 2006, pp. 250–66.

Kelly-Riley, Diane, and Norbert Elliot. "The 'WPA Outcomes Statement,' Validation, and the Pursuit of Localism." *Assessing Writing*, vol. 21, 2014, pp. 89–103.

Kelly-Riley, Diane, and Carl Whithaus, editors. *Theory of Ethics for Writing Assessment.* Special issue of *Journal of Writing Assessment*, vol. 9, no. 1, 2016, journalofwritingassessment.org/archives.php?issue=19. Accessed 4 Dec. 2019.

———, editors. *Two-Year College Writing Placement.* Special issue of *Journal of Writing Assessment*, vol. 12, no. 1, 2019, journalofwritingassessment.org/. Accessed 4 Dec. 2019.

Kelly-Riley, Diane, et al. "An Empirical Framework for E-Portfolio Assessment." *International Journal of E-Portfolio*, vol. 6, no. 2, 2016, pp. 95–116.

Kerschbaum, Stephanie. "Modality." *Multimodality in Motion: Disability and Kairotic Spaces, Kairos*, vol. 18, no. 1, 2013, kairos.technorhetoric.net/18.1/coverweb/yergeau-et-al/pages/mod/index.html. Accessed 4 Dec. 2019.

King, Lisa, et al. *Survivance, Sovereignty, and Story: Teaching American Indian Rhetorics.* Utah State UP, 2015.

Klenowski, Val, and Claire Wyatt-Smith. "The Impact of High Stakes Testing: The Australian Story." *Assessment in Education: Principles, Policy, and Practice*, vol. 19, no. 1, 2012, pp. 65–79.

Kraemer, Don. J. "The Good, the Right, and the Decent: Ethical Dispositions, the Moral Viewpoint, and Just Pedagogy." *College Composition and Communication*, vol. 68, no. 4, 2017, pp. 603–28.

Kuh, George, et al. *Knowing What Students Know and Can Do: The Current State of Student Learning Outcomes Assessment in US Colleges and Universities.* University of Illinois and Indiana University, National Institute for Learning Outcomes Assessment (NILOA), 2014.

Kurian, George T. *Datapedia of the United States, 1790–2005.* Bernan Press, 2001.

Ladson-Billings, Gloria. "Toward a Theory of Culturally Relevant Pedagogy." *American Educational Research Journal*, vol. 32, no. 3, 1995, pp. 465–91.

Latham, Christine L., and Nancy Ahern. "Profession Writing in Nursing Education: Creating an Academic-Community Writing Center." *Journal of Nursing Education*, vol. 52, no. 11, 2013, pp. 615–20.

Lavelle, Ellen, and Kathy Bushrow. "The Writing Approaches of Graduate Students." *Educational Psychology*, vol. 6, 2007, pp. 807–22.

Lavelle, Ellen, and Nancy Zuercher. "The Writing Approaches of University Students." *Higher Education*, vol. 42, no. 3, 2001, pp. 373–91.

Lavelle, Ellen, et al. "The Writing Approaches of Nursing Students." *Nurse Education Today*, vol. 33, no. 1, 2011, pp. 60–63.

Lee, Carol. "Cultural Modeling as Opportunity to Learn: Making Problem Solving Explicit in Culturally Robust Classrooms and Implications for Assessment." Moss et al., pp. 136–69.

Lee, Harper. *Go Set a Watchman.* Harper Collins, 2015.

———. *To Kill a Mockingbird.* Harper Perennial Modern Classics, 2006.

Leijten, Mariëlle, and Luuk van Waes. "Keystroke Logging in Writing Research: Using Inputlog to Analyze and Visualize Writing Processes." *Written Communication*, vol. 30, no. 3, 2013, pp. 358–92.

Leijten, Mariëlle, et al. "Writing in the Workplace: Constructing Documents Using Multiple Digital Sources." *Journal of Writing Research*, vol. 5, no. 3, 2014, pp. 285–337.

Liebowitz, Cara. "I Am Disabled: On Identity-First versus Person-First Language." *The Body Is Not an Apology*, 20 Mar. 2015, thebodyisnotanapology.com/magazine/i-am-disabled-on-identity-first-versus-people-first-language/.

Lindemann, Erika. "Freshman Composition: No Place for Literature." *College English*, vol. 55, no. 3, 1993, pp. 311–16.

———. "Three Views of English 101." *College English*, vol. 57, no. 3, 1995, pp. 287–302.

Linton, Simi. "What Is Disability Studies?" *PMLA*, vol. 120, no. 2, 2005, pp. 518–22.

Liu, Ou Lydia, et al. "Measuring Learning Outcomes in Higher Education." *Educational Researcher*, vol. 41, no. 9, 2012, pp. 352–62.

Loeb, Susanna, et al. "Descriptive Analysis in Education: A Guide for Researchers." United States, Department of Education, Institute of Education Sciences, National Center for Education Evaluation and Regional Assistance (NCEE), Mar. 2017. NCEE 2017-4023.

Long, Thomas. L., and Cheryl T. Beck. *Writing in Nursing: A Brief Guide*. Oxford UP, 2017.

Lu, Min-Zhan. "Conflict and Struggle: The Enemies or Preconditions of Basic Writing?" *College English*, vol. 54, no. 8, 1992, pp. 887–913.

Lucena, Juan, et al. *Engineering and Sustainable Community Development: Synthesis Lectures on Engineers, Technology, and Society*. Morgan and Claypool Publishers, 2010.

Lundstrom, Kristi, and Wendy Baker. "To Give Is Better than to Receive: The Benefits of Peer Review to the Reviewer's Own Writing." *Journal of Second Language Writing*, vol. 18, no. 1, 2009, pp. 30–43.

Lunsford, Andrea A., and Lahoucine Ouzgane. *Crossing Borderlands: Composition and Postcolonial Studies*. U of Pittsburgh P, 2004.

MacArthur, Charles, and Steve Graham. "Writing Research from a Cognitive Perspective." *Handbook of Writing Research*, edited by Charles MacArthur et al., The Guilford Press, 2016, pp. 24–40.

MacDonald, Barry. "Evaluation and the Control of Education." *Curriculum Evaluation Today: Trends and Implications*, edited by David A. Tawney, Macmillan, 1976, pp. 125–36.

Markman, Ellen M. "Realizing That You Don't Understand: Elementary School Children's Awareness of Inconsistencies." *Child Development*, vol. 50, no. 3, 1980, pp. 643–55.

Martin, Linley, and Marian Mahat. "The Assessment of Learning Outcomes in Australia: Finding the Holy Grail." *AERA Open*, Jan.–Mar. 2017, vol. 3, no. 1, pp. 1–19.

Maxwell, Scott E. "Sample Size and Multiple Regression Analysis." *Psychological Methods*, vol. 5, no. 4, pp. 434–58.

McConnell, Kathryne Drezek, and Terrel L. Rhodes. *On Solid Ground: VALUE Report 2017*. Association of American Colleges and Universities (AAC&U), 2017.

McLeod, Michael, et al. "Designing Effective Reviews: Helping Students Give Helpful Feedback." *Elireview.com*, 2014, elireview.com/content/td/reviews/. Accessed 4 Dec. 2019.

Melynk, Bernadette M., and Ellen Fineout-Overholt. *Evidence-Based Practice in Nursing and Healthcare: A Guide to Best Practice*. Wolters Kluwer, 2015.

Merleau-Ponty, Maurice. *Phenomenology of Perception*. Routledge, 2013.

Messick, Samuel J. "The Interplay of Evidence and Consequences in the Validation of Performance Assessments." *Educational Researcher*, vol. 23, no. 2, 1994, pp. 13–23.

———. "Test Validity and the Ethics of Assessment." *American Psychologist*, vol. 35, no. 11, 1980, pp. 1012–27.

———. "Validity of Psychological Assessment: Validation of Inferences from Persons' Responses and Performances as Scientific Inquiry into Score Meaning." *American Psychologist*, vol. 50, no. 9, 1995, pp. 741–49.

Meyer, Jan H. F., and Ray Land. *Overcoming Barriers to Student Understanding: Threshold Concepts and Troublesome Knowledge*. Routledge, 2006.

Michigan State University. "What Is the 'T'?" *T-Academy 2018*, tsummit.org/t. Accessed 4 Dec. 2019.

Middaugh, Michael F. *Planning and Assessment in Higher Education*. Jossey-Bass, 2010.

Miller, Carolyn R. "Genre as Social Action." *Quarterly Journal of Speech*, vol. 70, no. 2, 1984, pp. 151–67.

Mislevy, Robert J. "Postmodern Test Theory." *Transition in Work and Learning: Implications for Assessment*, edited by Alan M. Lesgold et al., 1997, pp. 180–99.

———. *Sociocognitive Foundations of Educational Measurement*. Routledge, 2018.

Mislevy, Robert J., and Norbert Elliot. "Ethics, Psychometrics, and Writing Assessment: A Conceptual Model." *After Plato: Rhetoric, Ethics, and the Teaching of Writing*, edited by John Duffy and Lois Agnew, Utah State UP, 2020, pp. 143–62.

Mislevy, Robert J., and Geneva D. Haertel. "Implications of Evidence-Centered Design for Educational Testing." *Educational Measurement: Issues and Practice*, vol. 25, no. 4, 2006, pp. 6–20.

Mislevy, Robert J., et al. "A 'Conditional' Sense of Fairness in Assessment." *Educational Research and Evaluation*, vol. 19, nos. 2–3, 2013, pp. 121–40.

Mislevy, Robert J., et al. "Design and Analysis in Task-Based Language Assessment." *Language Testing*, vol. 19, 2002, pp. 477–96.

Montenegro, Erick, and Natasha A. Jankowski. "Equity and Assessment: Moving Towards Culturally Responsive Assessment." National Institute for Learning Outcomes Assessment (NILOA), Jan. 2017. Occasional Paper 29.

———. *Focused on What Matters: Assessment of Student Learning Outcomes at Minority-Serving Institutions*. National Institute for Learning Outcomes Assessment (NILOA), 2015.

Moody, Anne. *Coming of Age in Mississippi*. Bantam, 1968.

Morrison, Kristan A., et al. "Operationalizing Culturally Relevant Pedagogy: A Synthesis of Classroom Based Research." *Equity and Excellence in Education*, vol. 41, no. 4, 2008, pp. 433–52.

Moss, Pamela A., et al., editors. *Assessment, Equity, and Opportunity to Learn*. Cambridge UP, 2008.

Moxley, Joe, et al. "Writing Analytics: Conceptualization of a Multidisciplinary Field." *Journal of Writing Analytics*, vol. 1, 2017, wac.colostate.edu/jwa/archives/vol1/. Accessed 4 Dec. 2019.

Murray, Elizabeth A., et al. "The New Work of Assessment: Evaluating Multimodal Compositions." *Computers and Composition Online*, Spring 2010.

"Myths vs. Facts." *Common Core State Standards Initiative*, 2019, www.corestandards .org/about-the-standards/myths-vs-facts/.

NANDA International (formerly North American Nursing Diagnosis Association). *Nursing Diagnoses: Definitions and Classification, 2015–17*. Wiley-Blackwell, 2014.

National Academies of Engineering. *The Engineer of 2020: Visions of Engineering in the New Century*. The National Academies Press, 2004.

National Research Council. *Education for Life and Work: Developing Transferable Knowledge and Skills in the Twenty-First Century*. Edited by James W. Pellegrino and Margaret L. Hilton, National Academies Press, 2012.

"N.C. A&T Remains Top Producer of African American Engineers at All Levels." *North Carolina A&T State University*, 2017, www.ncat.edu/news/2017/09/african -american-engineers%20.html. Accessed 4 Dec. 2019.

Neel, Jasper. *Options for the Teaching of English: Freshman Composition*. Modern Language Association of America, 1978.

Neff, Joyce Magnotto, and Carl Whithaus. *Writing across Distances and Disciplines: Research and Pedagogy in Distributed Learning*. Routledge, 2009.

Negretti, Raffaella. "Metacognition in Student Academic Writing: A Longitudinal Study of Metacognitive Awareness and Its Relation to Task, Perception, Self-Regulation, and Evaluation of Performance." *Written Communication*, vol. 29, no. 2, 2012, pp. 142–79.

Nelson, Sioban. *Say Little, Do Much: Nursing, Nuns, and Hospitals in the Nineteenth Century*. U of Pennsylvania P, 2008.

Nicol, David, et al. "Rethinking Feedback Practices in Higher Education: A Peer Review Perspective." *Assessment and Evaluation in Higher Education*, vol. 39, no. 1, Jan. 2014, pp. 102–22.

"Nurse Practice Act: Rules and Regulations." *National Council of State Boards of Nursing* (NCSBN), 2019, www.ncsbn.org/npa.htm. Accessed 4 Dec. 2019.

Oliveri, Maria Elena, et al. "After Admissions: What Comes Next in Higher Education?" *Higher Educational Admission Practices: An International Perspective*, edited by Oliveri and Catherine Wendler, Cambridge UP, 2020, pp. 347–75.

Ollis, David F., et al. *Liberal Education in Twenty-First Century Engineering: Responses to ABET/EC 2000 Criteria*. Peter Lang, 2004.

O'Meara, KerryAnn. "Advancing Graduate Student Agency." *Higher Education in Review*, vol. 10, 2013, pp. 1–10.

O'Neill, Peggy. "Moving Beyond Holistic Scoring through Validity Inquiry." *Journal of Writing Assessment*, vol. 1, no. 1, 2003, pp. 47–65.

———. "Reframing Reliability for Writing Assessment." *Journal of Writing Assessment*, vol. 4, no. 1, 2011, journalofwritingassessment.org/article.php?article=54. Accessed 4 Dec. 2019.

Ong, Walter J. "The Writer's Audience Is Always a Fiction." *PMLA*, vol. 90, no. 1, 1975, pp. 9–21.

"Outcome." *Oxford English Dictionary*, Oxford UP, July 2018, www.oed.com/view/Entry/133513. Accessed 4 Dec. 2019.

Paretti, Marie C., and Katrina M. Powell, editors. *Assessment of Writing*. Association for Institutional Research, 2009. Assessment in the Disciplines 4.

———. "Bringing Voices Together: Partnerships for Assessing Writing across Contexts." Introduction. Paretti and Powell, *Assessment*, pp. 1–10.

Parkes, Jay. "Reliability as Argument." *Educational Measurement: Issues and Practice*, vol. 26, no. 4, 2007, pp. 2–10.

Patchan, Melissa M., and Christian D. Schunn. "Understanding the Benefits of Providing Peer Feedback: How Students Respond to Peers' Texts of Varying Quality." *Instructional Science: An International Journal of the Learning Sciences*, vol. 43, no. 5, 2015, pp. 591–614.

Patton, Martha. *Writing in the Research University: A Darwinian Study of WID with Cases from Civil Engineering*. Hampton Press, 2011.

Paunesku, David, et al. "Mind-Set Interventions are a Scalable Treatment for Academic Underachievement." *Psychological Science*, vol. 26, 2015, pp. 784–93.

Peirce, Charles. *Letters to Lady Welby*. Edited by Irwin C. Lieb, Whitlock, 1953.

Perryman-Clark, Staci, et al., editors. *Students' Right to Their Own Language: A Critical Sourcebook*. Bedford / St. Martin's, 2015.

Petry, Lucile. "US Cadet Nurse Corps." *American Journal of Nursing*, vol. 42, no. 8, Aug. 1943, pp. 704–08.

Phelps, Louise Weatherbee, and John M. Ackerman. "Making the Case for Disciplinarity in Rhetoric, Composition, and Writing Studies." *College Composition and Communication*, vol. 62, no. 1, 2010, pp. 180–215.

Philippakos, Zoi A., and Charles A. MacArthur. "The Effects of Giving Feedback on the Persuasive Writing of Fourth- and Fifth-Grade Students." *Reading Research Quarterly*, vol. 51, no. 4, 2016, pp. 419–33.

Poe, Mya. "Making Digital Writing Assessment Fair for Diverse Writers." *Digital Writing Assessment and Evaluation*, edited by Heidi A. McKee and Dànielle Nicole DeVoss, Computers and Composition Digital Press / Utah State UP, 2013, ccdigitalpress.org/book/dwae/01_poe.html.

Poe, Mya, and John Aloysius Cogan, Jr. "Civil Rights and Writing Assessment: Using the Disparate Impact Approach as a Fairness Methodology to Evaluate Social Impact." *Journal of Writing Assessment*, vol. 9, no. 1, 2016, journalofwritingassessment.org/article.php?article=97. Accessed 4 Dec. 2019.

Poe, Mya, and Asao B. Inoue, editors. *Toward Writing as Social Justice*. Special issue of *College English*, vol. 79, no. 2, 2016.

———. "Toward Writing as Social Justice: An Idea Whose Time Has Come." Poe and Inoue, pp. 119–26.

Poe, Mya, et al. "The End of Isolation." Introduction. Poe et al., *Writing*, pp. 3–38.

Poe, Mya, et al. *Learning to Communicate in Science and Engineering: Case Studies from MIT*. MIT P, 2010.

Poe, Mya, et al. "The Legal and the Local: Using Disparate Impact Analysis to Understand the Consequences of Writing Assessment," *College Composition and Communication*, vol. 65, no. 5, 2014, pp. 588–611.

Poe, Mya, et al., editors. *Writing Assessment, Social Justice, and the Advancement of Opportunity*. WAC Clearinghouse / UP of Colorado, 2018.

President's Commission on Higher Education. *Higher Education for American Democracy*. United States Government Printing Office, 1947.

Price, Margaret. *Mad at School: Rhetorics of Mental Disability and Academic Life*. U of Michigan P, 2011.

Prior, Paul. *Writing/Disciplinarity: A Sociohistoric Account of Literate Activity in the Academy*. Routledge, 1998.

Procedures for Accreditation: Professional Degree Programs in Architecture, 2015 Edition. *National Architectural Accrediting Board* (NAAB), 2015, www.naab.org/wp-content/uploads/2016/03/Full-Document.pdf. Accessed 4 Dec. 2019.

Pryor, John, and Barbara Crossouard. "A Socio-cultural Theorisation of Formative Assessment." *Oxford Review of Education*, vol. 34, no. 1, 2008, pp. 1–20.

"Purchase College Fact Book 2019." Purchase College Office of Institutional Research, Nov. 2019, collaborate.purchase.edu/OIRreports/Fact%20Book/Factbook_2019.pdf.

"Quick Facts: WSU at a Glance." *Washington State University*, wsu.edu/about/facts/. Accessed 4 Dec. 2019.

Rawls, John. *Justice as Fairness: A Restatement*. Harvard UP, 2001.

———. *A Theory of Justice*. Oxford UP, 1999.

Reach Higher: Delivering on Common Core State Standards. College Board, 2012.

Reddy, Y. Malini, and Heidi Andrade. "A Review of Rubric Use in Higher Education." *Assessment and Evaluation in Higher Education*, vol. 35, no. 4, 2010, pp. 435–48.

Reichert Powell, Pegeen. *Retention and Resistance: Writing Instruction and Students Who Leave*. Utah State UP, 2014.

Reid, E. Shelley. "Peer Review for Peer Review's Sake: Resituating Peer Review Pedagogy." *Peer Pressure, Peer Power: Theory and Practice in Peer Review and Response for the Writing Classroom*, edited by Steven J. Corbett, et al., Fountainhead Press, 2014, pp. 217–31.

Reiff, Mary Jo, and Anis Bawarshi. "Tracing Discursive Resources: How Students Use Prior Genre Knowledge to Negotiate New Writing Contexts in First-Year Composition." *Written Communication*, vol. 28. no. 3, 2011, pp. 312–37.

Reisch, Michael. *Routledge International Handbook of Social Justice*. Routledge, 2014.

Relles, Stefani, and William Tierney. "Understanding the Writing Habits of Tomorrow's Students: Technology and College Readiness." *Journal of Higher Education*, vol. 84, 2013, pp. 477–505.

Reverby, Susan M., editor. *Annual Conventions, 1893–1899: The American Society of Superintendents of Training Schools for Nurses*. Garland, 1985.

Riley, Donna. "Employing Liberative Pedagogies in Engineering Education." *Journal of Women and Minorities in Science and Engineering*, vol. 9, no. 2, 2003, pp. 20–42.

Robertson, Liane, et al. "Notes toward a Theory of Prior Knowledge and Its Role in College Composers' Transfer of Knowledge and Practice." *Composition Forum*, vol. 26, Fall 2012, compositionforum.com/issue/26/troublesome-knowledge -threshold.php. Accessed 4 Dec. 2019.

Rogers, Peter, and Richard J. Freuler. "The T-Shaped Engineer." ASEE Annual Conference, Washington State Convention Center, Seattle, Washington, 16 June 2015. *ASEE Peer*, doi: 10.18260/p.24844.

Roozen, Kevin. "Tracing Trajectories of Practice: Repurposing in One Student's Developing Disciplinary Writing Processes." *Written Communication*, vol. 27, no. 3, 2010, pp. 318–54.

"Rose-Hulman Institute of Technology." *College Scorecard*, United States, Department of Education, collegescorecard.ed.gov/school/?152318-Rose-Hulman-Institute-of -Technology. Accessed 4 Dec. 2019.

Rosenfield, Patricia L. "The Potential of Transdisciplinary Research for Sustaining and Extending Linkages between the Health and Social Sciences." *Social Science Medicine*, vol. 35, no. 11, 1992, pp. 1343–57.

Ross, Valerie, and Ella Browning. "From Difference to Différance: Developing a Disability-Centered Writing Program." *Composition Forum*, vol. 39, Summer 2018, compositionforum.com/issue/39/u-penn.php. Accessed 4 Dec. 2019.

Russell, David R. *Writing in the Academic Disciplines, 1870–1990: A Curricular History*. Southern Illinois UP, 2002.

Rybczynski, Witold. "A Discourse on Emerging Tectonic Visualization and the Effects of Materiality on Praxis." *Slate*, 2 Feb. 2011, www.slate.com/articles/arts/ architecture/2011/02/a_discourse_on_emerging_tectonic_visualization_and _the_effects_of_materiality_on_praxis.html. Accessed 4 Dec. 2019.

Salvatori, Mariolina, and Patricia Donahue. *The Elements (and Pleasures) of Difficulty*. Pearson, 2005.

Scales, Katherine, et al. "Preparing for Program Accreditation Review Under ABET Engineering Criteria 2000: Choosing Outcome Indicators." *Journal of Engineering Education*, vol. 87, no. 3, 1998, pp. 207–10.

Scholes, Robert. *The Rise and Fall of English*. Yale UP, 1998.

Scholes, Robert, et al., editors. *Text Book: Writing Through Literature*. 3rd ed., Bedford / St. Martin's, 2002.

Scott-Clayton, Judith, and Olga Rodriguez. "Development, Discouragement, or Diversion? New Evidence on the Effects of College Remediation Policy." *Association for Education Finance and Policy*, vol. 10, no. 1, 2015, pp. 4–45.

Serafini, Frank. "Three Paradigms of Assessment: Measurement, Procedure, and Inquiry." *The Reading Teacher*, vol. 54, no. 4, Dec. 2000–Jan. 2001, pp. 384–93.

Shannon, Mary L. "Nurses in American History: Our First Four Licensure Laws." *American Journal of Nursing*, vol. 75, no. 8, Aug. 1975, pp. 1327–29.

Sharkey, Leslie, et al. "Outcomes Assessment of Case-Based Writing Exercises in a Veterinary Clinical Pathology Course." *Journal of Veterinary Medical Education*, vol. 39, no. 4, 2012, pp. 396–403.

Shaughnessy, Mina. *Errors and Expectations: A Guide for the Teacher of Basic Writing*. Oxford UP, 1977.

Shepard, Lorrie. "Classroom Assessment." *Educational Measurement*, edited by Robert L. Brennan, American Council on Education / Praeger, 2006, pp. 623–46.

———. "The Role of Assessment in a Learning Culture." *Educational Researcher*, vol. 29, no. 7, 2000, pp. 4–14.

Shipka, Jody. "Negotiating Rhetorical, Material, Methodological, and Technological Difference: Evaluating Multimodal Designs." *College Composition and Communication*, vol. 61, no. 1, 2009, pp. W343–W366.

Shipman, Debra, et al. "Using the Analytic Rubric as an Evaluation Tool in Nursing Education: The Positive and the Negative." *Nurse Education Today*, vol. 32, no. 3, 2012, pp. 246–49.

Shuman, Larry J., et al. "The ABET 'Professional Skills'—Can They Be Taught? Can They Be Assessed?" *Journal of Engineering Education*, vol. 94, no. 1, 2005, pp. 41–55.

Slomp, David. "An Integrated Design and Appraisal Framework for Ethical Writing Assessment." *Journal of Writing Assessment*, vol. 9 no. 1, 2016, www .journalofwritingassessment.org/article.php?article=91. Accessed 4 Dec. 2019.

Smit, David. *The End of Composition Studies*. Utah State UP, 2004.

Smith, Dorothy. *Writing the Social: Critique, Theory, and Investigation*. U of Toronto P, 1999.

Smith, Linda Tuhiwai. *Decolonizing Methodologies: Research and Indigenous Peoples*. Zed Books, 2012.

smith, s. e. "Why Are Huge Numbers of Disabled Students Dropping Out of College?" *AlterNet*, 19 June 2014. *AlterNet*, www.alternet.org/education/why-are-huge -numbers-disabled-students-dropping-out-college. Accessed 4 Dec. 2019.

Snart, Jason Allen. *Hybrid Learning: The Perils and Promise of Blending Online and Face-to-Face Instruction in Higher Education*. ABC-CLIO, 2010.

Snively, Mary A. "Uniform Curriculum for Training Schools." Reverby, p. 27.

Snyder, Thomas D., editor. *120 Years of American Education: A Statistical Portrait*. United States, Department of Education, National Center for Educational Statistics, Office of Educational Research and Improvement, 1993.

Sorapure, Madeleine. "Between Modes: Assessing Student New Media Compositions." *Kairos*, vol. 10, no. 2, 2006.

Sparks, Jesse R., et al. "Assessing Written Communication in Higher Education: Review and Recommendations for Next-Generation Assessment." *ETS Research Report No. RR-14-37*, 2014.

Spinuzzi, Clay. *Tracing Genres through Organizations: A Sociocultural Approach to Information Design*. MIT P, 2003.

Spurlin, Joni E., et al., editors. *Designing Better Engineering Education Through Assessment: A Practical Guide for Faculty and Department Chairs on Using Assessment and ABET Criteria to Improve Student Learning.* Stylus Press, 2008.

Stake, Robert E. *Program Evaluation, Particularly Responsive Evaluation.* Center for Instructional Research and Curriculum Evaluation, 1975.

Standards for Educational and Psychological Testing. American Educational Research Association / American Psychological Association / National Council on Measurement in Education, 2014.

Steele, Claude M., and Joshua Aronson. "Stereotype Threat and the Intellectual Test Performance of African Americans." *Journal of Personality and Social Psychology,* vol. 69, 1995, pp. 797–811.

Stein, Gertrude. *Tender Buttons.* Green Integer, 2007.

Stemler, Steven. E. "A Comparison of Consensus, Consistency, and Measurement Approaches to Estimating Interrater Reliability." *Practical Assessment, Research, and Evaluation,* vol. 9, no. 4, Mar. 2004, pp. 1–11.

Stewart, Mary K., et al. "Collaborative Course Design and Communities of Practice: Strategies for Adaptable Course Shells in Hybrid and Online Writing." *Transformative Dialogues: Teaching and Learning Journal,* vol. 9, no. 1, 2016, www .kpu.ca/sites/default/files/Transformative%20Dialogues/TD.9.1.9_Stewart_et _al_Collaborative_Course_Design.pdf. Accessed 4 Dec. 2019.

Stowe, Harriet Beecher. *Uncle Tom's Cabin.* Wordsworth Editions, 1999.

Strauss, Anselm, and Juliet J. Corbin. "Grounded Theory Methodology: An Overview." *Strategies of Qualitative Inquiry,* edited by Norman K. Denzin and Yvonna S. Lincoln, Sage, 1998, pp. 158–83.

Street, Brian. "At Last: Recent Applications of New Literacy Studies in Educational Contexts." *Research in the Teaching of English,* vol. 39, no. 4, 2005, pp. 417–23.

Sullivan, Daniel F., and Kate Drezek McConnell. "It's the Assignments—A Ubiquitous and Inexpensive Strategy to Significantly Improve Higher-Order Learning." *Change: The Magazine of Higher Learning,* vol. 50, no. 5, 2018, pp. 16–23.

Sullivan, Patrick, et al., editors. *Deep Reading: Teaching Reading in the Writing Classroom.* National Council of Teachers of English (NCTE), 2017.

Supiano, Beckie. "Traditional Teaching May Deepen Inequality. Can a Different Approach Fix It?" *The Chronicle of Higher Education,* 6 May 2018.

"Supporting Linguistically and Culturally Diverse Learners in English Education." Position statement. National Council of Teachers of English (NCTE), 2005, www .ncte.org/cee/positions/diverselearnersinee. Accessed 4 Dec. 2019.

Sutherland, Suzanne. "Introduction to Quantitative Research." *The Practice of Nursing Research,* edited by Jennifer R. Gray et al., Elsevier 2017, pp. 39–40.

Tardy, Christine M. "Crossing, or Creating, Divides? A Plea for Transdisciplinary Scholarship." *Crossing Divides: Exploring Translingual Writing Pedagogies and Programs,* edited by Bruce Horner and Laura Tetreault, UP of Colorado, 2017, pp. 181–89.

A Test of Leadership: Charting the Future of U.S. Higher Education. United States, Department of Education, 2006.

Thaiss, Chris, and Terry Myers Zawacki. *Engaged Writers / Dynamic Disciplines: Research on the Academic Writing Life.* Boynton/Cook, 2006.

Thibodeaux, Tilisa, et al. "Factors that Contribute to E-Portfolio Persistence." *The International Journal of E-Portfolio,* vol. 7, no. 1, 2017, pp. 1–12.

Thompson-Robinson, Melva, et al., editors. *In Search of Cultural Competence in Evaluation: Toward Principles and Practices.* Special issue of *New Directions for Evaluation,* vol. 102, 2004.

Tinberg, Howard. "Teaching for Transfer: A Passport for Writing in New Contexts." *Peer Review: New Frontiers in Writing,* vol. 19, no. 1, Winter 2017, www.aacu.org/ peerreview/2017/Winter/Tinberg. Accessed 4 Dec. 2019.

Torrance, Harry. "Assessment as Learning? How the Use of Explicit Learning Objectives, Assessment Criteria and Feedback in Post-secondary Education and Training Can Come to Dominate Learning." *Assessment in Education,* vol. 14, no. 3, 2007, pp. 281–94.

——. "Formative Assessment at the Crossroads: Conformative, Deformative, and Transformative Assessment." *Oxford Review of Education,* vol. 38, no. 3, 2012, pp. 323–42.

Toulmin, Stephen E. *The Uses of Argument.* Cambridge UP, 1958.

"Transparency Framework." *National Institute for Learning Outcomes Assessment* (NILOA), 2011, www.learningoutcomesassessment.org/ourwork/transparency -framework/. Accessed 4 Dec. 2019.

Troxler, Marilyn H., et al. "How Baccalaureate-Nursing Programs Teach Writing." *Nursing Forum,* vol. 46, no. 4, Oct.–Dec. 2011, pp. 280–88.

Turley, Eric D., and Chris Gallagher. "On the *Uses* of Rubrics: Reframing the Great Rubric Debate." *English Journal,* vol. 97, no. 4, 2010, pp. 87–92.

Two-Year College English Association (TYCA) Executive Committee. "TYCA White Paper on Placement Reform." *Teaching English in the Two-Year College,* vol. 44, no. 2, 2016, pp. 135–57.

"UC Davis Profile." *University of California, Davis,* 7 Mar. 2019, www.ucdavis.edu/sites/ default/files/upload/files/uc-davis-student-profile.pdf. Accessed 4 Dec. 2019.

United States, Department of Education. *Dear Colleague Letter: Resource Compatibility.* Office for Civil Rights, 2014, www2.ed.gov/about/offices/list/ocr/letters/ colleague-resourcecomp-201410.pdf. Accessed 4 Dec. 2019.

"VALUE Rubrics." *Association of American Colleges and Universities* (AAC&U), www.aacu .org/value-rubrics. Accessed 4 Dec. 2019.

Vieregge, Quentin D., et al. *Agency in the Age of Peer Production.* National Council of Teachers of English (NCTE), 2012.

Villanueva, Victor. "Maybe a Colony: And Still Another Critique of the Comp Community." *JAC,* vol. 17, no. 2, 1997, pp. 183–90.

Vitruvius. *Ten Books on Architecture.* Translated by Morris Hickey Morgan, Harvard UP, 1914.

Vygotsky, Lev S. *Thought and Language*. MIT P, 1962.

Walls, Douglas M., and Stephanie Vie, editors. *Social Writing / Social Media: Publics, Presentations, and Pedagogies*. WAC Clearinghouse / UP of Colorado, 2017.

Walters, Shannon. "A Different Kind of Wholeness: Disability Dis-closure and Ruptured Rhetorics of Multimodal Collaboration and Revision in *The Ride Together*." *Composition Forum*, vol. 39, Summer 2018, www.uc.edu/content/dam/uc/journals/composition-studies/docs/backissues/43-1/43.1%20Walters.pdf. Accessed 4 Dec. 2019.

Walton, Gregory M. "The New Science of Wise Psychological Interventions." *Current Directions in Psychological Science*, vol. 23, no. 1, 2014, pp. 73–82.

Walvoord, Barbara, and Lucille McCarthy. *Thinking and Writing in College: A Naturalistic Study of Students in Four Disciplines*. National Council of Teachers of English (NCTE), 1990.

Wardle, Elizabeth. "'Mutt Genres' and the Goal of FYC: Can We Help Students Write the Genres of the University?" *College Composition and Communication*, vol. 60, no. 4, 2009, pp. 765–89.

Warland, Jane. "Using Simulation to Promote Nursing Students Learning of Work Organization and People Management Skills: A Case-Study." *Nurse Education in Practice*, vol. 11, no. 3, 2011, pp. 186–91.

Warnock, Scott. *Teaching Writing Online: How and Why*. National Council of Teachers of English (NCTE), 2009.

Watson, C. Edward, et al. "Editorial: E-Portfolios—The Eleventh High Impact Practice." *International Journal of E-Portfolio*, vol. 6, no. 2, 2016, pp. 65–69, www.theijep.com/pdf/IJEP254.pdf. Accessed 4 Dec. 2019.

Weeks, Clara S. *A Textbook of Nursing for the Use of Training Schools, Families, and Private Students*. D. Appleton, 1885.

Wertsch, James V. "The Primacy of Mediated Action in Sociocultural Studies." *Mind, Culture, and Activity*, vol. 1, no. 4, 1994, pp. 202–08.

Western and Northern Canadian Protocol for Collaboration in Education. Rethinking Classroom Assessment with Purpose in Mind. Manitoba Education, Citizenship and Youth, 2006.

White, Edward, M., et al. *Assessment of Writing: Politics, Policies, Practices*. Modern Language Association of America, 1996.

White, Edward M., et al. *Very like a Whale: The Assessment of Writing Programs*. Utah State UP, 2015.

Whitehurst, Grover J. *Identifying and Implementing Educational Practices Supported by Rigorous Evidence*. United States, Department of Education, Institute of Education Sciences, 2003.

Wiggins, David. *Ethics: Twelve Lectures on the Philosophy of Morality*. Harvard UP, 2006.

Wigmore, John H. *The Science of Judicial Proof*. 3rd ed., Little, Brown, 1937.

Williams, Julia M. "Evaluating What Students Know: Using the *RosE* Portfolio System for Institutional and Program Outcomes (Assessment Tutorial)." *IEEE Transactions on Professional Communication*, vol. 53, no. 1, 2010, pp. 1–12.

———. "Transformations in Technical Communication Pedagogy: Engineering, Writing, and the ABET Engineering Criteria 2000." *Technical Communication Quarterly*, vol. 10, no. 2, pp. 149–67.

Williams, Julia M., et al. "Communication Pedagogy in the Engineering Classroom: A Report on Faculty Practices and Perceptions." ASEE Annual Conference, Austin Convention Center, Austin, TX, 14 June 2009. *ASEE Peer*, peer.asee.org/5444.

Wills, Katherine V., and Richard Aaron Rice. *E-Portfolio Performance Support Systems: Constructing, Presenting, and Assessing Portfolios*. WAC Clearinghouse / Parlor Press, 2013.

Winkelmes, Mary-Ann, et al. "A Teaching Intervention That Increases Underserved College Students' Success." *Peer Review: Transparency and Problem-Centered Learning*, vol. 18, no. 1–2, Winter–Spring 2016, www.aacu.org/peerreview/2016/winter-spring/Winkelmes. Accessed 4 Dec. 2019.

Winsor, Dorothy A. *Writing like An Engineer: A Rhetorical Education*. Routledge, 1996.

Witte, Stephen P., and Lester Faigley. *Evaluating College Writing Programs*. Southern Illinois UP, 1983.

Wojahn, Patricia, et al. "Blurring Boundaries between Technical Communication and Engineering: Challenges of a Multidisciplinary, Client-Based Pedagogy." *Technical Communication Quarterly*, vol. 10, no. 2, 2001, pp. 129–48.

Wolfe, Joanna. *Team Writing: A Guide to Working in Groups*. Bedford / St. Martin's, 2010.

Wolfe, Joanna, et al. "Knowing What We Know about Writing in the Disciplines: A New Approach to Teaching for Transfer in FYC." *WAC Journal*, vol. 25, 2014, pp. 42–77.

Wood, Tara, et al. "Moving Beyond Disability 2.0 in Composition Studies." *Composition Studies*, vol. 42, no. 2, 2014, pp. 147–50.

Woolf, Virginia. *A Room of One's Own*. Penguin, 1989.

"WPA Outcomes Statement for First-Year Composition (3.0)." *Council of Writing Program Administrators*, 17 July 2014, wpacouncil.org/positions/outcomes.html. Accessed 4 Dec. 2019.

Yancey, Kathleen Blake. "College Admissions and the Insight Resume: Writing, Reflection, and Students' Lived Curriculum as a Site of Equitable Assessment." Inoue and Poe, pp. 171–86.

———. "Looking for Sources of Coherence in a Fragmented World: Notes toward a New Assessment Design." *Computers and Composition*, vol. 21, no. 1, 2004, pp. 89–102.

———. *Reflection in the Writing Classroom*. Utah State UP, 1997.

———. "Standards, Outcomes, and All that Jazz." *The Outcomes Book: Debate and Consensus after the "WPA Outcomes Statement,"* edited by Susanmarie Harrington et al., 2005, Utah State UP, pp. 18–23.

————. *Writing in the Twenty-First Century: A Report from the National Council of Teachers of English*. National Council of Teachers of English (NCTE), 2009.

Yancey, Kathleen Blake, et al. *Writing across Contexts: Transfer, Composition, and Sites of Writing*. Utah State UP, 2014.

Yergeau, Melanie. "Aut(hored)ism." *Computers and Composition Online*, 2009, cconlinejournal.org/dmac/html/persev/002.html. Accessed 4 Dec. 2019.

Yergeau, Melanie, et al. "Multimodal in Motion: Disability and Kairotic Spaces." *Kairos*, vol. 18, no. 1, 2013, kairos.technorhetoric.net/18.1/coverweb/yergeau-et-al/ pages/index.html. Accessed 4 Dec. 2019.

Young, Art. *Teaching Writing across the Curriculum*. WAC Clearinghouse Landmark Publications in Writing Studies, 2006, wac.colostate.edu/books/landmarks/ young-teaching. Accessed 4 Dec. 2019.

Young, Iris Marion. *Responsibility for Justice*. Oxford UP, 2011.

Young, Richard F. *Discursive Practice in Language Learning and Teaching*. Wiley-Blackwell, 2009.

Zawacki, Terry Myers, and Karen Gentemann. "Merging a Culture of Writing with a Culture of Assessment: Embedded, Discipline-Based Writing Assessment." Paretti and Powell, *Assessment*, pp. 49–64.

Zawacki, Terry Myers, et al. "Voices at the Table: Balancing the Needs and Wants of Program Stakeholders to Design a Value-Added Writing Assessment Plan." *Across the Disciplines*, vol. 6, 2009, wac.colostate.edu/docs/atd/assessment/zawackietal .pdf. Accessed 4 Dec. 2019.

Zdenek, Sean. "Which Sounds Are Significant? Toward a Rhetoric of Closed Captioning." *Disability Studies Quarterly*, vol. 31, no. 3, 2011, dsq-sds.org/article/ view/1667. Accessed 4 Dec. 2019.

Zimmerman, B. J. "Development and Adaptation of Expertise: The Role of Self-Regulatory Process and Beliefs." Ericsson et al., pp. 705–22.